THE HEIDEGGER CHANGE

SUNY series in Contemporary French Thought

Edited by David Pettigrew and François Raffoul

THE HEIDEGGER CHANGE

On the Fantastic in Philosophy

Catherine Malabou

Translated and Edited by
Peter Skafish

© 2004 Éditions Léo Scheer
Le Change Heidegger

Published by State University of New York Press, Albany

© 2011 State University of New York

For information, contact State University of New York Press,
Albany, NY
www.sunypress.edu

Production by Diane Ganeles
Marketing by Fran Keneston

Library of Congress Cataloging-in-Publication Data

Malabou, Catherine.
  [Change Heidegger. English]
  The Heidegger change : on the fantastic in philosophy /
Catherine Malabou ; translated and edited by Peter Skafish.
       p. cm. — (SUNY series in contemporary French thought)
  "Bibliography of Heidegger's works"—P.
  Includes bibliographical references and index.
  ISBN 978-1-4384-3955-6 (hardcover : alk. paper)
  ISBN 978-1-4384-3954-9 (paperback : alk. paper)
  1. Heidegger, Martin, 1889–1976. 2. Change. I. Skafish,
Peter. II. Title.

  B3279.H49M271213 2011
  193—dc22   2011007665

                    10 9 8 7 6 5 4 3 2 1

My mind leads me to speak now of forms changed
    into new bodies:
O gods above, inspire this undertaking (which
    you've changed as well)
and guide my poem in its epic sweep
from the world's beginning to the present day.

—Ovid, *Metamorphoses* I, 1–4

Contents

x   Contents

Translator/Editor's Preface

Bringing Catherine Malabou's philosophy into English form involves very different problems than did the translation of the generation of intellectuals and philosophers associated with "French theory." Not only does Malabou belong to a moment (which she calls *"la génération d'après"*) when long, intricate sentences and self-referential language no longer provide the basic structure of theoretical thought, but her work itself abandons one of the chief presuppositions that made that its preferred form. Making the capacity of things to give, receive, and change their own and each other's forms the basic character and condition of the real results in a very different understanding of things than one that grants differences that role. The power of each individual to resist and change the other becomes just as important as (if not more crucial than) the capacity to be affected by the other. What fails to withstand the other will never be able to integrate enough from it to undergo change.

The consequences for writing and translation are almost immediate. Language that is stable, not so much polyvalent as subtly ambiguous, and even closed down to certain meanings turns out to be more effective at conveying this new ontological and politico-ethical status of identity than the old fragmented and plurilinear style. Malabou thus often renders her prose (especially in this book and her part of *Contre-Allée/Counterpath*[1] in terms so deliberate that the polysemy necessary for its reading and interpretation is kept from feeding back on and endlessly amplifying itself. As for translation, the common practice of inflecting the host language with strong traces of the cadence, tone, and grammatical structure of the original language is no longer self-evidently good. Reminding readers of the inadequacy of translation and thus the always-lost specificity of the original becomes less useful for transmitting its thoughts than bending them into idioms more ordinary in the other language. Cast in such familiar language, the translation takes on the sort of sharp definition that made the original distinctive; when the duplicity or untranslatability of the original needs to be exposed, the translation is strong enough to sustain punctures and gaps.

Translating in such a "plastic" fashion allowed the character and meaning of Malabou's writing to emerge more than would have the methods, whether literalist or fideist, commonly applied to philosophical texts. So while precision was my concern throughout, I preferred whenever possible natural phrasings over constructions whose "accuracy" would have mostly stiffened the original's sense. What was initially most important to me was to preserve the distinctiveness of Malabou's voice. At once personally unassuming and philosophically demanding, calm and volatile, and invitingly open and unyieldingly stern in its refusals—simultaneously "modest" and "cunning" was how Jacques Derrida put it—readers who have encountered Malabou in person know this contradictory affect to be the source of her credibility as a thinker. Instead of conveying genius through intellectual speed and agility, or philosophical authority through "classical" (and anachronistic) remove, she balances her fighting streak with a humility that suggests the point of philosophical sparring is to share in wisdom, not attain academic triumph. Because her voice is particularly evident here—the reader is both ordered and anticipated by it through the form of direct address employed for the entirety of the book—it seemed best to render it into an English disencumbered of heavy Gallicisms. These would have made it seem literally foreign instead of the internally uncanny force I believe it would be in many languages.

A less estranged English also proved suitable to the book's novel line of thought. Malabou's contention here is that Heidegger offers a conception of change that can more effectively think difference, the other, ethics, the gift, and time than the philosophies of his greatest and also most critical readers. This claim (which even sympathetic readers will no doubt find controversial) hinges on his persistent use of three words—*Wandel*, *Wandlung*, and *Verwandlung (W, W, & V)*—in nearly everything he wrote after *Being and Time*. Heidegger employs these terms, which more or less correspond to "change," "transformation," and "metamorphosis," to express how each of the various philosophical dispensations through which being is revealed in and as history is the transformation of the dispensation it succeeds (such that being is a continuous, unbroken transmission). But he also ends up using *Wandel*, *Wandlung*, and *Verwandlung* to make other, more radical claims about change and being that are rarely ascribed to him: the "it" in the "it gives" (*es gibt*) with which he eventually characterizes being never transcends what it gives; the series of dispensations that is the history of being is thus substitutive (and even prosthetic) in nature;

and change is therefore originary, without being able to anywhere begin.

Yet despite how much being thus turns out to be, as Malabou puts it, nothing but its changes, Heidegger never fully elaborates this thought or comments on what this text calls "the triad of change." *Wandel*, *Wandlung*, and *Verwandlung* are instead just left dangling, some of the loosest, most neglected threads in his writings (although more promising than others, like *Geist* and *Gestalt*, at the center of the French debates over Heidegger). Malabou even characterizes the triad as "textual pulp," leftover philosophical matter so unrefined that even careful, independent readers (when they have managed to notice them) are unable to connect to the major problems of his work. One instead ordinarily gleans from them (this was at least true for me) only a picture or image of the processes of change and transformation they express—a "fantastic," almost hallucinatory vision of the real as metamorphosis that analysis, argument, and concept are initially foreign to and can only afterward express.

So even as Malabou was only able to perceive the triad's significance because of her prior work on Hegel and plasticity, she approaches them less by tracking how they both exclude and open certain philosophical possibilities in Heidegger's texts than by simply conveying this strange vision. This required of her a poetic style rich enough to evoke a vivid picture of transformation but unobtrusive enough to not make the image seem like an artifact of language. The text's routine, argumentative sentences and adorned, performative phrases alike thus benefited from simple renderings that would not distract readers from this image of change.

This is not to say, however, that the text's marked words, technical expressions, and neologisms could somehow be simply transferred into English. Terms like *l'articulation migratoire-metamorphique* and *la cinéplastique de l'être*—which emphasize that change and molding are movement (and movement therefore change)—or *l'édition imaginale de la présence*, which plays on the fact molding leaves the prints or imprints so important in deconstruction, required the same mixture of fidelity and abuse that more technically difficult philosophical translations do. But these are not so rife in the text as to have made my method impossible. (Where they prove particularly "untranslatable," the originals are kept in brackets.)

The word that features the most this way is the French noun *change*; it carries a double meaning—both "change" and "exchange"—nearly impossible to evoke with the English substantive "change," and Malabou frequently plays on both senses throughout the text, sometimes even using the term interchangeably with two other frequently appearing words: *changement*, "change," and *échange*, "exchange." Since there was thus no way to consistently translate the term, I most often resort to "(ex)change," while occasionally using "change" (and placing *change* in brackets) when the meaning or rhythm of a sentence calls for it. In certain cases where *change* appears in close proximity to *changement* and *échange*, the latter terms also appear in brackets next to their cognates. The reader should be aware, then, that *The Heidegger Change* is also an "exchange," and that the politico-economic sense the French title would thus seem to insinuate is indeed intended. ("The Heidegger (Ex)Change," though, would not have made for much of a title.)

One recurrent and particularly untranslatable phrase—*donner le change* or *donner le change originaire*—deserves special note. *"Donner le change"* carries the figurative meaning of "to throw off the scent," and Malabou has in mind both this sense and the more literal one of "to give change" when she uses the phrase to convey that the changes being makes prevent it from ever following an entirely predetermined, teleological path. The phrase is thus usually rendered as "to throw off the trail and give change."

The same basic strategy also worked, finally, for what might have otherwise been the most linguistically and technically demanding dimension of this translation. Heidegger is, as is well known, the most difficult of the canonical modern philosophers to translate, and the problem is only compounded when texts that are already working between his German and another language have themselves to be translated. Even if Malabou does not for the most part focus on the significance different ways of translating Heidegger's lexicon have for understanding him, both the breadth of her engagement with his texts—most of the major published works are read closely or examined—and the sheer number of quotations from them (400+) result in a book that engages nearly the whole gamut of his principal concepts and terms. Deciding on how to render all the central and peripheral terms and even retranslating the passages from Heidegger used here obviously would have been huge tasks unto themselves. There was, however, rarely a compelling need for either thing. Malabou's focus on *Wandel*, *Wandlung*, and *Verwandlung* has her stressing and often retranslating elements of the quotations that concern these themes and their consequences and deemphasizing major terms, like *Sein*, *Seyn*, *Lichtung*, and *Ereignis*, whose different senses and implications thus become less important. The existing English translations could therefore be used here; the modifications to them that would have been necessary to bring out Malabou's argument bear on their renderings of the triad and related terms, which she is usually already compensating for in her own translations and retranslations of Heidegger. Small adjustments to the English texts, then, were usually sufficient for bringing out what she stresses in the originals.

Translating with more "disloyal loyalty" to the French than the "loyal disloyalty" preferred by the best translators of the old theoreticians had much to do (as some readers may by now suspect) with the recently "(ex)changed" statuses of French and American thought. A phase of obeisance to French literature, human science, and philosophy is no longer the almost obligatory aspect of an intellectual formation in the United States that it was even ten or fifteen years ago. Americans are no longer, as Deleuze once implied we had become, the "credulous Americans" that often greeted deconstruction and "French theory" as almost permanent truths, its figures as prophets, and indigenously American ideas as démodé. Theory has ceased to be, for the most part, a foreign import, and we Americans, having extricated it from Continental philosophy and transferred it into critical theory and other manifestly political modes of analysis, are no longer at risk, as William James put it, of "listening to the French and not talking back" ("the French" not now always having much to offer to such endeavors). The situation thus reversed, what is left of French thought needs to be rearticulated in an idiom that, however estranged from itself (philosophy will probably never sound right in any language), is far closer to English, and perhaps especially a generally American English, than yesterday's "translationese." Otherwise, its foreignness will most likely leave it unheard.

But not for good reasons. Although there are certainly justifications for the low currency being accorded French thought, the current aversion to it has much more to do with an aversion to theory (a new resistance to theory) than the politics on which it is supposedly based. The newly incredulous America has become so incredulous that theoretical invention (and sometimes theory itself) is often greeted as gratuitous pretention, as if the revolution were over, nothing new could be added to its guiding ideas, and analyses based on them were all there is left to do. Even when the books sell well and the lecture halls are full, new theoretical ideas—not just those of "French philosophers" like Malabou and Stiegler or Rancière and Badiou but those of younger "Americans" producing critical theories of globalization or decolonial thought (like Pheng Cheah and Nelson Maldonando-Torres)—are not seriously engaged in some of the very quarters that distinguish themselves as "theoretical" (but where analyses guided by a few nearly canonical theoretical writers usually suffice for the title). This has undoubtedly had the effect of freezing theoretical inquiry by restricting its chief references to (some) French thought circa 1970, Benjamin and sometimes Adorno, a few modern canonical philosophers (Nietzsche and some Hegel), and the anti- or post-philosophical theoreticians (Marx and Freud). Whatever the exact conditions for this—the recent retrenchment into the disciplines, the climate of fear and severe economic hardship of the 00's, the continued predominance of analytic philosophy in philosophy departments, the basically ideological fetishization of local questions—the notion that new French theory and philosophy is not receiving a wide reception because it is politically backward is highly dubious. More likely, the situation is that theory as such does not receive such a reception because theory—thought of a scope so general that it illumines contexts exceeding those of its own problems—is useless, even perturbing, when it is mostly particular questions that are being asked. "French theory," because its style is an index (and its form of thought still exemplary) of the theoretical, is thus easily rejected.

My hope, then, is that some part of theory-weary "America" will feel addressed enough by this translation to allow back some of its old credulity, and thus the possibility that the myriad, mostly delinked questions it works on can indeed be illumined by a general, theoretical vision. Although the question remains open as to whether the exact kind of broad view needed for such a vision can be found in "Continental philosophy" (especially when it includes "Heidegger"), attempting to create one out of empirical research alone is proving quite dangerous. The cosmopolitan and often polyglot space of thinking that America in fact is often took critical distance from French philosophy precisely when the latter failed to recognize racism, the legacy of colonialism, the neocolonial character of global capitalism, and thus epistemic pluralism as profound questions. Yet the United States' own neglect of developing philosophical approaches to these issues is often making it, I believe, far more epistemically European than were (whatever their political limits and failures) the European philosophers.

The problem is not that the histories, literatures, and thought of the many peoples once or still dominated by Europe often remain objects of scholarly neglect. Rather, the problem is that what attention is paid them is usually far too scholarly, and therefore far from the still philosophical kind of thinking that could dialogue with and eventually cede them authority in the humanities. Now that capitalism, political liberalism, and technoscience have become the chief modes of thought of much of the planet, it should be apparent that an approach to thinking capable of

engaging anything outside them will have not only to
critique their basic categories (this of course happens)
but to operate both at and beyond the limits of the
metaphysics on which they are based. "Subjects,"
"histories," and "truths" not belonging to the West
can be listened to and understood only if the concepts (of the subject, of history, and of truth) used
to interpret them are enough at the borders of metaphysics to cross them and thereby become estranged
by the other. The general tendency in the humanities, however, is to assume that such basic terms
of analysis can be employed (even simply "applied")
without being revised. The disturbing result is the
silent and thus all the more insidious reinstatement
of metaphysics, a situation that ideologically reflects
the basic condition of the "new world order"—"the
impossibility," as Malabou characterizes it, "of any
exotic, isolated, or geopolitically marginal event," and
the neutralization and "exhaustion of the outside."[2]
A "terrible" time in which it seems that "everything
has already happened" that could and when, one can
add, intellectual thought seems destined to remain
forever European.[3]

The aspect of this book bearing on this situation
is its rehabilitation and transformation of the Heideggerian question of being. Primary among Malabou's
claims is that the fact certain profoundly transformable beings, the commodity and technology, reveal
being *qua* change entails that being and beings—*that*
there is something and *what* each element of it is—
have effectively become indistinguishable. The only
means of accessing and bespeaking the thatness of
things—change—is through the whatness of a specific being, meaning the changes or mode of change
specific to it. This condition severely undermines the

capacity of beings to be distinct from each other, and thus even to be beings. No matter how various and radical the changes beings are made to undergo (shifts in global power, "Change We Can Believe In," religious conversions, transgenderings, cultural hybridizations, biotechnologies . . .), nearly all of them have already been brought into "conformity" with (techno-)capitalism's regime and form of value, which thus renders them mere tradable equivalents. *What* their transformations involve is of almost no importance given *that* they occur along a route that almost automatically converts them into exchange and surplus value (or "standing reserve"), and thus mere "content changes." Beings become merely formal and thus almost completely indistinguishable.

Countering this situation requires showing that transformation is a power inherent to each being, which in turns necessitates the development of a new, ontic approach to ontology. The fact that capitalism relentlessly forces beings to transform into each other nonetheless also foregrounds their capacity, which is irreducible to the value derived from it, to change themselves and the other. Viewed apart from its economic recuperation, this plasticity entails that what a being is changes as it integrates into itself characteristics of the other (through a process of habituating itself to these and thereby becoming estranged from itself). What beings are, then, is defined neither by an ultimate genre nor a corresponding fundamental form but by the sheer fact that they will always transport each other out of their present genres and into other forms. Their changes, once again, show that what beings are is just (that there is . . .) change. But this is no longer a purely ontological or capitalist statement. Being-as-change never entirely transcends specific changes. There is nothing about being that prevents specific beings from pretending to its position: change as such can only be said through specific change, and any change could end up playing that role. In fact, the plasticity of beings only seems ontological because the beings now masquerading as being cast the character of every specific change in techno-economic terms. Yet when seen from outside those value-forms, such changes show that plasticity is a capacity that belongs to beings as beings. What beings can become is not entirely or primarily determined by being, and being itself is always in turn subject to being changed by beings. Our greatest resource against capitalism therefore rests in our power to integrate from and impose on each other forms, which can deliver us from given, apparently inevitable forms.

Making this power explicit, however, requires opposing the ontologico-capitalist form of transformation with a counterform. Although it could seem that deconstructing the reigning form would be enough to liberate change, the pervasiveness and self-evidence of "ontological capitalism" instead requires that a renewed and metamorphosed version of the question of "being"—given that there is change, not just, what change now passes for it?, but also, what change will instead?—be constantly, vigilantly addressed. Thinking thus becomes the double task of expressing, first, that the "fact" that there is change can only be said by means of a specific change, and of finding a change, second, that can say this without at the same time casting all other changes in its terms alone. Such an "ontico-ontological" mode of thought would preserve the uniqueness of each change by conceiving change as a "global" form whose shape is always in tension with the casts of its local parts.

The reader will have to discover for herself why Malabou regards biological life, and the plasticity of the brain specifically, as the being whose mode of change most fits this bill. But it should now be apparent why Malabou elsewhere conceives the plasticity of life as the image of a future "alter-globalism" in which people(s) will "exercise transformative effects on each other through the demands of recognition, domination, and of liberty."[4] If disputation and dialogue across historical and epistemic lines—exchanges of thought—are to take place under the current ontological conditions, the reciprocity of understanding and changes in perspective sought will have to be carefully distinguished from the coercive universalization of perspective typical of capitalism. Not only will the humanities have to stand down from their dominant, effectively ontological position, but dialogue will have to take a form in which the terms of discussion—the "neutral" terms by which divergent and often incommensurate positions could speak to and change each other—can be furnished by all and negotiated along the way. Conceptions of what might be minimally common to all thought will be needed, not thinking that all thoughts are already shared in common.

Although what such common "concepts" could in the end be is largely unforeseeable, the idea that thought can always cast itself into form at the same time as it is being profoundly shaped by the other might be one. It would certainly allow modern theory to enter the negotiations confident of its survival. But plasticity might also prove an assumption basic to other formations of thought, which may in their own ways agree that being productively estranged by the other occurs only when it can also be integrated to some degree. If this concept is indeed germane across different "epistemes," some translations would indeed be best done in a spirit of resistance. The original could be more easily received by its audience, which would thus be left strong enough for the profound and dangerous transformations ahead of it.

The philosophy of plasticity may thus turn out to have been one of the theories most suited to holding together what was left of metaphysics so that it could open out to and take back in thoughts from other "philosophies" that were never part of it. "Philosophies" that will all, should we together survive the next decades, someday constitute with it the thinking—divergently unified and continuously mobile—of a free, (ex)changing, and ever metamorphosing planet. And "Heidegger"—Malabou's and perhaps even he himself—may in that fortunate event be looked back on as one of the weathered women who played midwife to the terrible agony of its birth.

Introduction

Wandel, Wandlung, and *Verwandlung*

The Heidegger change is a machine that accomplishes changes (*Wandeln*), transformations (*Wandlungen*), and metamorphoses (*Verwandlungen*). It operates in thought as a converter (*Wandler*), an instrument of variable structure that can function as a retort transforming cast iron into steel, as a grist mill that turns groats into flour, and as a converter of tension—both analog to digital and digital to analog—and of monetary value.

The Heidegger change carries out conversions of ontological, symbolic, and existential regimes: the mutation of metaphysics, the metamorphosis of man, the metamorphosis of God, the change of language, the transformation of the gaze, and even the molting of Heidegger himself.

Because it operates at once *in* and *on* Heidegger's thought, the Heidegger change both belongs to it and does not. It works within and beyond it. In fact, the Heidegger change is an invention resulting from a decision of reading—my own. This decision consists in the *empowerment* (*Ermächtigung*) of three linked notions that, although omnipresent in his texts, seem to sleep in them on account of the conceptual penumbra that holds them together. It concerns precisely

1

the notions of *Wandel, Wandlung*, and *Verwandlung*—
"change, transformation, and metamorphosis"—which
constitute what I will call *the triad of change*, and
which I will most often simply designate with their
initials: *W, W, & V.*

Still unnoticed despite its decisive importance
and never distinguished by Heidegger himself, the
triad has been left waiting its *exegetical switching-
on.* I am borrowing the word "empowerment" from
the 1931–32 lecture course on Plato entitled *On
the Essence of Truth.* The Good, Heidegger declares
there, is "empowerment" in the sense that it makes
able, capable, and *possible.* "The proper and original
meaning of ἀγάθον refers to what is good (or suitable)
for something, what can be put to good use. 'Good!'
means: it is done! It is decided! (*es wird gemacht! es
wird entschieden!*). . . . The good is the sound, the
enduring."[1] Constituted as a philosophical machine
and through that empowered, the triad *W, W, & V*
would then be what confers on Heidegger's thought
its power and vigor, and what at the same time
makes it *good for something* and *fit for something
else,* an energy greatly needed in the world of today
for reasons the present work has the task of *developing, reaffirming,* and *remobilizing.* The Heidegger
change—It is done! It is decided!

It is done through *us*—meaning by you and me.
The Heidegger change can only be put to work on
condition of a shared mode of speach. In effect, *to
address the reading, to speak of Heidegger to someone* already comes down to engaging his philosophy,
the very one said to be completely void of address
(of the "you" [*toi*] and "all you" [*vous*]), in its own
transformation(s), its actual *opening to the other.*
The other: the one that you are, and the one you
will be.

You—neither "Heideggerian" nor "anti-Heidegge-rian," you all know about "the affair." You came to Heidegger only after these damning, unappealable biographical and political revelations, and you know them in detail. So having doubts or illusions about them is unacceptable to you. Nevertheless, you have the strange feeling that Heidegger's thinking is always right before you, holding itself back like a shadow waiting to be freed. It is high time, then, for a new perspective on what is waiting there. You are not guilty for wanting to continue to think, you are not guilty for realizing you cannot make it without Heidegger or for being a philosopher, and you are not afraid to move against consensus—you are free.

More Than a Title

THREE "CHANGES" IN ONE

Let's unpack, in order to start, the polysemia of this strange title—*The Heidegger Change*—which is above all made possible by its syntactic mutability. "Change" at once has the value of a substantive and a verb, and three principal ways of understanding the formula, then, are possible. If change is taken as a noun, "the Heidegger change" expresses, first, a genitive tie: the change *of* Heidegger; secondly, it indicates a trade name: the change called Heidegger; and third, if change is heard as a verb, "the Heidegger change" then designates a device whereby Heidegger is changed.

Genitive tie. In Old French syntax, the elision of the preposition "*de*"—as in "*le Change [de] Heidegger*," the first, French title of the book—expresses a relation of belonging. Read in this manner (the change *of* Heidegger), the title announces a study devoted to the Heideggerian concept of change, which is to say, first of all, to Heidegger's understanding of change.[2]

Trade name. "The Heidegger change" can be just as much interpreted as a trademark or proprietary name. In chess, there is "the Fischer defense," while the steel industry has "the Bessemer converter," particle physics has "the Geiger counter," and economics, "the Tobin tax." A proper name becomes a sort of common noun bearing the imprint of a style or idea. Seen from this point of view, the title can be read as the name given a unique and particular change. *The Heidegger change* announces, then, a project that aims to discover what Heidegger, and he alone, has changed—to the point that it can be given his name.

Verb machine. If the "change" in "the Heidegger change" is understood to be the imperative form of the verb "to change," the title can be characterized as a means of commanding Heidegger to transform or change, through another, magic formula hidden within it: *"Heidegger, change!"* The success of this utterance is confirmed by the French title, since *"change"* can be understood to be in the present indicative there: *"Heidegger change,"* that is, "Heidegger changes." Announced, then, is an exegetical approach that will construct, page-by-page, this change-machine.

At this inchoate stage of the inquiry, you begin to understand that touching upon the triad of change, inquiring into the Heideggerian understanding of change, and taking stock of what Heidegger has changed and how he himself is now changing comes down to *changing, transforming, and metamorphosing the interpretation of Heidegger's thought in its entirety.*

It is urgent that we proceed today to this metabolic crossing.

AN UNTRANSLATABLE DISCRETION

Quite surprisingly, this crossing and resource for change [*change*] in and of Heidegger's thought has never really been examined. Although the triad *W, W, & V* touches the essential—in its relating to being, beings, *Dasein*, God, language, and metaphysics—it has not yet been made the object of a thematic analysis.

It is true that Heidegger does not offer the least specification of the meaning of *Wandel, Wandlung,* and *Verwandlung.* He frequently makes use of the three terms in the same paragraph or phrase, but does so without distinguishing between them or specifying their import. He never submits them to etymological research or a thinking translation, nor does he have recourse to High German, derivations, or interpretations. Even though he constantly *mobilizes* these words, he seems not to *vest* them. The names for change never partake in the glorious destiny of "historical decisions" but instead remain, from his oeuvre's start to its finish, *ordinary words.* In a disquieting manner, they seem to keep at a respectful distance from the traditional, technical concepts of change (*Änderung, Veränderung, Werden/* becoming) as well as from those *changes to a new time* that promise "the other thinking": the turning (*Kehre*), the playing-forth (*das Zuspiel*), and the leap (*Sprung*).[3]

The nontechnical, hypocategorical status of *W, W, & V* no doubt explains why the translators do not pay any particular attention to the triad. They contend with it in a perfectly casual manner, as though they were unburdened of all care for exactitude. In *The Fundamental Concepts of Metaphysics,* for example, the term *Verwandlung* is sometimes translated as transformation, sometimes as mutation, and sometimes as modification. In *The Essence of Truth, Wandlung* is variously translated as "revolution, change, or turning" without any explanation or justification. As we will very often see, there is no concern for consistency in the translation of the three notions of the triad—neither inside each text, nor from one translator to the other.[4]

This looseness can be easily understood. It is in fact no easier to establish in German a rigorous distinction between *Wandel, Wandlung,* and *Verwandlung* than it is to make apparent the differences between, in French, *changement* and *transformation,* and, in English, change and transformation, or even those between, in both languages, *mutation, metamorphosis,* and *muer* or molting/turning into. Moreover and reciprocally, every attempt at subjecting the triad to a uniform translation produces quite contestable effects. This becomes evident when reading, for example, the American translation of *Beiträge zur Philosophie— Contributions to Philosophy*—where all three notions are rendered as "transformation."

The point is not to fault the translators but to express surprise that they neither noticed nor commented on this *baseline untranslatability,* nor attempted to examine it closely. A sort of textual pulp, the triad defies capture and says in its own way—without dazzle but very surely, between slackness and rigidity and at a distance from major philosophemes—what, however, happens to major philosophemes: *they change.*

THE BASIC OCCURRENCES OF W, W, & V

Now that you are beginning to make out in the penumbra the uncanny tentacles of the triad, you see that you are before an infinitely flexible aptitude, an incredible capacity for mutability and convertibility, an unsuspected suppleness that has foiled the vigilance of the commentators and translators. You are beginning to understand that *W, W, & V* could be the *secret agent* of Heidegger's philosophy, what *sustains and clandestinely guides* the destiny of the essential. In which case you understand as well that our work will not consist in brutally summoning this agent and making it appear in full day. Since it has been trying to get our attention, it demands being treated as merits it—*to be recognized*, that is, *without being presented*. It is up to us, then, *to create an unprecedented approach to change*; to take account of it without filling it in or betraying it with the discrepancy that exists between the at first glance loose and vague use Heidegger makes of the triad and the decisive importance of what it is tied to. Such an approach, as much through its form as by what it moves toward, opens, as the double foundation of Heidegger's philosophy, the mysterious space of *the fantastic in philosophy*.

Before circumscribing this space, however, it would be useful to adumbrate the basic domains where the triad is deployed.

MAN'S METAMORPHOSIS INTO *DASEIN*

In the first place, *Wandel, Wandlung,* and *Verwandlung* express *what happens to man*. Man is going to change, man is going to metamorphose. In *The Fundamental Concepts of Metaphysics* or the 1929 lecture "What Is Metaphysics?" Heidegger announces *the metamorphosis of man into its* Dasein: "This requires [*hierzu wird verlangt*] that we actively complete the transformation of the human being into its *Dasein* [*die*

Verwandlung des Menschen in sein Da-Sein . . . nach-vollzieben]."⁵ This metamorphosis is just as much a recurrent motif in *Contributions to Philosophy*: "Man metamorphoses [*der Mensch verwandelt*]," Heidegger declares there. Prepared with "the other beginning" is "the metamorphosis of man himself [*die Verwandlung des Menschen selbst*]" or the "transformation of man itself [*vollige Verwandlung des Menschen*]."⁶

THE DESTRUCTION OF METAPHYSICS AND THE
METAMORPHOSIS OF PHILOSOPHY

The metamorphosis of man into *Dasein* is inseparable, furthermore, from the overcoming (*Überwindung*) and transformation of metaphysics: "If our thinking should succeed in its efforts to go back into the ground of metaphysics, it might well help to bring about a change in the human essence [*einen Wandel des Wesens des Menschen mitveranlassen*], a change accompanied by a transformation [*Verwandlung*] of metaphysics."⁷

But this metamorphosis and transformation are also confounded with the movement of the *Destruktion* or destruction of metaphysics. In "What Is Philosophy?" Heidegger insists on the positive meaning of the *Destruktion* that had already been brought to light in *Being and Time*; destruction, he says, is not annihilation but *metamorphosis* (*Verwandlung*). "We find," he declares, "the answer to the question, 'What is philosophy?' not through historical assertions about the definitions of philosophy but through conversing with that which has been handed down to us as the being of being. The path to the answer to our question is not a break with history, no repudiation of history, but is an appropriation and metamorphosis of what has been handed down to us

[*Aneignung und Verwandlung des überlieferten*]. Such an appropriation of history is what is meant by the term 'destruction' [*solche Aneignung der Geschichte ist mit dem Titel 'Destruktion' gemeint*]."[8] Destruction should be understood, then, as a *transformative rupture*, as the movement by which thinking henceforth "prepares its own transformation [*seine eigene Wandlung vorbereitet*]."[9]

MUTATION OF THE RELATION TO BEING

Wandel, Wandlung, and *Verwandlung* are also used to characterize the mutation of the relation to being that arises with the other thinking, a simultaneous mutation of the metamorphosis of the human and its *Dasein*, and the transformation of metaphysics. "The relation to being . . . changes [*der Bezug zu Sein wandelt sich*]," Heidegger declares in *Contributions to Philosophy*. What promises itself to thought is "a complete change of the relations to beings and to being [*ein volligen Wandel der Bezüge zum Seienden und zum Seyn*],"[10] a motif presented for the first time in the conclusion of "The Essence of Truth" and taken up again in the "Summary" of the seminar on *Time and Being*. In *Contributions*, Heidegger again affirms that "metamorphosed" *Dasein* is capable of "transforming" the "separation" of being from beings into a "simultaneity [*Gleichzeitigkeit*]."[11]

THE TRANSFORMATION OF LANGUAGE

The coming of this simultaneity or contemporaneousness, the announcement of "the other thinking," implies, too, a "metamorphosis of language." In *Contributions*, Heidegger asks: "Can a new language for Being be invented? No. [*Kann eine neue Sprache für*

das Seyn erfunden werden? Nein.]" It is only possible
to metamorphose [*verwandeln*] the sole language that
would be available to us: "the language of beings."
What would thereby appear is a "transformed saying [*gewandelte Sagen*]."[12] In *The Question of Being*,
he wonders: "In which language does the basic outline of thinking speak which indicates a crossing of
the line?" This crossing carries with it a "necessary
metamorphosis [*Verwandlung*] of language and a
mutation in the relation to the essence of language"
[*ein gewandeltes Verhältnis zum Wesen der Sprache*].
But Heidegger specifies that "this metamorphosis
[*Verwandlung*] does not come back to the exchanging of an old terminology for a new one."[13] Imposing
itself here is the idea of a *metamorphosis of language
right on language.*

METAMORPHOSIS OF THE GODS

At last, the gods: if they return, they will return
changed, so that no one recognizes them. Heidegger
effectively announces their "hidden metamorphosis
[*ihre verborgene Verwandlung*]." The last God appears
at the crossing of the arrival and flight of the ancient
gods. It does not arise as would a *new* divinity but
is born from *the secret transformation* of the previous
gods. In *Sojourns*, Heidegger affirms: "The gods of
Greece and their supreme god, if they ever come, will
return only transformed to a world [*nur Verwandelt in
eine Welt verkehren*] whose overthrow [*umstürzende
Veränderung*] is grounded in the land of the gods of
ancient Greece."[14]

THE FANTASTIC, OR THE WEIGHT OF LIGHTNESS

You can see that locating the trace of *W, W, & V* in
Heidegger's texts immediately raises a formidable dif-

ficulty. The triad clearly carries, on the one hand, the heavy burden of expressing, once again, *the change of man, of thinking, of the relation to being, of God,* and *of language.* But what is just as clear is that it *bears this load lightly.* In fact, as I have already indicated, Heidegger never pauses over it. It is up to us, then, to produce its *gravity* by determining exactly in what way man, thinking, the relation to being, God, and language are for Heidegger transformable and convertible instances; it is left to us to unfold *the general economy of this mutability.* This task corresponds precisely to an elaboration of "the Heidegger change." Empowering *W, W, & V* entails conferring the reality proper to them on the philosophical system that, much like the mystery of a body—its energetic expenditures and phenomena of assimilation and degradation—regulates the *changes, exchanges,* and *substitutions* at work in Heidegger's thought, the very conditions of its mobility and life. Empowering the triad grants us access to the *ontological metabolism* that renders possible all its changes, mutations, and transformations. I call such a point of access *fantastic.*

Simultaneously a mode of visibility and manifestation, the fantastic here designates the phenomenality of ontico-ontological transformations—those of man, god, language, etc.—which unveil the originary mutability of being while revealing at the same time that being is perhaps nothing . . . but its mutability.

To the extent that the mutability of being is not—not, that is, a being—its reality is necessarily imaginary, if by imaginary we understand, as Heidegger invites us to, a nonobjective modality of presence free of every reference and referent. Such a reality, visibility, and phenomenality form and determine in the same move a philosophical inquiry aimed at these. Seeing the change of being—being as (ex)change [*change*]—seeing that which changes, seeing the incision of the other in man, God, and thinking is only possible for the philosopher if she invents a manner of ensconcing herself in this hole or cavity in thought that always refuses itself to concepts and that the triad, through the very emptiness of its name—*W, W, & V*—constantly invites investing as merits it: otherwise. Otherwise than conceptually, that is, which means two things: otherwise than through recourse to traditional philosophical techniques, and otherwise than through the Heideggerian philosophemes that are nonetheless immediately available for expressing change in the full day of the text— time, historicality, *Ereignis*, and all the figures of the turning or leap.

Constructing the Heidegger change therefore demands that we both locate and create *the level of intelligibility specific to the change required by the structure of Heidegger's thinking itself* inasmuch as it opens in itself this distance or gap between the manifest character of its aims (the overcoming of metaphysics, time, history, *Ereignis*) and *the scarcely nameable—W, W, & V*—background movement that is their obscure support and indispensable accomplice. What matters is that we experience and test *the metabolic potential* of this thought, the sole one to have only ever spoken to us, from the forgetting of being to the coming of the other thinking, of *what is never seen.*

Both the mode of visibility of ontological metabolism and the intelligibility and evidence of the never seen, the fantastic "in philosophy" designates at once a kind of approach to change and the very strangeness of what changes and is going to change. It also manifests, by consequence, the uncanniness of the fantastic to itself: its irreducibility to a genre or

category of discourse, its resistance to every relega-
tion of itself to a conventional domain, to what Roger
Caillois calls "the fantastic of principle or obligation."[15]
The philosophical fantastic is contemporary with the
bringing to light, in the twentieth century, of the onto-
logical difference and, by way of consequence, the
possibility of thinking being without beings. It never
designates "an element exterior to the human world"
(that of "composite monsters, infernal fawns, the irrup-
tion of demonic, grotesque, or sinister creatures"), but
describes the foreigner on the inside, the whole of the
metabolic force that sleeps without sleeping in what
is, the very face of being that concepts cannot say
without losing face.[16]

As an imaginary production without referent and
pure ontological creation, the fantastic characterizes
the apprehension *and* the regime of existence of *what*
cannot be presented, of, that is, what can only ever
change. Eclipsed by the metaphysical tradition and
only *prepared* by the other thinking, change *risks*
being an unprecedented mode of being.

Constructing the Heidegger change therefore
involves elaborating the schematizing instance that
will alone permit us to perceive, with Heidegger and
beyond him, this *conceptually depatriated* place—
the very enigma of our philosophical moment—*this*
point of rupture and suture between metaphysics and
its other that imposes upon philosophy, whether
it admits it or not, its limit; a limit that it also
its *reality. This point is the phantasm of our philo-*
sophical reality. Lodged at the heart of the triad, it is
what gets displaced with it; unlocatable, undat-
able, and unthinkable, it is nonetheless the motor of
thought. I would like us now, you and me, to engage
together its unforeseeable, constantly changing
motility.

The Situation of the Question of Change in Heidegger's Thought

"Change": Change, Exchange, Substitution

This surprising image of an ontological metabolism in which the dividing line of change (which runs between the ancient and the new) is constantly changing is what imposed the title *The Heidegger Change* on me. I felt that the French word *change* had the merit of exactly situating the space of deployment of the essential significations of the triad *Wandel, Wandlung,* and *Verwandlung* in Heidegger's thinking—an intermediary space between *change, exchange,* and *substitution*. The substantive *change* in effect signifies, first, change in the sense of *succession, alternation,* or *variability*: that of seasons, moods, affections, and objects of desire. Second, it designates (a sense largely missing in English) barter, the *exchange* of one object for another, and what is given *for* and can also replace what one gives up or be through that its equivalent; "change" is also of course given following transactions that involve paper money. By extension, it is in French a name for the place where economic negotiations are carried out, such as *le marché des changes* or foreign exchange market (the Bourse's stockbrokers thus being *agents de change*). An old term of venery, *change* designates, finally, the *substitution* of a new animal for the one initially put out for the hunt. This last signification can still be heard in the expression *donner le change*—to dissimulate, in the sense of throwing off the scent or trail, as well as to pass the torch or to relay.

It must nonetheless be admitted that these French significations of exchange (*Tauschung*), barter, currency exchange or change (*Wechsel*), and substitution (*Austauschen*) do not precisely coincide in German, as etymology immediately shows in the case of *Wandel, Wandlung,* and *Verwandlung.* Why then am I authorized to make use of the word *change,* which in French allows for the conflation of significations that German distinguishes more clearly?

ANOTHER READING HAS ALREADY BEGUN

My response is to say that tracking Heidegger's thinking of change necessarily leads one to take account of an *exchange.*

An exchange, first of all, of a center of gravity. Now that your attention has been drawn to the triad, the same thing will happen to you as did me: you will see it and nothing else but, and no longer be able to ignore it—you will see it everywhere in Heidegger's oeuvre, throughout each of his books and lecture courses. From here out, the triad will predominate in your readings. In fact, another reading has already begun. In letting yourself be taken by the strange rhythm of the triad, in letting yourself be put under the spell of the leitmotif of *W, W, & V*—by the fantastic announcement of a change of man, god, being, language, and philosophy—you are already in the course of reaching *another Heidegger. An almost imperceptible but nonetheless vertiginous difference has begun to open up right on the ontological difference. This self-difference of difference is nothing but its ontological dimension.*

From the moment you decided to follow the occasional pulsation of change, you have without noticing it been distracted from the difference between being and beings. It no longer monopolizes or snatches up, as was its habit and as you had been taught it should, all your energy as a reader [*lecteur/lectrice*] of Heidegger; it no longer holds you. Henceforth, you will no longer be able to keep in focus the difference between being and beings but only the difference between *differing* and *changing*. The center of gravity of your reading has already been displaced. You have, without realizing it, *exchanged difference for change*.

An ontological exchange, secondly. In spite of this, you have not abandoned difference. Quite the opposite: you are about to discover that *exchange* is its origin. Meaning? From within the clear-obscure fantastic that has become our abode, you start to make out the silhouette of a sort of *go-between. W, W, & V* progressively draws your attention to this traveler, this runner or mule [*passeur*] that until now you would have only ever distractedly glanced at: *essence* or *Wesen. The difference between differing and changing directs your gaze to the difference between being and essence—for to behold essence is to witness change.*

When Heidegger heralds the change, metamorphosis, and mutation of man, gods, being, the relation to being, language, and philosophy, he does not have in mind a transformational event that would suddenly come to affect from the outside instances that would have first been originally intact and identical to themselves. Man, God, philosophy, and the rest indeed are, as we saw, *changing and changed from the outset*, which is to say *originally exchanged*. What else is metaphysics besides *the history of an exchange*—Heidegger calls it *eine Verwechslung*, a confusion—*between being and beings*? "From its beginning to its completion, the propositions of metaphysics have been strangely involved in a persistent confusion of beings and being," one reads in "Introduction to '"What Is Metaphysics?'"[17] Heidegger further specifies, in a note added to the text in 1949, that what must be heard in *Verwechslung* is change, *Wechsel*, and exchange, *Auswechslung*. "Confusion: remaining tied to passing over to Being and back to beings [*das Hinüber zu Sein und das Herüber zu Seiendem*]," he writes. "One always stands *in* the other and *for* the other [im *anderen und* für *das andere*], 'interchange' [*Wechsel*], 'exchange' [*Auswechslung*], first this way, then the other [*bald so, bald so*]."[18]

Difference, then, presupposes the exchangeability, and thus the nondifferentiation, of instances that differ. Ontological difference therefore remains unthinkable outside the very possibility of its occlusion; that is to say, outside the originary possibility of being and beings changing into each other. Now essence is precisely their point of convertibility. Throughout the metaphysical tradition, Heidegger writes, "essence is only the other word for being,"[19] and essence, he furthermore says, must be understood as "beingness," *Seinendheit*. Beingness takes being's place, which "enters its service."[20] This originary (ex)change—ontological mastery and servitude—corresponds to the going-in-drag [*travestissement*] of essence, and is the most basic resource of metaphysics.

This being-in-drag corresponds to a transformation (*W, W, & V*) of originary mutability into immutability, *Unwandelbarkeit*. The essence of a thing is effectively what in it does not change. This exchange of mutability for its opposite is exactly what originally *gives change [donne le change] in philosophy, throwing it off the trail.*

Although the difference between being and essence is different from that between being and beings, it should nonetheless, you must grant me, not be located within the foyer of *another* difference—

neither within some other ontological difference nor within a difference different than the ontological difference. *The problematic of change brings to light a differing that is not the alternative to ontological difference, but which constitutes the site of Heidegger's thinking of change.*

TOWARD AN ONTOLOGICAL REVOLUTION

The mutation (*W, W, & V*) of the mutable into the immutable that presides over metaphysics' destiny will, Heidegger declares, undergo yet another change: the *putting back into play of originary mutability* that occurs with the transformation of man, god, the relation to being, language, and philosophy.

What takes place at the end of metaphysics is not, as could be believed, the end of exchange but rather *an (ex)change of the first change—a new exchangeability of being and beings*. A new exchangeability that does not occlude their difference but instead frees essence from the burden of its old immutability so that it is rendered forever *unrecognizable*. The entirety of Heidegger's thinking is thus devoted to uncovering the conditions of a new ontological exchange. An exchange without violation [*rapt*], usurpation, and domination but an exchange nonetheless—one that *Ereignis* prefigures.

The Heidegger change, understood once more as a trade name ("the change called Heidegger"), is nothing less than the instrument of *an ontological revolution.*

I invite you to discover all the surprises that Heidegger's thought has in store when read as a thinking of mutation, and to see everything that difference and consequently destruction owe to transformability.

The Migratory-Metamorphic Articulation

This transformability is even more difficult to think because of the fact it governs a double economy. You have perhaps caught on that there are effectively *two (ex-)changes*. One where essence *doubles* being—is given for it—and another where essence is the coming and advent of being itself. *Each of these (ex-)changes also shelters a metabolic regime that is proper to it* . . . and yet both express it using the same words: *W, W, & V*. Heidegger conceives, for instance, the history of metaphysics' epochs as a sequence of "transformations [*Abwandlungen*]" and "mutations [*Wandlungen*]," while "the other thinking" is also said to open a "transformation [*Wandlung*] of Western history."[21]

The dividing line between the two (ex-)changes is nonetheless decisive—relentlessly imprinting and effacing itself, it threatens to appear and disappear.

FORM AND PATHWAY

How, then, can this line be rigorously apprehended? We will consider more closely our three terms *Wandel, Wandlung,* and *Verwandlung.* All three obviously signify change, transformation, mutation, turning-into, conversion, and commutation. . . . We immediately realize, however, that these significations are ordered along two principal axes that together reveal a fundamental articulation constitutive of all change: a *migratory* axis, and a *metamorphic* one—as though "change" always means at once *change of route* and *change of form.*

A certain proximity indicated by the dictionaries ties *Wandlung*—transformation—to *Wanderung,*

migration or peregrination. *Wandern* signifies traveling without destination, strolling about, and incessant and directionless change, as happens in the
Wanderhalle, the concourse or waiting area [*salle de
pas perdus*]. Heidegger himself insists on the kinship
between *wandeln* and *wandern* that Hölderlin brings
out in his poem *"Der Ister."* Apropos the "migration
[*Wanderung*]" of "the *stream*" that Hölderlin calls
"the changing [*der Wandelnde*]," Heidegger declares:
"Change has here the sense of migrating, going, but
at the same time of becoming other [*Wandeln hier
als Wandern und gehen, aber zugleich als Ändern,
Fortnehmen*]."[22] Change takes shape, then, as a way
forward while paths, reciprocally, are revealed to be
continually changing.

  Wandeln and *wandern* are, moreover, iterative
forms of *wenden*, which means to turn; *die Wende*
also signifies turning,[23] and *Wandeln* is to change
by following a series of bends and turns or reversing course. The triad of *W, W, & V* outlines, then,
the trace of a development that weaves around and
tacks, a progress without aim. We can see, too, that
Wandel, Wandlung, and *Verwandlung* always for Heidegger convey an *advance* that is at the same time
a *turning back*, a progression that is also a *roaming*
or *rambling*.

  Wandel, Wandlung, and *Verwandlung* are equally
employed in contemporary German to designate
processes of metamorphosis. If the register of form
(μορφή) is not present in the etymology of the three
terms, there is nonetheless little difference in German between the usages of *Metamorphose* and *Verwandlung*. This is what elsewhere authorizes Kafka's
Verwandlung to be translated into French as *La Méta-
morphose* and into English as *The Metamorphosis*. In
the same manner, the title of a chapter from *Thus*

Spoke Zarathustra, "*Von den drei Verwandlungen*," is generally translated as "*Des trois Métamorphoses*" or "On the Three Metamorphoses." The *Dudden* dictionary also clearly emphasizes the synonymy of *Verwandlung* and *Metamorphose* and specifies that the two can signify: "*First*, the development of the egg from an independent larval state to the maturity specific to it (among insects, for example), or the transformation of the basic form of a vegetable organ into an organ endowed with a particular function; *second*, the fantastic transformation of a being into an animal, plant, or stone."[24] *Wandel* and *Wandlung* can also express these two senses of metamorphosis as biological phenomenon and, in the tradition of Ovid and Apuleius, as the incarnation of a man or god in another being, most often an animal. Hence one can read, under *Wandel*: "1. to become other, to receive another form or figure; 2. to be metamorphosed into something; to become something else [*1. sich verändern, eine andere Form, Gestalt, bekommen; 2. zu etwas sich verwandeln; zu etwas anderem werden*]."[25]

For Heidegger, every real change is partly comprised of a metamorphic dimension. So that in each new epoch of metaphysics—first (ex)change—"an essential metamorphosis [*wesentliche Verwandlung*]"[26] is accomplished, while in the same way—second change—"the grounding-question" that orients the other thinking "transforms in itself [*einverwandelt*] the guiding-question," which is that of metaphysics.[27] This is to say that Heidegger characterizes metaphysics as a "form [*Form*]" that changes form from epoch to epoch by being re-formed, even as he just as much promises "the other thinking" to be a *transformation* in the literal sense—a *passage* or *transition* to another form.

While it should be acknowledged that Heidegger never employs the word *Metamorphose*, this is perhaps only because *Verwandlung* offers, in its proximity with *Wandlung*, the advantage of rendering change of route and change of form indistinguishable from each other. Just as Kafka's *Verwandlung* is indissociable from a *Wanderung* around a room, the *Verwandlung* announced by Heidegger is indissociable from a *Wanderung* in the world. Reciprocally, just as Kafka's *Verwandlung* is indissociable from a change of form, the *Wandlung* announced by Heidegger as pathway and turnaround always doubles as an adventure of *trans-formation*.[28] The two changes are correlative: each loop of the road has its corresponding form (*Form*) or figure (*Gestalt*), while every formal mutation is, inversely, a change of itinerary.

The other (ex)change is likewise structured according to the double, migratory and metamorphic, articulation presiding over the destiny of *W, W, & V*. Hence, for example, the metamorphosis of man appears as a displacement and a transformation. On the one hand, the "transformation of humanness [*Verwandlung des Menschseins*]," is in effect "a displacing [of] its site among beings [*Ver-rückung seiner Stellung im Seienden*]."[29] On the other, this renewal involves, in its about-turns and changes of course, the abandonment and re-formation of the traditional form (*Form*) of man: the form of the rational animal, "*das 'vernüftige' Tier, animal rationale.*"[30] The other beginning is likewise presented as an "*ändersförmig*" or different form at the same time as it is cast as following "another direction."[31] As for the gods, we "need a preliminary thought of the field of their arrival under a transformed figure [*gewandelte Gestalt*]"[32]—a figure that would itself be given in the movement of a very singular migration, one that would be at once an arrival (*Ankunft*) and flight (*Flucht*).[33] What we will have to analyze is the movement of this future metamorphosis to come, which, from *Dasein* to language, being to thought, and beings to god, enters the adventure of form at a curve in the road.

ONE TRIAD, TWO CHANGES

Are these analyses actually helpful? If the first, metaphysical change shares the diction of its kinesis (*W, W, & V*) with the second—the other thinking—then we again find ourselves before our problem. How can we establish *the dividing line between change and change*? If one and the same articulation (the migratory-metamorphic) governs the economy of the two changes, how can we establish *the dividing line between self-metamorphosis and self-metamorphosis, between migration and migration*?

If man, being, beings, God, and language all change, must they be understood as exchanging their traditional determinations for others that have not yet appeared, and this only by grace of the metaphysical metabolism that holds one last surprise in store for them? Or must one, on the contrary, presume that the very idea of an ontological metabolism emerges *only once things have changed*, only after there is acceptance of the clearly ultrametaphysical idea that ontology designates nothing other, at bottom, than *the structure of transformation*?

Will we ever know this? Will we ever know if we have changed? Will we ever know if migration and metamorphosis have already taken place, or if they remain always to come?

These questions cast Heideggerian thought in a strange, disquieting light. From the one change

[*change*] and regime of exchange [*échange*] to the other, a metabolic circulation takes place between man and *Dasein*, God and god, being (*Sein*) and be-ing (*Seyn*), and essence (*Wesen*) and essencing or swaying (*Wesung*), a circulation that can appear to be absolutely uncontrollable because it has neither limits nor strict determinations. *W, W, & V* are doubtlessly, then, what endow Heidegger's thought with its vertiginous dimension, what is both fascinating and dangerous about it. With *W, W, & V*, in fact, we verge on danger itself—on *ontological transformability, the both migratory and metamorphic mutability of everything that is. We touch the core of this plasticity, where every other changes into every other, but without at the same time knowing from whence comes the other or if, in truth, there could be another way of changing.*

The Janus-Head *Gestell*

The only exposition manifestly devoted to the terms *Wandel, Wandlung,* and *Verwandlung* themselves is found in "The Summary of a Seminar on the Lecture *Time and Being*." It alone may help us here, despite its brevity. The succession of the epochs of being is presented there as "the abundance of the transformation [*Wandlungsfülle*] of being," and the sense of these "transformations" is precisely what the seminar focuses on. "The sixth and last session concerned at first some questions raised, which had to do with the meaning that lies in the words 'transformation' [*Wandlung*], 'transmutation' [*Verwandlung*, metamorphosis] when the fullness of the transformation of being is spoken about [*wenn von der Wandlungsfülle des Seins gesprochen wird*]."[34] The *same terms,* continue the authors, characterize *at once* both the course of metaphysics (the succession of epochs that unfurl upon the substitution of beingness for being and the occlusion of this substitution) and the advent of the other beginning or other change [*change*]. "Transformation, transmutation [*Verwandlung*, or metamorphosis], is, on the one hand, predicated within metaphysics about metaphysics."[35] All the different philosophical doctrines constitute through time "the changing forms [*wechselnden Gestalten*] in which being shows itself [*zeigt*], epochally and historically."[36] Each epoch of the history of being thus accomplishes a *Wandlung* or *Verwandlung* of metaphysics's guiding question.

However, "[w]e must sharply distinguish from this meaning of transformation, which refers to metaphysics, the meaning which is intended when we say that being is transformed—to *Ereignis* [*das Sein verwandelt wird—nämlich in das Ereignis*]. Here it is not a matter of a manifestation [*Manifestation*] of being comparable to the metaphysical formations [*Gestalten*] of being and following them as a new manifestation."[37]

"The abundance of the transformation [*Wandlungsfülle*] of being" should be heard, then, in *two radically different senses*. Yet how can the same words, *Wandel*, *Wandlung*, and *Verwandlung*, express *both* of the two (ex)changes?

The "Summary" provides this decisive response: "Between the epochal formations of being and the transformation of being into Appropriation stands Enframing [*Ge-stell*]. The Enframing is an in-between stage [*Zwischenstation*], so to speak. It offers a double aspect, one might say, a Janus head. It can be understood as a kind of continuation of the will to will, thus as an extreme formation of being. At the same time, however, it is a first form of *Ereignis* itself."[38]

If the *Gestell* plays this role of the go- and in-between for the philosophemes of the two (ex)changes—between, again, essence and essence, beings and beings, God and god, man and *Dasein*, language and language, and being and being—then our inquiry should borrow from it its power of *machination* and *liberation*. Constructing our approach (the Heidegger change) as a *writing-Gestell* will therefore enable us to attempt to precisely account for the changes in Heidegger's thought.

Heidegger and the Others

Yet what does insisting on the change in Heidegger's oeuvre, you ask me, really at bottom change? Perhaps nothing, perhaps everything. My ambition with this inquiry is at once modest and inordinate: I believe it is possible to assert that *until now, philosophers have merely paralyzed Heidegger's thought in an immobile apparatus by seeking, above all, to identify it.*

To identify means both *to recognize*—like when a naturalist recognizes plants or mineral samples—and *to consider something identical, to assimilate it*. I permit myself to place, under the classificatory heading of the first sense, all the attempts at a *periodization* of Heidegger's work—those analyses that aim to date, situate, and fix the modifications, displacements, evolutions, or ruptures constituting the living tissue of his thought. Those asking where and when should the turning (*Kehre*) be located?, what mutations does *aletheia* undergo?, does the question of being truly get abandoned in the last texts?, but without precisely relating these transformations to Heidegger's understanding of transformation itself.[39]

Secondly, I also include within this first sense those essays claiming an *ontologico-political* periodization, all of which intend to reveal, *right on the philosophemes themselves*, Heidegger's involvement with Nazism, and to determine through that its duration and significance but without taking account of the fundamental role of the triad.[40]

I consider last, under the heading of the second meaning of recognition, analyses that aspire to make Heidegger look like a thinker of the identical. Heidegger's thinking, even though it has difference at its core, supposedly lacks the other, and lacks it for not making it, exactly and explicitly, its decisive question. This is the powerful—ethical *and* metaphysical—objection that his most eminent readers will address to him in different ways during the second half of the twentieth century; his thought will for this reason only be for them, at bottom, a *supplementary version of metaphysics*.

Exploring the motif of change in Heidegger's oeuvre, following, that is, its multiple migratory and metamorphic turns as well as the destiny of the triad *Wandel, Wandlung, and Verwandlung,* should allow us to discover (counter to all these identifications), first, that it is impossible to *immobilize the evolutions of his thought*, and, second, that *a question concerning the other* is very much in evidence in it—an other irreducible to the same but irreducible as well to absolute alterity, the Other so fecund in Levinas's thinking. If there is something other in Heidegger, it is something other than the Other. *The phenomenon of this other alterity should be sought in the tight articulation uniting change and difference.*

So as to discover this other, I invite you to *have an experience of and with Heidegger.* "To undergo an experience with something," Heidegger writes, "be it a person, a thing, or a god, means that this experience befalls us, strikes us, comes over us, overwhelms us, and transforms us [*daß es un widerfährt, daß es un trifft, über uns kommt, uns umwirft und verwandelt*]."[41]

I invite you, therefore, to see just how Heidegger metamorphoses and turns us upside down, and at the same time to take measure of what a migration and a metamorphosis in philosophy can be.

READING HEIDEGGER CHANGING

But how are we going to read Heidegger *changing*? How are we going to traverse the densities of his thought, respecting its constant molting while not dividing it into rigid stages? My proposal is that the steps of our itinerary be situated in the paradoxical space opened by *two great changes that happened in Heidegger's thinking of change.*

First, the change that happened to the very lexicon of change, and second, the change in his understanding of the origin of change.

Change of lexicon. I said earlier that it is possible to see *W, W, & V* at work in all of Heidegger's books and lecture courses. But this is not exactly true: one work, *Being and Time*, is an exception to the rule, the triad being found nowhere in it. The existential analytic knows nothing of *Wandeln, Wandlung,* or *Verwandlung*; only *Modifikationen* (modifications). The vocabulary of modification is in fact constantly present in *Being and Time*, with the change in the lexicon of change taking place immediately after its 1927 publication. Beginning with "What Is Metaphysics?" there is effectively a transfer of power from *Modifikation* to *W, W, & V*. We should therefore attempt to determine exactly what the difference separating *modification* from *migration* and *metamorphosis* is.

Change in the understanding of change. In the lecture entitled *The End of Philosophy and The Task of Thinking*, Heidegger confides that he had previously regarded the commencement of the metaphysical tradition as proceeding from a "transformation of the essence of truth" (*Wesenswandel der Wahrheit*). He had therefore long perceived a coincidence between the forgetting of being and the change or mutation of the essence of truth, those founders of metaphysics—or the first (ex)change.

Now it is to this conception that philosophy returns, to close: "[W]e must acknowledge," he declares, "the fact that ἀλήθεια, unconcealment in the sense of opening of presence, was originally only [*sogleich und nur*] experienced as *orthotes*, as the correctness of representations and statements. But then the assertion about the essential transformation of truth, that is, from unconcealment to correctness, is untenable. Instead we must say: *Aletheia*, as opening of presence and presencing in thinking and saying, originally comes under the perspective of *homoiosis* and *adaequatio*, that is, the perspective of adequation in the sense of the correspondence of representing with what is present."[42] There would not be a *mutation princeps* of the essence of truth, since being and truth are from the outset given only in their withdrawal. We see that this new consideration, far from leading Heidegger to expulse change from the sphere of the origin, allowed him, on the contrary, to envisage the retreat of being itself as a power of originary change. *As if it must be supposed that being has an originary aptitude for giving change.*

So as to envisage these changes, I will scramble chronological order by taking as my point of departure Heidegger's reversal of his views on the subject of originary change, and by keeping for the end an analysis of modification in *Being and Time*.

The inquiry will unfold through three principal moments, entitled *Metamorphoses and Migrations of*

Metaphysics, The New Ontological Exchange, and *At Last—Modification.* From one exchange to the other, we will let ourselves be guided and diverted, transformed and disoriented by the fantastic caprices of the point of suture and rupture between (ex)change and (ex)change.

*Burrowed away in our writing-*Gestell, *we will ask ourselves what changing can mean in the epoch when epochal changes mean nothing anymore.*

We will ask ourselves what transformation and transformability mean when history is over.

The Heidegger change: Onward! It is decided!

Part I

Metamorphoses and Migrations of Metaphysics

In the west, philosophy has been reigning [*waltet*] and transforming itself [*wandelt sich*] since the sixth century B.C.

—Heidegger, *The Principle of Reason*

Change at the Beginning

It all starts with a change. The foundational event of metaphysics is, indeed, a *mutation*. A "change of the essence of truth" [*Wandel des Wesens der Wahrheit*] comes to pass.[1] Plato, that is, brings about "a transformation in the essence of truth."[2] "Truth becomes ὀρθότης, the correctness of apprehending and asserting,"[3] and "ἰδέα gains dominance over ἀλήθεια," the latter coming "under the yoke [*unter das Joch*]" of it.[4] *With replacement the inaugural force, the exchange takes place.*

In this turn—or revolution—of the first (ex) change, change is immobilized; *essence molts into an immutable instance.* So goes the organization of the economy of the confusion (*Verwechslung*) of being (*Sein*) and beingness (*Seiendheit*). This ontological fixity of substitution—"being as immutability" [*Sein als Unwandelbarkeit*]—which is necessarily accompanied by a blindness to the ontological dignity of substitution,

31

constitutes for Heidegger the *form* and *guiding idea* of metaphysics.

Never stopping, this form *changes forms*; not stopping, the guiding idea *changes place*. The history of metaphysics is a long metamorphosis and migration of the immutable. According to a paradox that can only be apparent, *the occlusion of the metabolic origin of metaphysics decides the metamorphic and migratory structure of metaphysics*. The history of philosophy is very much that of a transformation (*Wandlung*).

In *What is Called Thinking?* Heidegger states that "it remains obscure how the shaping of the essence [*Wesensprägung*] of traditional thinking takes place [*ereignet*]."[5] Nonetheless, he continues, "the essential nature of thinking, the essential origin of thinking, the essential possibilities of thinking that are comprehended in that origin—they are all strange to us, and by that very fact are what gives us . . . thought before all else and always."[6]

I invite you to consider the impossible possibility of *grasping hold of the living tissue of metaphysics in the course of its taking* . . . its *taking form*—Heidegger in fact always characterizes metaphysics as either a form (*Form*) or a figure (*Gestalt*)—and its *taking a direction*: Heidegger also always in effect characterizes metaphysics as a *pathway* [*Weg*]. We will contemplate the build of the solidarity between the re-formation and displacement of metaphysics through asking ourselves exactly what makes possible the at once *morphological* and *topographical* perspective through which Heidegger views the tradition.

The Double Process of Schematization

It is impossible to envisage the first change and the transformations proceeding from it without interrogating the conditions of *visibility* of the structural whole of metaphysics. How can the articulation of the migratory and metamorphic, the conjunction of form and pathway soldered together in(to) the tradition, *appear*? It is imperative for you, who refuse to regard the reduction of "the tradition" and consequently its *Destruktion* as self-evident operations, that these questions be posed.

What matters is to show that *the appearance of the structure of metaphysics is the result of a double—archi- and ultra-philosophical—process of schematization that sews and tears the very same tissue.*

The first side of this process, the sewing, is immanent to metaphysics. If there is a *phenomenon of metaphysics* (of its form and meaning), it must be that metaphysics possesses, at the beginning, *the power to make itself appear.* It is in this way that metaphysics is, for Heidegger, an auto-schematizing instance, one that renders into an image its own transformations and peregrinations. From the beginning, the beginning is *(self-)*given to being seen, in a picture. It is to this scenic fascination of the origin that Heidegger devotes his great text "Plato's Doctrine of Truth," which analyzes the emergence of metaphysics as the arising of a *way of seeing*—which is also to say, of *not seeing*—the primordial (ex)change from which it proceeds.

From the cavern to the mountain peak and from the prisoners of the shadows to Zarathustra's silhouette, metaphysics will not stop its auto-imaging until all the *figures* and *displacements of ontological confusion* (*the human form and its migrations, the form of the divine and its migrations, and those of the relation to being, of thought and of philosophical language . . .*) meet their end by being forced to appear before their own eyes, and expose there their *skin*.

But if the far path of this *self-envisaging molting* is to be followed, there must be another gaze, come of late and freed *by* and *from* this chrysalis-play, which pits its own power to imagine against the old scheme and stages *anew* a scene of the *Ereignis* of the beginning. The appearance of the structure of metaphysics is thus the result of a second process of schematization that has been somehow *fitted* to the first, therein also transforming and displacing it. What this double perspective constitutes is precisely the *fantastic* intimacy of Heideggerian thought.

For the entirety of metaphysics to appear, the other has to be given with the same and the uncanny included (*eingerückt*) in the familiar—the basic definition Heidegger gives of the *Ein-bilden* of "imagining" in "Poetically Man Dwells." "The genuine image," he says there, "as a sight or spectacle, lets the invisible be seen and so imagines the invisible in something alien to it."[7] The image of the birth of metaphysics is thus always, in a certain way, *another image* at the same time as it is the *image of something other* than metaphysics.

This union of the familiar and the alien alone permits for understanding, in all its complexity, the meaning of "transformation" in the West. On the one hand, in effect, metaphysics appears, in place of the fantastic convergence of the two schemas, as the reworking and revision of one and the same form and the continual reverting to this one same path: metaphysics, writes Heidegger, "remains what it is across its transformations [*durch alle Abwandlungen hindurch bleibt*]." On the other, this transformation (*Wandlung*) names the secret labor of difference—intervals, false starts, and formal, figural, and topical heterogeneities—which *also* constitutes the metabolic resource of the history of being. "If changing [*weschselnde*] fundamental positions of metaphysical thinking develop," Heidegger also writes, "then their manifoldness only confirms the unchanging unity of the underlying determinations of being. However, this unchangingness is only an illusion under whose protection metaphysics occurs as the history of being."[8]

It is through casting this double gaze upon transformation, then, that we will follow the sharp turns of the first change. In departing from the initial event of the change that arose in the essence of truth, I will enter with you into the serpentine windings of philosophical metamorphosis and migration (*W, W, & V*) up to the advent of the change in the direction, the form of meaning, and the form of metaphysics, until that turnaround sets off in the same move the *W, W, & V* of man, being, God, and the rest . . .

As we go, essence will take shape as the place of exchange between the two images. Along our way, this locus of exchange will reveal itself as the secret foyer of the Heideggerian imaginary.

1

The Metabolism
of the Immutable

"We ought not . . . overlook the fact that philosophy from Aristotle to Nietzsche, precisely because
of these changes [transformations/ *Wandlungen*]
throughout their course, has remained the same.
For the transformations [metamorphoses] are the
warranty for the kinship in the same [*denn die
Verwandlungen sind die Bürgschaft für die Ver-
wandschaft im Selben*]."[1]

You suggest that I begin by exposing, in their simultaneity and contemporaneousness, *the turning point
of a first exchange, the emergence of a form,* and *the
trail of a displacement.* These are the three terms of
the taking place of metaphysics, *the three constitutive
instances of the first (ex)change.*

There exists between these instances a *solidarity,* one Heidegger subjects to the morphological and
topographical gaze that has continued to divert so
many of his readers. This gaze shows the unity of
metaphysics to be both the continuity of a form that
gets deformed and reformed *without changing form,*
and the stability of a road that opens out *without
changing direction.* This close articulation of form and
meaning attests to the historical cohesion endowing
upon the entirety of the tradition *the exchange of*

being for beingness—the understanding of essence as immutability.

The Structural Traits of Philosophy

A MOBILE CONFIGURATION

A question (*Frage*), a direction (*Richtung*), an imprint (*Prägung*): these are, enumerated as succinctly as possible, the essential morphological and topographical characteristics of metaphysics.

They take form in being "*in eins mit*"—"at one with"—"each other."[2] In effect, the substitution of beingness—*Seiendheit*—for being forms the form of metaphysics, and determines from the outset its guiding question, or *Leitfrage*. An orienting that strikes and fashions, an imprint, *Prägung*, capable of setting itself running, the first change literally *impresses its movement upon metaphysics*.

So at the beginning, path and direction are confused, the pathway sealed, the type set on its way . . . until the end. In *Contributions to Philosophy*, Heidegger writes: "If we inquire into beings as beings and thus inquire into the being of beings in this starting point [*Ansetzung*] and direction [*Richtung*], then whoever inquires stands in the realm of the question that guides the beginning of Western philosophy and its history up to its end in Nietzsche. Therefore we call this question concerning being (of beings) the guiding question. Its most general form [*ihre allgemeinste Form*] received its imprint [*Prägung*] from Aristotle, as τί τὸ ὄν; what is οὐσία as the beingness of a being? Being here means beingness. This says at the same time that, despite rejection of the species-character, being (as beingness) is always and only meant as the κοινόυ, i.e. what is common and thus common for every being."[3]

A GENERAL IDEA

You see it: *the form of metaphysics in general is intimately linked to the elaboration of generality as form.* Metaphysics is the "determination of essence (*quiddity*) as essentiality of being (ούσία)" and the community of all beings of the same genre.[4] Essence, so changed into formal immobility, sees its own history cast in the form of a form.

The expression "form of metaphyics," then, designates at once the *structure* of the tradition and the *fixed concept* of form immanent to this same tradition. In both cases, form is what perdures, ίδέα. "Ίδειν," Heidegger tells us in "On the Question of Being," is "a word that Plato uses to refer to a looking that catches sight not of that which is changeable and can be perceived by the senses, but of the unchangeable, being, the ίδέα."[5] The "idea" or form of a thing is what is stable and constant in it: *"Das 'Sein' als Unwandelbarkeit"*—" 'being' as immutability."[6] Such is the constant result of the first exchange.

"In accordance with metaphysics," he continues, "all beings, changeable and moved, mobile and mobilized, are represented from the perspective of a 'being that is at rest,' and this even where, as in Hegel and Nietzsche, 'being' (the actuality of the actual) is thought as pure becoming and absolute movement."[7] At rest, then, at its source, "[m]etaphysics is in all its forms [*Gestalten*] and historical stages a unique . . . fate [*einzige Verhängnis*]."[8] Of what does this fate consist? *Contributions* furnishes the following response: "In all variations and secularizations [*in allen Abwandunglen und Verweltlichungen*] of Western metaphysics, one again recognizes [*erkennen*] that being is at the service of beings, even when being appears to be dominating as cause [*das Sein in Dienste des Seienden, auch wenn es als Ursache scheinbar die Herrschaft hat*]."⁹ It is therefore always in the direction of *a servitude that throws off the trail, giving change,* that those particular philosophical thoughts spread out which never cease, "from Anaximander to Nietzsche,"¹⁰ reviving the imprint, solidifying the form (*Form*), and refiguring the figure (*Gestalt*).

"FROM DESCARTES TO HEGEL . . ."

A "RE-FORMULATION"

This being so, the historical change that arises with each new epoch of metaphysics appears a simple "reformulation" (*Unformung*) of the same form. In *Contributions*, a major affirmation of this can be found: "From Descartes to Hegel, a renewed reformulation, but no essential change [*von Descartes bis Hegel, eine erneute Umformung aber kein wesentlicher Wandel*]."¹¹ And then, slightly further down: "What lies between Hegel and Nietzsche has many shapes but is nowhere within the metaphysical in any originary sense—not even Kierkegaard [*was zwischen Hegel und Nietzsche liegt ist vielgestaltig, nirgends ursprünglich im Metaphysische, auch Kierkegaard nicht*]."¹²

"No essential change" should here be understood to mean "no change in essence." Each philosophy, once again, is a simple reformulation of the preceding. The verb *umformen* signifies "to give a new form [*eine andere Form geben*]," "to change in form [*in der Form verändern, umändern*]," or "to formulate otherwise [*anders formulieren*]." Yet the *Unformungen* or *reformulations* of metaphysics in effect change it without affecting it, reform it even as they confirm it. *W, W, & V* thus designate here a metamorphosis and migration that brings about an identity instead of altering it.

A DISPLACEMENT

Each epoch of metaphysics makes its appearance, then, as a *transformation* but also as a *displacement in(to) the identical* of the preceding one. Every new epoch, Heidegger in fact says, is a "displacement [*Verlagerung*] of the structure of essence [*Wesensfüge*] of the preceding [*vormalige*]."[13] So that in the same way the form of metaphysics depends on the metaphysical concept of form, the route of metaphysics depends on the metaphysical conception of a "change of location [*Ortwechsel*]."

The wealth of meanings of Aristotlelian μεταβολή finds itself reduced in the epoch of modernity to a single one of its modalities: local movement: φορά. The very mobility of the concept of mobility is thereby lost. "Today, with the predominance of the mechanistic thinking of the modern sciences," Heidegger declares, "we are inclined both to hold that the basic form of movement is movedness in the sense of motion [*Forthebung*] from one position in space to another; and then to 'explain' everything in terms of it. That kind of movedness—κίνησις κατὰ τόπον, movedness in terms of place or location—is for Aristotle only *one* kind [*Art*] of movedness among others, but it in no way counts *as movement pure and simple*."[14] Modernity carries out *the reduction of the metabolic to the phoronomic*. Henceforth movement is understood on the basis of the mover, which is in turn known as what provides the energy required for a displacement, that is a change of place." Displacement, change of place (*Ortwechsel*), transportation from location to location, change of position (*Lageänderung*) henceforward, then, appear to be original, veritable forms of movement. This restriction occludes the metabolism of μεταβολή and restrains the movement of its different identity.[15]

What must nonetheless be seen is that this transformation (*Wandlung*) of the concepts of movement and change is, in reality, already prepared within Aristotle's philosophy itself. In *Contributions*, Heidegger affirms that the impoverishment and decline of μεταβολή into φορά (which the Greeks nevertheless regard as something quite different from rectilinear trajectory) constitutes "the kernel of Aristotle's ontology [*der Kern der "Ontologie" des Aristotles*]."[16] The change (*Wandlung*) of change (μεταβολή) never properly commenced. *It started at the beginning*

This can even be discerned in the Presocratics. In *The Basic Concepts of Ancient Philosophy*, Heidegger shows that the pre-Socratic understanding of change (*Wandel*) as "generation and corruption [*Enstehen und Vergehen*]" and "mixing and separating [*Mischung und Entmischung*]" is already inhabited by an "ontological tendency [*ontologische Tendanz*]" which makes it so that change's "characteristics of being [*Seinscharakteristik*] . . . cannot be thought as change." Notions of the "multiform [*mannigfaltig*]" and "self-changing [*sichwandelnder*]" are at the very outset distanced from every discourse on "unity [*Einheit*], uniqueness [*Einzigkeit*], wholeness [*Ganzheit*], and immutability [*Unveränderlichkeit*]."[17]

It is evident, then, that the reduction of the metabolic to the phoronomic (inscribed as it is from the beginning) governs, on the basis of this fundamental "tendency," the traditional understanding of the "displacement" of the structure of essence that takes place in each new epoch of the history of philosophy. The metaphysical conception of metamorphosis as a simple *Umformung*—reformation or reformulation—necessarily works in tandem with metaphysics' conception of migration as a simple passage from one place to another. *W, W, & V*, when they are in charge of expressing the movement of metaphysics, seem then to conjugate the placidness of a "*capax mutationum*" that does not itself change, and the energy of a "mover," an instance that "provides the energy for a displacement, that is a change of place."[18]

The Whole-Form and Its Particular Trajectories

TRANSCENDENCE AS THE STRUCTURAL UNITY OF METAPHYSICS

"Transcendence" is the name Heidegger gives the "immutable" articulation of the mutable and the mover, of the form and meaning of metaphysics. Transcendence indeed appears as "the inner form of metaphysics [*die innere Form der Metaphysik*],"[19] which remains invariable despite its reformulations. Yet transcendence is at the same time a *migration*, it *leads* and *passes toward*. "Transcendence," Heidegger writes, "refers to the relation proceeding from beings and passing over to *being*, and which transpires between the two [*die hinübergehende Beziehung zwischen beiden*]. At the same time, however, transcendence refers to the relation leading from changeable beings [*verändlichen Seindes*] to an *entity that is at rest* [*ruhenden Seienden*]."[20]

This analysis of transcendence as the solidarity between a form and displacement which neither deform nor displace the substitution from which they proceed will lead Heidegger to specify that the very meaning of this substitution is *structure*. It is in this sense that he will speak of "*the ontotheological structure of metaphysics.*" The morphological-topographical gaze has for its task "turn[ing] our thought to the essential origin of the onto-theological structure of all metaphysics (*die Wesenherkunft der ontotheologischen Struktur aller Metaphysik*),"[21] and this essential origin is, precisely, the inaugural exchange of being for beingness: "Metaphysics is in a twofold and yet unitary manner, the truth of beings in their universality and in the highest being. According to its essence, metaphysics is at the same time both ontology . . . and theology."[22]

Elaborating, Heidegger specifies that "[t]his ontotheological essence of philosophy proper . . . must indeed be grounded in the way in which the ὄν opens up in it, namely as ὄν. Thus the theological character of ontology is not merely due to the fact that Greek metaphysics was taken up and transformed [*umgebildet*] by the ecclesiastic theology of Christianity. Rather it is due to the manner in which beings as beings have revealed themselves from early on."[23] Hence the upheaval producing the sudden appearance of Christianity is for Heidegger merely the reformulation (*Umformung*) and phoronomic displacement of the Greek spiritual universe. *No historical innovation is susceptible to disorganize the ontotheological structure.* Right at the start, "beings enter philosophy" as "the deity enters"[24] too, and *there they stay*. Whether Greek or Christian, the common source of ontology and theology fixes itself in place, forming thereby, but without any essential upset, "the twofold character [*Zweigestaltung*]" and guiding thread (*Leitfade*) of metaphysics.[25]

"THE FUNDAMENTAL METAPHYSICAL POSITIONS"

Just what, then, is a particular epoch of metaphysics? How is the general movement of transformation economized in it? Responding to these questions, Heidegger tells us, requires that we account for how "the meaning is changing at any particular time and to how the meaning in history becomes fixed at any particular time [*inwiefern jeweils die Bedeutung sich wandelt und sich jeweils geschichtlich festliegt*]."[26] Each epoch of the tradition constitutes a "fundamental metaphysical position [*metaphysische Grundstellung*]" that corresponds to "a particular interpretation of beings [*eine bestimmte Auslegung Seienden*]" providing the principle or "ground of its essential shape [*Wesensgestalt*]."[27] This principle "comprehensively governs all decisions distinctive of the age."[28]

The "essential shape" of an epoch consists of four basic elements. "What is essential to a fundamental metaphysical position," Heidegger writes, "embraces [*umfaßt*]

1. The manner and way in which man is man, that is, himself [*die Art und Weise, wie der Mensche Mensch und dh. er selbst ist*]: the essential nature of selfhood [*die Wesensart der Selbstheit*]. . . .

2. The essential interpretation of the being of beings.

3. The essential projection of truth [*den Wesensentwurf der Wahrheit*].

4. The sense in which, in any given instance, "man is the measure" [*Maß ist*]

None of the essential moments of the fundamental metaphysical position can be understood apart from the others [*läßt sich abgesondert von den anderen begreifen*]. Each, by itself, indicates the totality."[29]

What is decided in each epoch of metaphysics is: *the manner of being of man; the concept of being*, namely the particular *way* being is understood in terms of beings; as a consequence, *the essence of truth* sustaining this understanding; and, finally, the *measure, sense*, or *orientation* of this truth. Every fundamental metaphysical position thus in itself represents a change of man and of the relation to being, a change as well in the relation to transcendence, beings in general, and God, and also an alteration of the relation to thought and the determination of the essence of philosophy.

Change—and Change

THE SAME, "ESSENTIALLY TRANSFORMED"

So if it is true that metaphysics is a unique sense, a form, an inevitability, and a singular historical cohesion, and if it true as well that every fundamental philosophical position reproduces and guarantees the essential structure of philosophy, why speak of transformation (*Wandlung*)?

Just as you ask this question, you notice a certain trembling pass through *W, W, & V*. The triad expresses, in effect, the reformulation and maintenance of metaphysical direction even as it sends this into the swerve of a radical mutation. Heidegger affirms this in saying that "[t]he history of being is . . . not some rolling-on series of transformations of a detached, self-subsistent being [*kein abrollender Verlauf von Verwandlungen eines losgelöst für sich bestehenden Seins*]."[30] Historical metamorphoses are not the avatars of one substantial form. "All great and genuine philosophy," a passage in *The Fundamental Concepts of Metaphysics* reads, "moves within the limited sphere of a few questions which appear to common sense as perennially the same, although in fact they are necessarily different [*anders*] in every instance of philosophizing. Different not in any merely external sense, but rather in such a way that the selfsame [*das Selbe*] is in each case essentially transformed [*verwandelt*] once more. Only in such transformation [*Verwandlung*] does philosophy possess its genuine selfsameness. This transformation lends a properly primordial historicity to the occurrence of the history of philosophizing."[31] Transformation into the identical at the same time opens the identical to its alterity. But then what, exactly, is the meaning and true import of the triad of change?

SOME METAMORPHOSES AND MIGRATIONS

What must be seen is that the gaze through which Heidegger views the structural whole of metaphysics splits, so that he is *seeing double.*

"MOVING SIDEWALKS"

On one side, Heidegger has a vision of the continuous "shrouding" of the meaning of being, to the profit of beingness: particular philosophies are only the byways of one and the same forgetting. Hence, for example, "[t]he metaphysical foundation of Descartes' position is taken over [*getragen*] from Platonic-Aristotelian metaphysics. Despite its new beginning, it attends to the very same question: what is being? That this question is not explicitly posed in Descartes' *Meditations* only goes to prove how essentially the fundamental position determines a transformation in the answer to it [*abgewandelte Antwort*]. It is Descartes' interpretation of beings and of truth which first creates the preconditions for the possibility of a theory or metaphysics of knowledge."[32] Metamorphoses and displacements affect only the *responses* that have been provided to the question of being, not the question itself.

Continuing, Heidegger says that "the essential modifications [metamorphoses] of Descartes' fundamental position [*die Verwandlungen der Grundstellung Descartes*] which have been achieved by German thinking since Leibniz in no way overcome this fundamental position. They only expand its metaphysical scope and establish the preconditions of the nineteenth century—still the most obscure of all the centuries up to now. They indirectly reinforce Descartes' fundamental position in a form [*Form*] that is scarcely recognizable [*fast unkenntlich*], yet not, on that account, any the less real [*aber deshalb nicht weniger wirklich*]."[33] Descartes' successors, just as Descartes himself did in his era, metamorphose the fundamental position they inherit so that it is no longer recognizable—*despite its not having essentially changed.*

This change (of the) immutable is exactly what authorizes Heidegger to draw up so frequently his

lists of the metamorphoses and migrations of metaphysics, those brief inventories which summarize in
a mere few lines twenty centuries' worth of the history of philosophy.[34] In reading these, did you ever
recall Proust's characterization of Flaubert's style as
a "moving sidewalk"?[35] Have you never realized that
Heidegger likewise *scrolls* through historical change?
I will limit myself to just one example of this, which
is the exposition, in *Contributions*, of the way different philosophers "interpret" essence as "beingness"
but without thereby changing its sense:

> Oriented by this mindfulness, we can initially
> discuss the historical consequence of the
> concepts of essence, as they appear within
> the history of the guiding question, as guid-
> ing threads for the questions of beingness:
>
> 1. οὐσία as ἰδέα
>
> 2. οὐσία in the Aristotelian discussion in
>   Metaphysics ZHΘ
>
> 3. the *essentia* of the Middle Ages
>
> 4. *possibilitas* in Leibniz (Leibniz seminars)
>
> 5. the "condition of possibility" in Kant, the
>   transcendental concept of essence
>
> 6. the dialectical-absolute idealistic concept
>   of essence in Hegel."[36]

Such "guiding threads," through *following* closely a
certain understanding of essence, enable the essential
to be unwound by displaying, *on the same sidewalk*,
the continuous movement of a metamorphosis and
migration of thought.

THE OTHER QUESTION

The other vision opened up by Heidegger nonetheless and *at the same time* allows these transformations of the same to be considered *otherwise* than as simple additions to it. Aristotle, for instance, does not complete Parmenides' thought in bringing out new significations of being. *He actually changes the question.* As Heidegger asks, "does Aristotle deny and disavow the first decisive truth of philosophy as expressed by Parmenides? No. He does not renounce it, but rather first truly comprehends it. He assists this truth in becoming a truly philosophical truth, that is, an actual question. . . . Those who believe that Aristotle merely added other meanings onto a meaning of being are clinging to appearances. It is a matter not just of embellishment but of a *transformation* of the entire question [*eine Verwandlung der ganzen Frage*]: the question about ὄν as ἕν comes into sharp focus here for the first time [*das Nicht-seiende*]. . . . Plato attained the insight that nonbeing [*Unseinde*], the false, the evil, the transitory—hence unbeing—also is. But the sense of being thereby had to shift [*so mußte sich der Sinn des Seins wandeln*]."[37]

And apropos Descartes and the change of meaning (*Bedeutungswandel*) the concepts of subject and object are forced to undergo with him, Heidegger states that "this reversal of the meanings [*Umkehrung der Bedeutungen*] of the words *subjectum* and *objectum* is no mere affair of usage; it is a radical change of *Dasein* [*Grundstürzender Wandel des Daseins*], i.e. the illumination [*Lichtung*] of the being of what is on the basis of the mathematical. *It is a stretch of the way of history* [*Geschichte*] *necessarily hidden from the naked eye*, a history which always concerns the openness [*Offenbarkeit*] of being—or nothing at all."[38]

Each epoch of metaphysics cannot, therefore, consent to be apprehended only as a reformation or reformulation of one same form or a reversal of course that stays the (same) course, since it is also a rupture and radical overturning of this logic of reorganization itself. *Each epoch is at once the maintenance of a roadblock and a way through opened by its being run.* In each one, essence essentializes—immobilizes some more—its immutability; but in so doing, it is paradoxically deployed as what, in truth, it is: *changing.*

This double vision shows that it is only possible to account for the structure of metaphysics, as I asserted at the outset, when it is surpassed. Heidegger, moreover, says so overtly: "Why and to what extent the selfhood of man, the concept of being, the essence of truth, and the manner of standard giving determine in advance a fundamental metaphysical position, sustain metaphysics as such, and make it the articulation of beings themselves, are questions that cannot be asked by and through metaphysics."[39]

Metaphysics truly has exhausted these forms and trails. It "is completed [*vollendet*]. Which means: it has gone through the sphere of prefigured possibilities [*das will sagen: sie hat den Umkreis der vorgezeichneten Möglichkeiten absgeschritten*]."[40] So that its form, like its route, becomes *visible.*

This brings us, though, back to the same difficulty as before. In effect, form "is 'metaphysical power,'"[41] and would seem for that reason to be meaningful only from within the limits of metaphysics. So would it, in that case, even be possible to envisage metaphysics as a form without remaining prisoner to this same form?

Not unless taking account of the metamorphic and migratory structure of metaphysics liberates both *formal resources that no longer belong to the hylemorphic heritage and other, metabolic resources not coming from its sole φορά. Such a nonmetaphysical surplus of form and migration would alone allow metaphysics to be envisaged as a form and migration.*

You now see, I think, how the triad of W, W, & V functions as a historical interchange, one capable of carrying out, in the shadows and unostentatiously—the same words, always—the conversion of two guises of change that structure: the structure, and its excess.

2

The Mound of Visions*

Plato Averts His Gaze

What remains unsaid [*was ungesagt bleibt*] in Plato's thinking is a turnaround [*Wendung*] in what determines the essence of truth. The fact that this turnaround does take place, what it consists in, and what gets grounded through the change of the essence of truth [*was durch diesen Wandel des Wesens der Warheit begründet wird*]—all of that can be clarified by an interpretation of the allegory of the cave.

—*Plato's Doctrine of Truth*[1]

The crossing of the two (ex)changes is where I am now inviting you to proceed—the very place where the commencement and overcoming of metaphysics appear together, in a startling contemporaneousness.

Come, let me take you to this peak, this rise in the exposition. Come to the place where being juts up in its structure, where it lets itself be seen. Come with me to the mound of visions, to the fantastic point where "a change takes place [ein Wandel ereignet]*."*[2]

As we go, remember this: what I call the fantastic is the visibility of being granted by the latter's molting,

---

La Butte aux Visions (1952) is the title of a painting by Jean Dubuffet.

*the visibility of the molt of being through which being
is revealed to be nothing—but its mutability.*

Come with me to the mound of (ex)change. "The
change [*Wandel*] is brought about in the determination
of the being of beings as . . . ἰδέα."[3] We will enter the
movement of the "turnaround" of truth, which leads
to the origin of the exchange, to the first ontological—metamorphic and migratory—transaction, that
which creates the form and direction of philosophy.
*Follow me into the cave, which has been fantastically
reopened by the Heidegger change.*

The myth or allegory of the cave opens up for
us a glimpse of "the change of the essence of truth":
"henceforth, the essence of truth does not, as the
essence of unhiddenness [*Unverborgenheit*], unfold
from its proper and essential fullness, but rather
shifts to the essence of the ἰδέα. The essence of truth
gives up its fundamental trait of unhiddenness."[4]

*This myth is the primal scene of the exchange
of essences.*

*Come. Glide with me to this point where the
phantasm of historicity plays upon two living pictures.*

"Heidegger's Doctrine of Truth"

THE "CAVE," OR THE GIFT OF DOUBLE VISION

Of the several texts devoted to the question of "the
change of the essence of truth," *Plato's Doctrine of
Truth* is the most fascinating.[5] This text effectively
stages the scene of *an exchange of vision(s) in the
very place of the first ontological exchange. The ultrametaphysical gaze catches metaphysics in the act
of constituting itself into a gaze.* The emergence of
a certain kind of ontological visibility—that of the

idea, the leitmotif of "the myth of the cave"—is thus in turn scrutinized through an imaging agency that does not fall under its jurisdiction. These two gazes encounter each other and exchange in the heart of the change of the essence of truth, and their respective phantasms converge in their very heterochrony, which marks throughout the text the very particular usage Heidegger gives the triad of change. The triad is needed to describe both what takes place *in* the myth of the cave—the change brought about *in* the soul of the prisoners by their *formation* (παιδεία/*Bildung*)—and the change taking place *with* the myth of the cavern, which is the change of the understanding of truth that founds metaphysics. "The 'allegory,'" Heidegger declares, "not only illustrates the essence of education [formation: *Bildung*] but at the same time opens our eyes to a change of the essence of truth [*sondern es öffnet zugleich den Einblick in einem Wesenswandel der 'Wahrheit'*]."[6] The cave allegory, then, is transformed into a strange textual phenomenon, one under a double authority: Plato's, as well as Heidegger's.

Heidegger acknowledges, moreover, that he displaces and changes the subject of the myth. "Plato's assertion," he says, "is clear: The 'allegory of the cave' illustrates the essence of 'education' [*Bildung*]. By contrast, the interpretation of the 'allegory' that we are now going to attempt means to point out the Platonic 'doctrine' of truth. Are we not then burdening the 'allegory' with something foreign to it [*wird so dem 'Gleichnis' nicht etwas Fremdes aufgebürtet*]? The interpretation threatens to degenerate into a reinterpretation that does violence to the text. Let this appearance stand [*mag dies so scheinen*] until we have confirmed our insight that Plato's thinking subjects itself to a transformation in the essence of truth [*bis sich die Einsicht gefestigt hat daß Platons Denken sich einem Wandel des Wesens der Wahrheit unterwirft*]."[7]

We should, then, simultaneously track both the movement of *the formation of the soul in(to) the truth*, which "metamorphoses" it, and the movement of *the formation of truth into its new form*, which "transforms" truth. Their articulation together is rendered possible by a fantastic convergence of gazes. Or, more exactly, by a fantastic convergence of the turning [*détour*] of these gazes. In effect, Heidegger catches Plato looking away at the very moment he reveals that access to truth rests on the possibility of an "averting" or "shifting of the gaze [*Wegwendung des Blickes*]."[8] This averting or "turning away" (*Umwendung*) has a double meaning. It corresponds, first, to the prisoners' need to tear themselves from the shadows in order to contemplate the idea. But it designates as well *a way of not seeing constitutive of metaphysical visibility*: Plato looks away just as he is forming the philosophical gaze. *The fantastic thus emerges here from the way Heidegger imagines Plato shielding his eyes from the change he is staging.* The possibility of this concord of averted gazes is in both cases guaranteed by the unity of the migratory and metamorphic expressed throughout the text by the triad of change. Whether what is at stake is the (ex) change of the soul into and for its truth (Plato) or the (ex)change of truth itself (Heidegger), *W, W, & V* always designate *the conjunction of a change of form and a change of route.*

GENESIS OF FORM/BIRTH OF DISPLACEMENT

Heidegger specifies that what is in question in the cave allegory is only "passages [*Übergangen*]": "the movements it recounts," he says, "are movements of passage [*Übergange*]."[9] The *passage, progress,* or *process* of *Bildung* is both the shaping of a form and the constitution of an access. The passage is in itself and quite literally *meta-physical*—the possibility of going beyond.[10] It is thus through its being figured as a passage that metaphysics receives and gives to itself its proper form: "[t]he 'philosophy' that begins with Plato has . . . the distinguishing mark of what is later called metaphysics. Plato himself concretely illustrates [*anschaulich macht*] the basic outline [*Grundgestalt*] of metaphysics in the story recounted in 'the allegory of the cave.'"[11] And we read, just after this, that "the coining of the word 'metaphysics' is already prefigured in Plato's presentation."[12]

We therefore witness, by (the schematic) virtue of the myth of the cave, the *mutant* and *migratory* coming of a truth announced *in the order of the imprint, figure, and form.*[13] The "change" coincides, in effect, with the emergence of form understood as essence, as, that is, idea (ἰδέα), aspect (εἰδος), or face (*Aussehen*). In general, what comes *once and for all* is the interdependence and solidarity *essence-idea-aspect-figure-configuration-image-picture* that constitutes at once both the meaning of the metaphysical concept of form and the very form of metaphysics. "[T]he way in which form [*Gestalt*], ἰδέα, and being belong together" indeed is, as Heidegger confides to Jünger, "metaphysical power" as such.[14] This figural cohesion of truth at the same time presupposes, as its necessary lining, an understanding of "formation [*Bildung*]" as a "fundamental change in direction [*Unwendung der Grundrichtung*]": "just as the physical eye must accustom itself . . . either to the light or to the dark, so likewise the soul . . . has to accustom itself to the region of beings to which it is exposed.

But this process of getting accustomed requires that
before all else the soul in its entirety be turned
around [*Umwendung*] as regards the fundamental
direction of its striving, in the same way as the eye
can look comfortably in whatever direction only when
the whole body has first assumed the appropriate
position."[15] Truth, then, also announces itself in the
order of displacement.

(Ex)CHANGE AT THE ORIGIN

We will now enumerate the consequences and decisive results of the change of the essence of truth,
this averting of the gaze or turnaround movement
in whose course essence takes the place of being,
throwing off the trail and giving change.

THE CHANGE OF BEING INTO ITS ESSENCE AS
ORIGIN OF BEINGNESS

"The movement of passage from one place to the
other," as Heidegger writes, "consists in the process
whereby the gaze becomes more correct. Everything depends on the ὀρθότης, the correctness of
the gaze. . . . What results from this conforming of
apprehension, as an ἰδεῖν, to the ἰδέα, is a ὁμοίωσις,
an agreement of the act of knowing with the thing
itself."[16] This transformation of truth into correctness
presupposes that "something can appear in its whatness and thus be present in its constancy."[17] This
permanence is the essence, or form, of the thing,
what in it is capable of being presented: "the visible form [*Aussehen*] has in addition something of
a 'stepping forth' whereby a thing presents itself."[18]
Henceforth, *the being of beings* will be conceived

as precisely this "self-evidence" of the aspect. *The first (ex)change is the emergence of the visibility of being.*

THE CHANGE OF THE ESSENCE OF *DASEIN* AS ORIGIN OF MAN

The emergence of the visibility of being corresponds to the emergence of the visibility of man. From its beginning, "[c]oncern with human being and with the position of humans amidst beings entirely dominates metaphysics."[19] If formation and education in the truth involve "transporting man toward a turning around of his whole being [*das Geleit zur Umwendung des ganzen Menschen in seinem Wesen*],"[20] then man must be understood not as pre-existing this formation but as *being formed in and with it. The change of the essence of truth makes the essence of man appear. Man starts with metaphysics.* "The beginning of metaphysics in the thought of Plato," Heidegger states, "is at the same time the beginning of 'humanism.' Here the word must be thought in its essence and therefore in its broadest sense. In that regard 'humanism' means the process that is implicated in the beginning, in the unfolding, and in the end of metaphysics, whereby human beings, in differing respects but always deliberately, move into a central place among beings. . . . Here 'human being' sometimes means humanity or humankind, sometimes the individual or the community, and sometimes the people [*das Volk*] or a group of peoples. What is always at stake is this: to take 'human beings,' who within the sphere of a fundamental, metaphysically established system of beings are defined as *animal rationale,* and to lead them, within that sphere, to the liberation of their possibilities, to the certitude of their destiny, and to the securing of their 'life.'"[21] *The first (ex)change marks in this way the birth of the first man.*

THE CHANGE OF PHENOMENA AS ORIGIN OF BEINGS

In the course of the formation, "everything that has been heretofore manifest to human beings, as well as the way it gets manifested, gets transformed [*anders werden*]."[22] "Whatever has been unhidden to human beings at any given time, as well as the manner of its unhiddenness, has to be transformed."[23] Phenomena are changed (*W, W, & V*) into beings (*Seiendes*). From then on, what will be revealed to the gaze are beings, whose provenance—that is, being—must necessarily, *in truth*, be interrogated. Beings as beings thus make, along again with the visibility of being and the origin of man, their entrance. *The first (ex) change makes it possible for the question of beings (in their being) to arise.*

THE CHANGE OF THINKING AS ORIGIN OF PHILOSOPHY

This becoming other of "unveiledness" marks the "beginning [*Beginn*]" of metaphysics.[24] "Outside the cave σοφία is φιλοσοφία. The Greek language already knew the word before the time of Plato and used it in general to name the predilection for correct astuteness. Plato first appropriated the word as a name for the specific astuteness about beings that at the same time defines the being of beings as idea. Since Plato, thinking about the being of beings has become . . . 'philosophy' "because it is a matter of gazing up at the ideas."[25] The change (*Wandel*) that arose with Plato marks the beginnings of "the history of metaphysics, which in Nietzsche's thinking has entered upon its unconditioned fulfillment."[26] *From the outset, the first (ex)change changes philosophy into the tradition.*

THE CHANGE OF GOD

The essential exchange of ἰδέα for being determines in the same move *the coming of god*. A certain form of god arrives (*ereignet*), in effect, with metaphysics. "Ever since being got interpreted as ἰδέα," affirms Heidegger, "thinking about the being of beings has been metaphysical, and metaphysics has been theological. In this case theology means the interpretation of the 'cause' of beings as God and the transferring of being onto this cause, which contains being in itself and dispenses being from out of itself, because it is the being-est of beings."[27]

In the course on *Parmenides*, Heidegger insists on the essential transformation (*wesentliche Wandlung*) the Roman understanding of truth represents in relation to the understanding of ἀλήθεια Plato founds. This mutation is nothing less than the *change (Wandel) of god*. The Christian God is the "Lord [*Herr*]" whose "figure [*Gestalt*]" accords with truth understood as "justice."[28] But this "transformation" only *prolongs* the Greek event of the first change. In effect, "the long Christianization of god [*die lange Verchristlichung des Gottes*]" is prepared with *the change of the essence of truth that occurs at the birth of philosophy*. The Christian God is only ever inscribed in "the origin of transcendence in its various shapings [*der Transzendenz in ihren verschiedenen Gestalten*]," which was rendered possible by the first change.[29] Transcendence is the " 'beyond' [of] those things that are experienced,"[30] and this "beyond" is, starting from Plato, nothing other than the ensemble of ideas that "are the suprasensible."[31] "And," Heidegger continues, "highest in the region of the suprasensible is that idea which, as the idea of all ideas, remains the cause of the subsistence and the appearing of all beings. Because this 'idea' is thereby the cause of everything, it is also the 'idea' that is called 'the good.' This highest and first cause is named by Plato and correspondingly by Aristotle το θειον, the divine."[32] Yet from the divine understood as the Good to the Christian God, there are, here again, only "reformulations" but "no essential change." *The first (ex)change is the condition of the immutable character of the gods of metaphysics.*

CHANGE IN SPEECH AS THE ORIGIN OF LATIN-GREEK

Henceforth, metaphysics will speak *its own* language. Between Greek ὁμοίωσις and Latin *adaequatio*, a bastardization may occur, but no decisive change. The understanding of truth as correspondence to its object, as exactness and correctness, governs the philosophical tradition in it entirety. Heidegger remarks that "the essence of truth as the correctness of both representation and assertion becomes normative for the whole of Western thinking. . . . For medieval Scholasticism, Thomas Aquinas's thesis holds good: *veritae proprie invenitur in intellectu humano vel divino* (*Quaestiones de Veritate, quaestio I, articulus 4, responsio*): 'Truth is properly encountered in the human or in the divine intellect.' The intellect is where truth has its essential locus. In this text truth is no longer ἀλήθεια but ὁμοίωσις (*adaequatio*)."[33] This idiomatic (ex)change is not a structural overturning. *The first change destines philosophy to speak but one language.*

Miming *Bildung*

In considering with me these consequences of the first (ex)change, you are at the same time beginning to understanding that *neither being nor beings, neither man nor god and not even ἀλήθεια exist prior to their change. The enigma of change stems from its originarity, from the fact that nothing precedes it, above all not (ex)change. The triad of W, W, & V enables Heidegger to express the contemporaneousness of the arising of what changes and the very movement of its change; the coincidence, that is, of exchangeability and the event* (Ereignis) *of exchange. Only through the veil of a mutation can there be a reading of pure unveiledness, of the pure possibility (or phantasm) of the mutation of unveiledness.*

The change invents what it changes. And it is just this that attests, in the allegory as Heidegger rereads it, to the very movement of formation, of *Bildung*. It is in effect through a sort of modeless mimeticism that *Bildung* conjures up what it occludes—through an imitation that neither perceives nor knows, in the economy of its proper mutability, the historical change from which it proceeds. Heidegger settles his gaze upon the locus of this fantastic correspondence between the metabolism of *Bildung* and the historical transformation that it makes appear without the latter realizing it.

When *Bildung* makes its first appearance in the allegory, it does so as a change of place. "Παιδεια," writes Heidegger, "means turning around the whole human being. It means removing human beings from the region where they first encounter things and transferring and accustoming them to another realm where beings appear."[34] This definition of *Bildung* as transfer makes fantastically visible, as if in negative, the change of the essence of truth as displacement. "The essence of truth . . . ," Heidegger writes, "is displaced [*verlagert*] to the essence of the ἰδέα,"[35] and "with this transformation of the essence of truth there takes place at the same time a change of the locus of truth [*Wechsel des Ortes der Wahrheit*]."[36] The distance the soul needs to cover to form into the truth is, then, what allows one to envisage, which is to say figure, exactly what its concept occludes: the historical migration of truth.

In the allegory, *Bildung* is also a power of metamorphosis. In fact, the transporting [*acheminement*] of the soul to essence involves the former's *Verwandlung*. "Plato . . . wants to show," we read, "that the essence of παιδεία does not consist in merely pouring knowledge into the unprepared soul as if it were some container held out empty and waiting. On the contrary, real education lays hold of the soul itself and transforms [*verwandelt*] it in its entirety by first of all leading us to the place of our essential being and accustoming us to it."[37] Conveyance to essence is, then, a thoroughly metamorphic process, and this *Verwandlung* allows an essential characteristic of the historical change of truth to be mimetically perceived: truth is only made through displacement; it *takes form*. Everything happens, in that event, as if the change of origin, the *changing of* origin (of origin as such), is itself schematized and brought into form starting with and by way of its occlusion.

It follows that the understanding of essence as idea, although it proceeds from the change of the essence of truth, appears to be the *cause* of this change.

It is just this that explains why one can never exactly know if Plato's philosophy *inherits* the change or instead *provokes* it. On the one hand, Heidegger

declares, "an essential relation holds between 'education' [formation, *Bildung*] and 'truth'" which "consists in the fact that the essence of truth and the
sort of transformation it undergoes here first make
possible 'education' in its basic structures."[38] We
are also later told that "Plato's thinking follows the
change in the essence of truth [*folgt dem Wandel
des Wesens der Wahrheit*]."[39] Again: "Whatever happens with historical human beings always derives
from a decision about the essence of truth that was
taken long ago and is never up to humans alone.
Through this decision, the lines are always already
drawn regarding what, in the light of the established
essence of truth, is sought after and established as
true and likewise what is thrown away and passed
over as untrue."[40] At the same time and on the
other hand, Heidegger affirms that Plato's philosophy is somehow at the origin of the change from
which it proceeds. "[T]he priority of ἰδέα and ἰδεῖν
over ἀλήθεια," he says, "results in a transformation
of the essence of truth."[41] *Plato's elaboration of his
philosophy results from the mutation he accomplishes.*
This strange situation consists in owing an inheri-
tance to a *changing (of the) origin.*

History and Change

TWO VERSIONS OF THE SAME TRANSFORMATION

How can we better define this ontological mimeticism,
which authorizes the two processes of schematization to converge?

On one side—that of the first picture—the schematization at work in the allegory of the cave is
symbolic. The cavern is the image, *Bild,* of the place

where men abide, and "the fire in the cave, which burns above those who dwell there, is the 'image' for the sun."[42] There are, between images and things, correspondences—*Entsprechungen*. The symbolic is, from this first point of view, the *Deutungskraft* or interpretive force of the myth.

On the other side—the second picture—*figuration brings into an image what absolutely exceeds the order of the symbolic*. This is, first, because Plato, as we just saw, does not see what he is in the process of figuring: the change of the essence of truth "remains unformulated [*ungesagt*]" in his thought. Second, and as a consequence, this is also because the retrospective figuration of this change no longer belongs to the order of symbolic idealization.

In order to think the ties between these two figurations and what sees itself, though unformulated and non-unveiled, nonetheless set into form and on its way, it must be recalled that accounting for the first change is only possible starting from *the other change*, which reverses the former's course. The expression "essence of truth" gets its meaning from its inversion (what is also sometimes called its *Kehre*): "the truth of essence." In the note appended to the lecture *On the Essence of Truth*, Heidegger makes this celebrated declaration: "The question of the essence of truth arises from the question of the truth of essence [*Die Frage nach dem Wesen der Wahrheit entspringt aus der Frage nach der Wahrheit des Wesen*]."[43]

Hence the gaze that discerns "the change in the essence of truth" in the Platonic gesture is itself possible only at the cost of a "change in the questioning [*Wandel der Fragens*] that belongs to the overcoming of metaphysics."[44] This change corresponds to "a transformed historical position [*eine*

gewandelte geschichtlichen Grundstellung]," which
reveals, precisely, the truth of essence occluded by
the traditional concept of the essence of truth—no
longer "correspondence" but *freedom* or *errancy*.

These analyses allow us to see with clarity that
the triad of change—*W, W, & V*—*expresses at once
both the change of the essence of truth and the change
of thinking, speaking, and questioning necessitated by
the truth of essence. The same words, then, characterize two events that are indeed structurally linked,
even while they have the opposite meaning:* on one
side, the mutation leading the originary understanding
of ἀλήθεια into the Platonic conception of truth as
adequation (ὁμοίωσις) and correctness (ὀρθότης), and,
on the other, the change of this change, which reveals
the very sense of change to be errancy or "ek-sistent
freedom."[45] Heidegger presents this last change as
a transformation of thinking (the "indication of an
essential connection between truth as correctness
and freedom uproots these preconceptions, granted
of course that we are prepared for a transformation
[*Wandlung*] of thinking"[46]), a transformation of the
relation to being ("the course of the [new] questioning
is intrinsically the path of a thinking that, instead of
furnishing representations and concepts, experiences
and tests itself as a transformation of its relatedness
to being"[47]), and, in a word and last, as a "metamorphosis [*Einverwandlung*] of humanity."[48]

Whether the one process of schematization or
the other, then, it is always *W, W, & V* . . . Yet
why accord such a considerable role to the triad, to
three words having *no particular (neither inaugural
nor terminal) historical status?*

*The fantastic, as I said before, is ever playing
upon two different pictures—the picture of metaphysics, and the wholly other scene—and the historical*

and philosophical neutrality of the triad is just what enables these two pictures to be converted into each other.

In entrusting these three words that have no particular destiny (W, W, & V, once more, are not philosophemes, and therefore do not form an essential link in the conceptual chain of the tradition) with the task of bringing into language, in the least inadequate fashion possible, the great historical turning points of a first (ex)change and the (ex)change of this (ex)change, Heidegger points toward the conceptually and historically depatriated place of the point of convertibility between metaphysics and its other.

This point, where the metamorphosis of metamorphosis or migration of migration is achieved, can only be invested with phantasms, with images of these extra- or hypo-historical processes. The enigma of history, in the double sense of Historie *and* Geschichte, *is the spatial and temporal location of the point of collision between philosophy and what it is not, between metaphysics and its destruction. W, W, & V inscribe in Heidegger's text the possibility of a fantastic margin where, in both the light and the shadows of the philosophical imaginary, the moment of the exchange takes place; the event of the exchange of the inaugural event—the first beginning—and the terminal event, the other beginning. An exchange of visions, an exchange of mutations.*

The fantastic of the visibility of being, then, stems not only from the metaphysical production of its image (of, that is, its essence) but also from the ultrametaphysical arrangement (Einrichtung) *of the image of this image as well.*

What is fantastic is the simultaneously *metaphysical and nonmetaphysical visibility of being.*

W, W, & V: Relief to the Historical

Conceiving the change that arose in the essence of truth as both the movement and result of a historical decision will illumine nothing so long as we do not ask what instance or authority guarantees the ontological convertibility of truth (which is inscribed in its essence) into *another* essence. This convertibility is by no means self-evident. It is not miraculously granted by some secret virtue of ἀλήθεια, through which the latter would render itself exchangeable in letting itself be occluded. How can we even keep to this stage of our inquiry, given that Heidegger will modify his position on this point by leaving his conception of a mutation originally befalling the essence of truth for an understanding of change conceived as the originary withdrawal of being? Permanently sheltering it behind historicality (*Geschichtlichkeit*) is no help. *Historicality would be nothing without the change (W, W, & V) constituting it.*

Heidegger of course recognizes that the formula "change of the essence of truth" designates the movement of historicity and nothing but. He states, in *Parmenides*, that " 'history,' conceived essentially, that is thought in terms of the ground of the essence of being itself, is the change of the essence of truth. It is 'only' this."[49] Moreover, it is almost impossible to pass over without comment another basic declaration of this: "to speak of 'the change of the essence of truth' [*Wandel der Wahrheit*] is admittedly only an expedient [*ein Notbehelf*]; for it is still to speak of truth in an objectifying way [*gegenständlich*] over and against the way it itself comes to presence and history 'is.' "[50]

What must nonetheless be admitted is that this "expedient" formula offers relief to the historicity whose metaphor it merely seems to be. Without the seeming philosophical grisaille of the triad, which, qua *ontico-ontological convertor, alone allows for imagining what something like a historical change could be, historicity would have to call for help. Without the formula and its relief, the historical would go without relief.*

Our inquiry into the triad of change is thus in no way incidental, since it enables us to discover that each of the two scenes at work in *Plato's Doctrine of Truth*—those whose mutual convertibility it ensures—includes in itself *an opening to its other.* Whether the one *W, W, & V* or the other, we find sheltered in the triad the possibility of a welcoming of the uncanny into the self, and this, precisely, is the potential for history. This possibility is *metamorphic and migratory possibility itself:* the changing of form, the taking leave of self. A little myth in history indeed . . .

Genuine images, remember, "are imaginings in a distinctive sense: not mere fancies and illusions but imaginings that are visible inclusions of the alien in the familiar [*als erblickbare Einschlüsse des Fremden in den Anblick der Vertrauen*]."[51]

The triad of change is precisely the imaginary dimension of the historical.

The *Einbildung*, do not forget, is *creative within the ontological order,* and one of the great motifs in Heidegger's thought.[52] In my eyes, it is the greatest of them all. But was it ever so in *his?*

What I am calling fantastic is precisely what cannot be seen through Heidegger's eyes.

First Incision*

Geltung

We have arrived before the astonishing economy of an exchange before exchange and prior to all economy; one prior to money, price, and sex—prior, even, to commerce.

Heideggerian philosophy unceasingly transports us back to this neither archaic, nor classic, nor mythic prior of the prior where everything seems (ex)changed. Where everything that comes comes about only to be exchanged, passing into the strange vestibule that is the first room, the very first, of the house of being.

Neither archaic nor classic nor even mythic, properly speaking, but fantastic. Such would be the image of this originary tendency toward convertibility necessarily accompanying, as its structural sibling, the difference between being and beings.

The fantastic: the locus of originary (ex)change can only be invested with images. The concept falls forever short of it. Because on the one hand, the commencement of metaphysics—the setting into form and on its way of the first (ex)change—coincides with the

---

*"Incision" translates only one of the senses of the French noun *incise* in play here; the term can also convey "phrase," "proposition," and, also of significance, "interpolated clause." The three "incisions" in this book can thus also be thought of as "insertions." —Trans.

vesting of the image as the inaugural event of being (exchanged): idea, essence, face, picture. But also because, on the other, the retrospective apprehension of this investment exceeds and breaches the conceptuality and metamorphic and migratory resources of metaphysics. It no longer belongs to them since it is possible only in the place of their disappearance, a posthumous image that can only touch up the colors of a picture of their birth.

The fantastic: the first change and exchange are themselves only imaginable, scenically possible for thought, at the moment when metaphysics itself is exchanged for its other. When convertibility is economized differently.

Reading Heidegger, then, always comes down to having one's gaze perturbed by two changes, whose difference is always at the same time mysteriously shrouded by the nondifferentiation and gray neutrality of the names of its mobility and pulsing, which are always, in every instance, Wandel, Wandlung, *and* Verwandlung (W, W, & V). *As if it was up to the reader to illumine, in the glow of the triad's own imaginary or "poetico-rational" investments, the epochal stratification of this bloc, and introduce distinctions into it.*

As if it was up to us, then, to you and me, to navigate visually, to cross through this space of the two exchanges, which is continually agitated by a double metamorphic and migratory wave that makes the apparent wisdom and gleam of the differentiating of difference tremble.

Always before, always after: such is the rhythm marking the time of our sojourn with Heidegger. The exchange of essences is archimonetary, archiprecious, archisocial, and archisexual, yet it could not be made out until the end of metaphysics. On account of the latter alone do we retrospectively understand that transformation is what makes identity, that a body, a gender, or a currency exists only by virtue of its transformability, exchangeability, and convertibility. And we so much better understand that this retrospective gaze is relieved by a prospective gaze that is freed by the former and directed at our essences, bodies, and genders, the merchandise we buy and sell, our objects of thought—all things promised, quite obviously, to other metamorphoses and other migrations.

If the locus of this first (ex)change is more originary than the taking place of every ontic exchange, this is not because it would itself be priceless or outside price, without and beyond value, or, in other words, sacred—all these being clichés ascribed today to alterity. In its turn, indeed, this locus has got to and will change. It has, it too, its value for exchange—its exchange value. Nothing, for Heidegger, escapes (ex) change or convertibility. It must be repeated: what Heidegger thinks under the heading of ontology is the structure of transformation alone. Being is nothing but (its) transformability.

Yet we find ourselves, with ontological transformability, touching up against something heavy, grave, and onerous. In effect, the complicity of change and difference is, in its first version, nothing but the origin of what must be dubbed ontological capitalism, "the ever-advancing world history of the planet."[1]

Was Heidegger, under the name "metaphysics," after anything but?

Ontological capitalism designates the economic system opened by the originary exchange of presence with itself: beings for being via the money of essence. The magnificent, sinuous movement of thought that gets deployed in "Anaximander's Saying" follows all the turns of this exchange: "To be the being of beings is to be the matter of being. The grammatical form of the enigmatically ambiguous genitive names a genesis, an origin of what is present out of presencing."[2] *Nevertheless, "presence"* (Anwesenheit, Anwesung) *and "present beings"* (Anwesendes) *have from the origin been exchanged—as though they were equal.* "From earliest times it has seemed as though presence and what is present are each something for themselves. Unintentionally, presence and what is present become something for themselves."[3] *This "becoming" is what our sights have been set on; this is what we call (ex) change, or metamorphosis and migration. From here out, which is to say at the same time and from the outset, present beings pass for presence, are of value for it:* "presence as such is not distinguished from what is present. It is taken to be only the highest and most universal of present beings and hence as one of them [*es gilt nur als das Allgemeinste und Höchste des Anwesendes und somit als ein solches*]. The essence of presence and the difference between presence and what is present remains forgotten. The oblivion of being is oblivion to the difference between being and the being."[4] *What difference owes to change is its forgetting. This forgetting has for its name "of value for, gelten."*

Keep the following in mind: gelten: *to be valid, in force and effective, to apply;* gelten für: *to be of value for;* gelten als: *to pass for. The verb* gelten *and the substantive* Geltung—*validity, worth, currency—are of considerable importance in Heidegger's texts. To be of value for, to pass for, to have the value of . . .*

The economy of the first (ex)change—ontological capitalism—is a system of generalized equivalence ruled by Geltung. *A fundamental complicity, moreover, links* Geltung *to* Wert *(value) in Heidegger:* "Taking the essence of truth as the correctness of the representation, one thinks of all beings according to 'ideas' and evaluates all reality according to 'values.' That which alone and first of all is decisive is not which ideas and which values are posited, but rather the fact that the real is interpreted according to 'ideas' at all, that the 'world' is weighed according to 'values' at all."[5] *Essence is of value for beingness, which is of value for being. Correctness is of value for truth, present beings of value for presence.* "The calculative process of resolving beings into what has been counted counts as the explanation of their being [*das Aufgehen der Rechnung mit dem Seienden gilt als die Erklärung seines Seins*]."[6]

The question raised by the end of metaphysics is that of its coincidence with the end of (ontological) capitalism. The end of the one is no more datable, locatable, or effective than the end of the other. This is, according to me, what explains Heidegger's recourse to the triad of change, which unceasingly displaces, as we have seen, the point of suture and rupture. The revolution will declare W, W, & V. But given that, it will also go by the very name of what it overturns. Its event will remain indeterminate. Do the other change and exchange remain to come? Will they ever arrive? Faced with these abyssal questions, we are left only with the enigma of our transformations. Is the revelation of the ontologically transformable character of everything ancient history or does it instead come from the future? The answer, Heidegger replies, is both: W, W, & V.

We have seen how vague instances were at the beginning, meaning in the cave, offered up to the exchange through which they received their determinations as beings, men, the divine, being, and truth. There is, at departure, a rush of presence to the door

*of exchange, a rush that is nothing if not a metamor-
phic and migratory influx. Prior to exchange, nothing.
Everything goes at the outset into the convertor. And
so it begins: difference.*

*Heidegger shows that this first offer—metaphys-
ics is what makes being a first offer—is something
irreducibly older than self-exposure in prostitution,
self-(ex)change in alienation, disguise, mendacity, or
imposture. Something more originary than a deal with
the devil. So that there would be bargaining and the
cutting of deals in being, so that being would at bottom
be this alone, and the first change would be the first
alliance, the passage into the convertor. All this is so
heavy, so grave and onerous. Which means that from
the dawn of the West, whoever announces himself by
declaring "I am" has always in reality been saying,
"I am originally changed." Whoever. And this is the
first coming. Man, god, truth, and the rest . . . I am
what I am, (ex)changed in advance.*

*Nothing and nobody ever comes or ever will
without being changed; without being, from the very
outset, exchanged.*

3

"Color, the Very Look of Things, Their *Eidos*, Presencing, Being— This Is What Changes"*

"Better to remain in debt than to pay with a coin that does not bear our image" says our sovereignty.

—Nietzsche, *The Gay Science* §252

I will now lead you to the critical point where the other form slightly surfaces from form, where another pathway takes shape, and the bulge of a turnaround rises in the middle of the road. We are headed to the place where Nietzsche and Heidegger meet, where one last look at metaphysics gets exchanged for a first vision of the other beginning.

This is the critical point where the other form can be seen emerging out of the first form, where a camel's hump breaks the long ribbon of the path, a place Nietzsche shows to be the result of something molting. From this molt, the first change or Wandel-Haütung, *he collects the molt, the dead skin or slough*

---

*Nietzsche Volume II: The Eternal Recurrence of the Same, translated by David Farrell Krell (San Francisco: Harper San Francisco, 1991), 131–32. *Nietzsche. G.A.* Bd 6.1, 353. Hereafter cited as NII.

(abgestreifte *Haut*) *that afterward remains, and welcomes it into metaphysics. Nietzsche is the first thinker of ontological transformability. For with him, metamorphosis makes for the first time its entrance into the scene of philosophy.*

> On the Third Shedding
> Already cracks and breaks my skin,
> My appetite unslaking
> Is fueled by earth I've taken in:
> This snake for earth is aching.[1]

*Heidegger nonetheless judges the migratory and metamorphic power of Nietzsche's thought to be incorrectly located (*erörtet*), its ontological source going unquestioned. Nietzsche does not in fact inquire into which of the essential changes the serpent is born from and thereby omits the "changing" (*wandelbar*) character of essence, the profound reason for philosophical mutation.* "Nietzsche does not pose the question of truth proper, the question concerning the essence of the true and the truth of essence, and with it the question of the ineluctable possibility of its essential transformation [*ihres Wesenswandel*]."[2] *In the course of his reading, Heidegger will for that reason superimpose the triad of* W, W, & V *over all the movements or "countermovements" (*Gegenbewegungen*) of inversion and transvaluation, hence over all the instances of metamorphosis and migration present in Nietzsche's texts. Although the triad is more vague in appearance than the Nietzschean determinations of change, it paradoxically enables the ontological import of the latter to be specified while also clearly affirming that* "Nietzsche's way of thought does not want to overthrow [*umstürzen*] anything—it merely wants to retake [*nachholen*] something."[3]

What does "retake" mean here? This retaking, which constitutes for Heidegger the veritable metamorphic and migratory force of Nieztsche's thought, should be understood as the result of *the strange tendency metaphysics has of reinvesting, at its close, its own traces*, of somehow coming back upon itself so as to "go beyond . . . the complete determination of its whole nature."[4] This retake, therefore, is a reinstallation, a reestablishment of the tradition, without which it would remain teetering and unstable. *The tradition goes back through its skin, experiencing, as would a molting animal, the crossing of its limits. Such reinvestment of self as change of self constitutes for Heidegger one of the most profound motifs of the doctrine of eternal return.*

Because of this repeating that traces and reforms— a repeating itself repeated in its reinterpretation by Heidegger—being is made to appear as it is: changed from its dawning. Without this image, the fantastic vision of this inaugural shedding, which is foremost present in Nietzsche, it would be impossible for the original gaze (Plato's) and the ultrametaphysical gaze (Heidegger's) to converge. The terminal image of metaphysics Nietzsche creates is the condition of the "inclusion of the uncanny in the familiar" that we previously encountered. In Nietzsche's thought, the beginning reappears "in a metamorphosed form [*in verwandelter Gestalt*],"[5] and "all the themes of Western thought, though all of them transmuted, fatefully gather together [*alle Motive des abendländischen Denkens, aber alle verwandelt, geschicklich versammeln*]."[6]

We arrive before the place of this gathering, where the streams at the same time separate. Where metamorphosis and migration are revealed to themselves. Where the signification of the fantastic is clarified

*as designating this regime of the visibility of being
granted by the repetition of the first change and the
exposure of its skin.*

W, W, & V, or the
Real Foundation of Inversion

WHAT HEIDEGGER SEES

The play of gazes between Nietzsche and Heidegger
is no less disturbing than the one we saw deep in
the cavern.

This disturbance is born from Heidegger's unceas-
ing denial of the importance of the motif of inversion
(*Umdrehung*) to Nietzschean thought. Inversion as well
as transvaluation in general are for him only effects
of a more profound, radical, and originary metabolic
dynamism. So that throughout the four volumes of
Nietzsche, inversion (*Umdrehung*), reversal (*Umkehrung*), transmutation, transvaluation (*Umwertung*),
transfiguration (*Verklärung*), and countermovement
(*Gegenbewegung*) are constantly referred to the triad
of change—*W, W, & V*—which is alone capable of
leading back to their foundation. "We are now asking what new interpretation and ordering of the sensible and nonsensible results from the overturning
of Platonism [*Umdrehung des Platonismus*]? To what
extent is 'the sensible' the genuine 'reality'? What
transformation accompanies the inversion? [*welche
Verwandlung geht mit der Umdrehung zusammen?*]
What metamorphosis underlies it? [*welche Verwandlung leigt der Umdrehung zugrund?*]"[7]

If Nietzsche's thought is in Heidegger's eyes the
most powerful thinking of change in the history of philosophy, this is primarily because this change always

concerns *something else besides what it changes* and thus resides elsewhere than in its abode. Heidegger's interpretive strategy consists in unceasingly exhibiting the alterity of change to itself and, by way of consequence, the alterity of Nietzsche to himself, but not at all to make manifest some "contradiction" in his thought, but in order, on the contrary, *to confuse it with its own metamorphosis.*

Heidegger states of "overturning" [*Umdrehung*] that "to be sure, Nietzsche himself often expresses the state of affairs that way . . . , although he is aiming at something else [*etwas anderes sucht*]."[8] He is not seeking to renew the content of the "old schema of hierarchy [*Ordnungschema*]" but to metamorphose (*verwandeln*) the value of this schema itself. *The metamorphosis of schematism*: for Heidegger, this is, in the last instance, the veritable reason for the *Umdrehung.*

This is a point on which I will have to insist: schematism will henceforth, with Nietzsche, no longer simply be a mechanism permitting the becoming-sensible and figuration of meaning, but a mechanism that also figures and schematizes *itself.* With Nietzsche, *schematism itself appears in its schemes.* The "philosopher-artist" puts to the proof the mutability of transcendental mechanisms and in the same move definitely displaces the economy and mode of formulation inherent to metaphysics.

HERACLITUS' NAME THROWS US OFF THE TRAIL . . .

Such an interpretive orientation allows us to understand why Heidegger never stopped contrasting the ordinary and "superficial" view of the affinity between Heraclitus and Nietzsche. "One often," he writes, "characterizes Nietzsche's thought as Heraclitean

and in citing this name dissimulates [*vorgeben*] having thought something."⁹ Heidegger refuses, as is
known, to accept that πάντα ῥεῖ—"everything melts
away," "everything is change"—is Heraclitus' master
phrase. In Heraclitus as well as Nietzsche, the source
of the motif of change is paradoxically enough not
to be found in the thought of flux, becoming, or
some term for change. *In Heidegger's eyes, becoming
strangely enough appears to be a concept devoid of
future. The fundamental question of change has its
origin not in the thought of becoming but in that of
the image.* In particular, in the thought that truth is
illusion. As Heidegger declares: "neither is Nietzsche
the Heraclitus of the waning nineteenth century, nor
is Heraclitus a Nietzsche for the age of pre-Platonic
philosophy. In contrast, what 'is,' what is still hap-
pening in Western history—hitherto, at present, and
to come—is the power of the essence of truth. In it,
beings as such show themselves. . . . What is and
what occurs consist in the strange [*Befremdliches*]
fact that at the beginning of the consummation of
modernity truth is defined as 'illusion.' The initial
fundamental decisions concerning thought are transformed [*verwandeln*] in this definition, but just as
decisively their dominion is established."¹⁰

Illusion of course has "image" as one of its primary meanings. Once again, Nietzsche's thinking of
change draws its resources from a singular understanding of both *schema* and *schematization,* via the
image and the *imagination.* It is this understanding
which imposes the distinctions between both the
stable and the changing and the immutable and the
moving, which call into question the relation between
the true and apparent worlds. Heidegger has no
doubt that the source of the Nietzschean signification of change is to be found in the determination of

essence as image, idea, aspect, and form, since this is already the case in Heraclitus's thought. Heidegger says, in effect, that "[f]or Heraclitus, knowing means to take hold of what shows itself, to guard the sight [*Anblick*] as the 'view' [*Ansicht*] that something proffers, the 'image,' in the designated sense of φαντασία [*phantasia*]. In knowing, what is true is held fast; what shows itself, the image, is taken up and into possession; what is true is the in-formed image [*die ein-gebildete Bild*]. Truth is imaging [*Wahrheit ist Einbildung*], the word thought now in a Greek way, not 'psychologically,' not epistemologically in the modern sense."[11]

Heidegger compares the first part of fragment 28 of Heraclitus—"for having views / is also / the knowing of the most highly regarded one, watching over / holding fast to a view [δοκέοντα γάρ ὁ δοκιμώτατος γινώσκει, φυλλάσσει]"[12]—with fragment 602 of "*The Will to Power*": "the honoring of truth is already the *consequence of an illusion* [*Illusion*]."[13] Illusion, *qua* image, is also something that shows, and shows itself. Δοκέοντα, Heidegger recalls, means "what shows itself," and δοκειν, "to show itself, to appear."[14] *The image is the (true) subject of change.*

Indeed, from the dawn of philosophy, presencing and birth are thought as appearances in the image, forms that show themselves. Originally, bringing into image and φύσις—growth, blooming—are one and the same thing. "What is image-like," Heidegger continues, "does not consist in what is fabricated, like a copied imitation [*das Bildhafte besteht nicht im Zurechtgemachten, etwa gar im nachgebilteden Abbild*]. The Greek sense of 'image'—if we may use that word at all—is a 'coming to the fore' [*zum Vorschein-kommen*], φαντασία, understood as 'coming to presence' [*in die Anwesenheit tretten*]."[15] The first metamorphosis, which corresponds to the first φαντασία, is just that: *passing into the state of presence.*

Change quite exactly has its source in the passing or being published into presence.

THE AMBIGUITY OF THE IMAGINAL

Heidegger shows, then, that the thinking of presence as image is at once both the originary locus of the formation of metaphysics—the image understood as idea, picture, and figure—and the very possibility of the break opening to the other thought, the image in that case not being related to any essential permanence. Hence the avowed *ambivalence* of Heidegger's reading of Nietzsche, who appears in it as both *the last philosopher*, the one accomplishing the history of metaphysics as the history of the idea, and *the first thinker*, of the metamorphosis and migration, that is, of the image.

On the one hand, Nietzsche can be situated, according to Heidegger, in the main line of the metaphysical interpretation of truth as correctness and of the image as idea. His thought is just one last "reformulation" (*Umformung*) of it:

> With the transformations [*Abwandlungen*] of the Greek concept of being in the course of the history of metaphysics, the Western concept of the image changes accordingly [*verwandelt sich*]. In antiquity, in the Middle Ages, in the modern 'period,' 'image' is different not only in regard to content and name but also with regard to essence. 'Image' means:

1. coming to presence [*Hervortreten in die Anwesenheit*];

2. referential [or significational] correspondence within the order of creation [*Verweidendes Entsprechen innerhalb der Schöpfungsordnung*];

3. representational object [*Vorstellender Gegenstand*].[16]

Nietzsche completes this final epoch by carrying to its term what Heidegger calls "the poetizing essence of reason."

What is this poetizing essence of reason? "Kant," writes Heidegger, "first explicitly perceived and thought through the creative [or poetizing] character of reason in his doctrine of the transcendental imagination. The conception of essence of absolute reason in the metaphysics of German Idealism (in Fichte, Schelling, and Hegel) is thoroughly based on the essence of reason as a 'formative,' 'creative' 'force' [*bildende, dichtende Kraft*]."[17] Nietzsche was not, then, the one who "first discovered" this figural force, which reveals that reason is "explicitly . . . the faculty that forms and images to *itself* everything that beings are [*was das Seiende ist,* sich selbst *zu- und ein-bildet*]."[18] Instead, he fulfilled its concept.

On the other hand, Heidegger shows that concealed at the same time under the name "the poetizing essence of reason" is what, in the history of metaphysics, from the very beginning looks, like an open window (which is closed in its very opening), toward metaphysics' other. The poetic essence of reason in effect points toward freedom understood as *the truth of essence*: "Freedom—in the simple and profound sense that Kant understood its essence—is in itself poetizing [*Dichten*]: the groundless grounding of a ground, in such a way that it grants itself the law of its essence."[19] And Nietzsche will carry this freedom to its highest expression.

Hence, to resume with these two movements, it is possible to say that with Nietzsche, the poetizing essence of reason appears in its *imaginal issue.*

You are, I am quite sure, unaware of the meaning of "imaginal." In zoology, imaginal designates the last stage of an organism's development toward metamorphosis. Coming after the embryonic and larval is the imaginal stage, which is separated from the first two by what is, properly speaking, a metamorphic crisis, and which designates the adult state of an animal, such as an insect, that has attained its definitive imago, or general form. The imaginal exists in certain species, from their larval period on, in the form of invaginations or discs which shelter the basic outline of the imago. Hence the caterpillar, for example, bears inside itself the imaginal discs of the wings of the butterfly.

I have coined the expression "imaginal issue of presence" in order to indicate both the formative outline of the image and its crisis. I would like to use this formula to account, on the one hand, for the way in which Nietzsche's understanding of change completes, at the conclusion of a long tradition, the formative outline of the image; I also want, on the other, to account for the critical, metamorphic moment that decides upon a new meaning of presence and the image and thereby transforms metaphysical metamorphosis itself.

In Heidegger's interpretation, the Nietzschean conception of the relation of truth and imagination would indeed appear to be both *the culmination of the structural imago of metaphysics* (the final term of its metamorphic migration) and *the overturning of the image*: catching a glimpse of itself, the fulfilled image gets displaced toward *another becoming-form*.

Given all this, we now have to figure out how the economy of imaginal exchange is organized in Nietzsche, which is to say the organization of the conversion of one image of thought into another. Guided by Heidegger, we will find the answer within the thought of the will to power, understood as a *historical convertor*.

The Will and Its Fashioning

According to Heidegger, *the plasticity of essence* appears for the first time in this device for self-perspectivalizing that is will as Nietzsche conceives it. Will to power is the name given the historical interchange within which the convertibility of being comes to light through the bringing into play of essence. Nietzsche omits "the changing character of essence," but he simultaneously reveals a distance of essence from itself wherein *the originally metabolic dimension of presence* resides.

Heidegger grants that Nietzsche's interpretation of the first (ex)change (which is insufficient, since the latter understands this change as a first inversion—of the sensible and the supersensible—and not as an exchange between being and beingness) appears in all its strength in the definition of the will. The will is *the very structure of change* and because of this shares something (of the) essential with organic metabolism: its "vascular changes, alterations in skin tone, temperature, and secretion"—its "changes in the body."[20] Heidegger insists on the astonishing proximity of the will and Aristotelian μεταβολή; in Nietzsche, he

writes, "basic determinations of being . . . are con-
joined in the essence of motion (κίνησις, μεταβολή)."[21]

If there is change, it is because *the will wants
it*—simply, *naturally. Will is only the (ex)change it wills.*
If men, beings, God, and even being are exchanged
in the inaugural cavern, if they acquire their essence
through exchange, this is because they want it, or
rather because it is wanted in them. Not through
the play of some intention, but through the originary
movement of a self-desire of desire which hurls and
catches itself midair. What Heidegger discerns in the
will to power is a device for *self-transformation* lacking
a first instance to transform. Will designates just this
change of self, this exchanging of the self for nothing.
"Self-assertion is original assertion of essence [*Selb-
stbehauptung ist ursprüngliche Wesenbehauptung*]."[22]

For Nietzsche, willing first and foremost signifies willing exchange, and willing exchange always
signifies willing a change of essence, a *changing of
essence* itself. If the will is the "revelation of essence
which unfolds of itself," it is in the sense that it
metamorphoses and displaces essence: "Willing proper
does not go away from itself [*ein Von-sich-weg*], but
goes way beyond itself [*ein Über-sich-hinweg*]; in
such surpassing itself [*sich-Überholen*] the will cap-
tures the one who wills, absorbing and transforming
[metamorphosing] him into and along with itself [*der
Wille den Wollenden gerade auffängt und in sich mit
hereinnimmt und verwandelt*]."[23]

Willing is not given before what it wills, which is
to say prior to (ex)change. The very present of what
is exchanged is carried off into its future: "willing
is to want oneself [*sich-Selbst-wollen*]," yet " 'oneself'
is never meant as what is at hand [*Vorhandene*],
existing just at it is [*Bestehende*]; 'oneself' means
what first of all wants to become what it is [*was

erst werden will, was es ist]."[24] What wants itself in willing, then, is always essence, but the will is what first gives itself essence *through casting the latter far from itself.*

So insofar as essence is in Nietzsche *changing through the self-casting of willing,* it is possible to consider the philosopher as having come very close to the *truth of essence,* which he would otherwise like to keep completely settled in itself. Nietzsche calls this play of essence with itself *creation.* Willing comes down to creating essence, which is to say at once *fulfilling* and *destroying* it until it becomes radically other, new: "will to power is something creative. . . . What is decisive is not production in the sense of manufacturing but *taking up [hinaufbringen]* and *transforming* [metamorphosing: *verwandeln*], making something other than [*dieses Anders als*] . . . other in an essential way [*und zwar im Wesentlichen anders*]."[25] The unity of destruction and creation within the will's metamorphic and migratory throwing allows us to understand why art is for Nietzsche the fundamental structure of the will to power.

The will is effectively the power of *ontological creation.* This power, which has been disclosed from Kant onward in the transcendental imagination, is deployed and transformed in Nietzsche in such a way that art must be understood as the possibility of *creating beings in their entirety.* The philosopher is only an artist "in that he gives form [*Gestalten*] to beings as a whole [*indem er am Seienden im Ganzen gestaltet*], beginning there where they reveal themselves, i.e. in man. It is with this thought in mind that we are to read number 795 of *The Will to Power:*

"The *artist*-philosopher. Higher concept of art. Whether a man can remove himself far enough from other men, in order to *give them form* [*um an ihnen zu gestalten*]."[26]

Ontological determination as the result of a creation: this is the Nietzschean version of *change* and *exchange*.

The Inclusion of the Thinker in What Is Thought

ANOTHER FIGURE

Heidegger shows that the metabolic structure of the will to power presiding over this creation brings into play a concept of form at once both traditional and unprecedented.

On the one hand, "Nietzsche explains such becoming-form [*das Form-werden*] . . . in an aside as 'giving itself up,' 'making itself public.' Although at first blush these words seem quite strange, they define the essence of form . . . , [as] the definition corresponds to the original concept of form as it develops with the Greeks."[27] "*Forma*," Heidegger continues, "corresponds to the Greek μορφή. It is the enclosing limit and boundary, what brings and stations a being into that which it is, so that it stands in itself: its configuration [or figure: *die Gestalt*]. Whatever stands in this way is what the particular being shows itself to be, its outward appearance, ειδος, through which and in which it emerges, stations itself there as publicly present, scintillates, and achieves pure radiance."[28]

On the other hand, "form" is not only the *form of things,* the *aspect* of such and such a being, but the *originary ontological fashionability of things, their plastic and mutable character. So that it is the form-*

ability or transformability of form that enters presence. So that it is schematization itself that shows itself. "The essence of form is not . . . immediately the form of the work" but is primarily the result of a process of schematization which constitutes its "inherent tension."[29] *The crevice that opens between essence and its fashioning in the orbit of the will to power allows the ontological anteriority of fashioning over essence to come into view.*

The schema's coming to presence in what it schematizes entails, as I said before, the mutability of the schematism itself. At the same time, the thinker *sees himself figured in his thought itself.* "What is to be thought recoils on [*schlägt . . . zurück*] the thinker because of the way it is to be thought, and so it compels the thinker. Yet it does so solely in order to draw the thinker into what has to be thought."[30] Thinking entails the thinker always being caught or included (*einrückt*) in the thought. The structure of this coiling is this schema of the schema, which enables the philosopher to understand that she henceforth has less business with her objects of thought than with the inclusion of her image in her thought. "That the one who wills, wills himself into his will, means that such willing itself, and in unity with it he who wills and what is willed, becomes manifest [*sich offenbar werden*] in the willing."[31]

THE PHYSIOGNOMY OF ZARATHUSTRA

Willed, exchangeable, and exchanged, essence shows itself to be what it is: *a figure.* One Nietzsche gives a name: Zarathustra. The power of repetition inherent to metaphysics, which leads it to go back through its own traces, concludes by *stripping essence of its character of generality.* Henceforth, the thinker can contemplate this molt, the molt of the first exchange, because it is first and foremost *her own*, the essence of "man," which appears to itself, at last, as *the physiognomy of a singularly general man.*

The thought of eternal return is indissociable from the prior creation of its thinker or doctor: "*To be* the initial and proper thinker of the thought of eternal return of the same *is the essence of Zarathustra.*"[32] Then, further on: "The communication of the thought most difficult to bear, the greatest burden, first of all requires the poetic creation of the figure who will think this thought and teach it."[33] We find these same analyses in "Who Is Zarathustra?" where Heidegger says, "The question now asks who this teacher is. Who is this figure which, at the stage of metaphysics' completion, appears within metaphysics? Nowhere else in the history of Western metaphysics has the essential figure [*Wesensgestalt*] been expressly created in this way for its respective thinker—or, to put it more appropriately and literally, nowhere else has that figure been so tellingly *thought* [*erdacht*]. Nowhere else—unless at the beginning of Western thought, in Parmenides, though there only in veiled outlines."[34]

The one who thinks sees himself appear this way in what he thinks. He also sheds in the same instant his idea—like a serpent. Zarathustra is the slough of the essence of man become visible through a singular man. Essence, man, and visibility that become, then, what they have never ceased to be: values. The products, that is, of a fashioning, an exchange, a change. One even God fails to escape. He is "sunk down [niedergeschlagen] to a value" and thus "killed [getötet]."[35] *Man at last sees his figure as well as those of being, the whole of beings, and God as the (exchange) values they all are. In that way, he experiences his own exchangeability and bids farewell to himself.*

But in the opening of the will to itself, essence is loosened up, and the other (ex)change prepared. Every evaluable instance is necessarily re-evaluable, convertible, mutable.

Hence the figure of Zarathustra is at once that of the old man and that of "another man [*anderer Mensch*]"[36] or a "transformed man [*gerwandelter Mensch*]."[37] Indeed, "the thinking of this thought [eternal recurrence] transforms [metamorphoses/ *verwandelt*] life in its very grounds and thereby propounds new standards of education."[38] The eternal return is the first thought to figure the metamorphic and migratory unity of the other change. This dual unity is symbolized by Zarathustra's two animals: the eagle, who unceasingly makes volte-faces, and the serpent, who endlessly changes his masks. "The eagle is the proudest animal. He lives always in the heights, and for them. Even when he plunges into the depths, these are depths among mountain heights, crevasses, not plains where all is flattened out and equalized. The serpent is the most discerning animal [*das klügste Tier*]. Discernment suggests the mastery of actual knowledge concerning the sundry ways in which knowing announces itself, holds itself in reserve, asserts itself yet remains flexible, avoiding its own pitfalls [*Schlinge*]. Proper to such discernment are the power to metamorphose and disguise oneself [*zu dieser Klugheit gehört die Kraft der Verstellung und Verwandlung*]—a power that cannot be reduced to vulgar falsehood [*niedrige Falschheit*]—and the mastery of masks [*die Herrschaft über die Maske*]. Discernment does not betray itself. It haunts the background while playing in the foreground; it wields power over the play of being and semblance."[39]

The *migration* is announced in Zarathustra's descent. "Downgoing [*Untergang*]," Heidegger affirms, "means two things here: first, transition as departure

[*Weggang als Übergang*]; second, descent as acknowl-
edgment of the abyss [*Hinuntergang als Annerkennung
des Abgrundes*]," and also, therefore, disappearance.[40]
Zarathustra is the *transitional*, the transition toward
the overman. "Prior man is unable actually to think
[eternal recurrence]. He thus must be made to
transcend himself [*über sich hinausgebracht*], to be
transformed [*verwandelt*]—into the overman."[41]

The Transformation of Transcendence

*As for metamorphosis, it is nothing less than a trans-
formation—a change of form, in fact—of metaphysics.*
What follows from this inclusion of the thinker in
what is thought, from this coming to presence of the
schema, is in effect *a transformation of transcendence*,
and hence *a change of the form of metaphysics*.

"In what way, within modern metaphysics,"
Heidegger asks in "On the Question of Being," does
"a thinking become necessary that represents Zarathustra as *Gestalt* [*das Zarathoustra als Gestalt vor-
stellt*]"?[42] "[T]he essential *Gestalt* of Zarathustra within
the metaphysics of the will to power," he continues, is
very well *the human form* become particular, become
merely one form among others.[43] Why has humanity
come to figure itself *in this fashion*? What necessity
is there to this speculation, this "appearing of the
objective subjectivity of the *subjectum*?"[44]

The answer is as follows: when the human form
is represented in a particular physiognomy, "transcendence is transformed [*sich wandelt*],"[45] and "the inner
form of metaphysics becomes transformed [*demzufolge
wandelt sich die innere Form der Metaphysik*]."[46] Heidegger explains: "the meta-physical in metaphysics—
transcendence—comes to be transformed whenever,

within the realm of these distinctions, the *Gestalt* of the human essence appears as the source that gives meaning [*die Gestalt des Menschenwesens als Quelle der Sinngeburg*]. Transcendence, understood in its multiple meanings, turns around [*kehrt sich um*] into a corresponding rescendance [*Reszendenz*] and disappears therein. The kind of descent via the *Gestalt* [*Rückstieg durch die Gestalt*] occurs in such a way that the presence of the latter represents itself, becomes present again in what is shaped by its shaping [*im Geprägten ihrer Prägung wieder anwesend wird*]."[47]

The integration of the thinker in the thought becomes visible and thinkable from the moment the coherence of structure destructures and disintegrates, when transcendence, become like an emptied skin, comes to its end by falling back in on itself.

This falling in or folding back, this self-reinvestment of metaphysics that renders possible its re-presentation, opens a double possibility. Two forms and pathways appear, which together mark not only all the "ontological ambiguity" of Nietzsche's thought but also, and above all, the ambiguity of our position in the world, we philosophers today.

The end of metaphysics is seen—concretely, really. So it is no phantom, but looks exactly like a molting, a metamorphosis. Man manipulates his slough, it being at last graspable and prehensible. It is then possible, and this is the first possibility, for *him to keep doing what, without knowing it, he has always been doing: being anthropologically modified.*

The form of man, become visible for itself, is imprinted on everything, everywhere. The world is stamped with the character of "humanity." The determination of man as a figure that apprehends itself—Heidegger calls this a "new type of humanity"—is

precisely the phenomenon of the achievement of metaphysics ("rescendance" imaging in some fashion "transcendence"): a continually growing "anthropologization"
of the being of beings, an increasingly pronounced
"humanization" of beings."[48] This humanization, which
is analyzed without respite in the second (German or
French) volume of *Nietzsche*, leads Heidegger to affirm
that "metaphysics as such is nihilism proper."[49] The
history of metaphysics in its whole entirety ends in
the understanding of the will to power as the efficacy
of "the self-fashioning [*Selbstprägung*] of man," which
aims at "absolutely empower[ing] the essence of power
for *dominion* over the earth."[50]

*It is at the same time possible—now the second
possibility—for a skin to grow back that would not be
that of "man" and that would allow for seeing that
"being is no fabrication [ein Gemächte] of human
beings and humanity no mere special case among
beings."*[51] It is possible that transformation and
ontological transformability ever remain unmaster-
able and authorless, change being neither our doing
nor our work.

*Imagine metaphysics shedding its skin, so that it
is exposing the latter. This is basically, for Heidegger,
how things happen, Nietzsche's philosophy setting up
this strange speculation. The skin is that of essence,
the image, value, and substitute for being that was
formed in exchange. Imagine metaphysics sloughing
off its (ex)change. Imagine metaphysics changing. Yes,
changing, as though it were undressing itself.*

*Imagine as well the schema of this vast machine
for forming images and giving change being you. The
particular modality, the figure or type, being you.
Yourself, inasmuch as you are a philosopher, being
a piece of the skin of metaphysics.*

In imagining this, you are already someone else and have already left this covering behind. You are in yourself double. As are we all. Double. A dual visibility whose concreteness, whose form and trait, I will to the end keep trying to outline.

Philosophizing today necessitates our finding our place between the two halves of the theoretical jaw that, once originary ontological fashionability has been acknowledged, represent, on the one hand, manipulation and, on the other, the opening to creative metamorphosis: mastery and disappropriation, flexibility and plasticity.

According to Callois, the fantastic "arises from a contradiction that bears on the very nature of life and achieves, by a vain but troubling prestige, nothing less than the apparent, momentary abolition of the border separating life from death."[52] My own belief is that the fantastic perhaps does not depend on the *abolition* of a border, but rather on *the emergence of its visibility. Thresholds, lines, partitions (we will later see the importance of the motif of the partition, or wall, in* Being and Time) *become visible like veins, like the vein separating, for instance, metaphysics from its other, its life from its death. These are thresholds of (ex)change. What is fantastic is that these thresholds can be seen, in you and me, sitting right out in full view.*

Like the ages of a shell inscribed in its form, like successive compartments melted together in calcite while remaining finely separate, ontological nautiluses are what we are—divided.

Is this complicity and divorce between historicity and the evolution of species, then, the dwelling place of philosophy?

Outline of a
Cineplastic of Being

A burden creates no new forces, while it does
change [*verwandelt*] the direction of their motion
[*indes verwandelt es ihre Bewegungsrichtung*],
thus creating for whatever force is available new
laws of motion [*neue Bewegungsgesetztze der ver-
fügbaren Kraft*].[1]

Who could tell what the difference is between a
structural, differential opposition and an imaginary archetype whose role is to differentiate itself?[2]

You protest. I've been speaking the whole time, you
say, of migration, metamorphosis, and the migratory
structure of metaphysics, but without ever truly clari-
fying what all this means. We have so far explored
together the economy of both the initial and terminal moments of the first change—the way went from
Plato to Nietzsche, from molt to molt—in an attempt
to make apparent the fundamental importance of
W, W, & V. Yet it is true that I have not asked which
kinetic and metabolic regimes govern metamorphosis
and migration. In fact, we do not yet know exactly
what Heidegger means by transformation, self-transformation, turning into, mutation, displacement, and
self-displacement. We also, moreover, indicated the

possibility of a bond between the historical and biological, but without specifying its stakes.

It must not be forgotten that Heidegger never
explains his constant use of the triad . . . that he
never reflects on the semantic proximity of the words
Verwandlung and *Metamorphose* . . . that he at no
point analyzes the passages in Nietzsche's work
explicitly devoted to metamorphosis—"The Three
Metamorphoses" (*Von den drei Verwandlungen*) in
Thus Spoke Zarathustra, for example, or the definition of the Dionysian as a power of metamorphosis
(*Metamorphose*) and displacement[3] . . . that he keeps
silent about the fate of "metamorphosed gods."[4] And
that he never turns toward the great tradition that,
from Ovid to Apuleius, imprinted onto metamorphosis
its fantastic character. And that he made no allu-
sions to Goethe's *Metamorphosis of Plants*. Or that
he just ignores Kafka, whose *Metamorphosis* (*Die
Werwandlung*) he doubtlessly never read.[5]

Nevertheless, Heidegger is doubtlessly the first
philosopher to accord a decisive, meaning *ontological*,
role to *Wandlung* and *Verwandlung*. The first to draw
out explicitly the possibility of *originary* transformation
and displacement. Yet if it is true that every great
thinking of change leaves to its reader the care of
mobilizing as she understands it the space of meaning it unfolds before her, then it is up to me, so as
to conclude this first analytical movement, to try by
my own might to bring out the broad outline of what
I will call *the Heideggerian ontological imaginary*.

Doing so will lead me to specify the use I have
made this whole time of my *Gestell* of reading and
writing—*the Heidegger change*—which has allowed me,
in surreptitiously borrowing from some forms and
pathways not strictly Heidegger's, to draw out and
schematize the metamorphic and migratory mobiles
proper to his thought. This fabulous alterity consti-

tutes, moreover, the core of the experiment which, drawing on all my poetico-rational powers, I am now undertaking, with both it and you.

What does "imaginary" mean here? I share Deleuze and Guattari's reservations when they question, in their joint book, the existence of a "Kafkaean imaginary." The imaginary, they say, can in no case designate a "symbolic" or "bestiary."[6] With them, and against such a conception, I defend *another* definition of the imaginary as *the opening of a line of flight, an originary glimpse of an exit or continuation; an imaginary that is necessarily cinematic—never thematic. A pure view onto movement.*

In order to characterize further this imaginary, I will allow myself to speak of a *Heideggerian "cineplastic."* The later term is used by Élie Faure, in a 1920 article concerning cinema.[7] He stresses there that the qualifier "plastic" is too often attributed to congealed configurations, even though it perfectly lends itself to the description of *forms in movement,* or *mobile figures.* The "cineplastic," because it brings about a displacement of plastic processes, precisely allows for an interrogation of *the plastic value of displacement.* In fact, as I declared above, form—*Form* or *Gestalt*—is always for Heidegger that of a pathway or peregrination. Inversely, every course, insofar as it crosses thresholds, is creative of forms.

The problem is that for Heidegger, this migratory and metamorphic solidarity doubles, since *W, W, & V* designate at once—first (ex)change—*the continuous passage from one form and loop of the path to another,* and—other (ex)change—*a dislocation of this very continuity.* There are then two cineplastics at the core of the Heideggerian cineplastic.

This duality has been our problem from the start. Heidegger winds forward, on the one hand, the long moving sidewalk of metamorphoses and migrations in(to) the identical, and reveals, on the other, the multiple, irreparable interruptions originally disturbing this series, interruptions that are themselves metamorphoses and migrations of another time and type. How can these two regimes of change coexist? This is what we now have to envisage.

From One Change to the Other: Persistence of Form and Trajectory

The question has not ceased haunting us this whole time: Why do the same words—*W, W, & V*—designate intra- and extra-metaphysical change? How is it possible for the inaugural gaze of metaphysics (Plato), its terminal gaze (Nietzsche), and the ultrametaphysical gaze (Heidegger) to fantastically converge in the very place of their divergence?

One thing is sure: from metaphysics to the other thought, the metamorphic and the migratory retain their primacy in determining the meaning of change. From the succession of epochs up to the upsetting of the very idea of the epoch or epochality, change always signifies for Heidegger changing form and direction. *The entire problem, then, is to know if changing form and changing direction have, as one goes from the one (ex)change to the other, the same meaning.*

The triad is therefore not reserved for the structural and historical description of metaphysics alone. On the contrary, one can only be struck, in reading the texts announcing "the other thinking," by both the frequency of its occurrence and the fact that *W, W, & V* continue to shelter the double, metamorphic and migratory, articulation of change. In *Contributions*, for example, the triad is constantly resorted to, since it characterizes, all at once, the change leading from metaphysics to the other thinking, the mobility specific to *Ereignis*, and the new exchangeability over which these preside. The passage from "the first beginning [*erster Anfang*]" to "the other beginning [*anderer Anfang*]"—"the passage from metaphysics to ontohistorical thinking [*Übergang von der Metaphysik in das seyngeschichtliche Denken*]"—is presented as a "great transformation [*große Wandlung*]." Heidegger declares that "[i]f the other beginning is still being prepared, then this preparation is concealed as a great transformation [*al seine große Wandlung verborgen*]; and the more hidden it is, the greater its occurrence [*umso verborgener je größer das Geschehnis*]."[8]

Now this change itself also consists in both a change of course—the windings of a path unfurled in the drift of a *Wanderung*—and a change of form. "*Contributions to Philosophy*," writes Heidegger, "enact a questioning along a pathway which is first traced out by the crossing [*Übergang*] to the other beginning, into which Western thinking is now entering [*erst gebahnt wird*]."[9] This "pathway" is also referred to as "an other form [*andersförmig*]."[10] Heidegger affirms that "[t]he work of thinking in the epoch of the crossing can only and must be a passage [*Gang*] in both senses of the word: a going and a way at the same time—thus a way that itself goes [*ein Gehen und ein Weg zumal, somit ein Weg, der selbst geht*]."[11] This itinerant ambiguity—a going and a way—is in some way *figured by the change of form of* Dasein. The "metamorphosis of *Dasein*" appears, in effect, at the edge of the text as *a change of figure taking place on the way*. A *mobile metamorphic decision*: "as transformed, man is shifted into the decision to be-there and be-away [*der Mensch verwandelt, in die Entscheidung des Da-seins und des Weg-seins*

gerückt]."[12] It is *on the way, en route,* that the form
of what has never before been shown begins to
appear. Heidegger speaks this way of "the emerging
shape of sheltering beings [*die aufscheinende Gestalt
des bergenden Seienden*]."[13] A figure breaks through
from beneath one that had been occluding it. A new
form comes forth, one that is always at the same
time precisely the index of an *itinerary,* the sign of
a new historical topography: "In the most hidden
shapes . . . is the spur for the utmost historicity
and the veiled ground for decidedness of the shortest
path [*in den verhülltesten Gestalten ist der Stachel
höchster Geschichtlichkeit und der geheime Grund der
Entschiedenheit zur kürzesten Bahn*]."[14]

*The metamorphosis of metaphysics lets another
form appear at a detour in its road.*

Continuity and Rupture

So if this form whose shape is decided along the way
or this way that takes form in being decided on are
wholly other than the form and path of metaphysics, if they are its metamorphosis and displacement,
could migratory and metamorphic structure itself be
identical within both their regimes?

DESTRUCTION, SAVING

It is undeniable that for Heidegger, change has continuity as one of its essential dimensions. If change
is to be *creative,* it cannot abandon what it changes,
but must instead carry it along with itself. The
philosophy "to come [*zukünftig*]," Heidegger writes,
"transforms [*verwandelt*] what is past into something
that is not lost [*das Vergangene in das Unverlorene*

verwandelt]."[15] Metamorphic displacement is never an absolute rupture. Heidegger establishes, moreover, an equivalence between *"Wandlung,"* transforming, and *"Rettung,"* or saving.[16] The other thinking cannot unceremoniously leave metaphysics "behind it [*hinter sich zu lassen*]" but on the contrary "must accomplish its end [*hinter sich zu bringen*]," which signifies, again, "grasping this end now for the first time in what is ownmost to it [*erst in seinem Wesen zu fassen*] and letting this be transformed and played into the truth of being [*d. h. und gewandelt in die Wahrheit des Seyns einspielen zu lassen*]."[17] It is well known that "the end of metaphysics" does not mean being finished and *done with it*.[18] The other thinking comprises, in a sense, metaphysics; "it contains [*einschließt*] within itself the transformed [*einverwandelt*] guiding question."[19]

But if the "wholly other" only arrives as a conservative "caesura [*Scheidung*]," is it still the "wholly other"?[20] It is clear that "the wholly other [*ganz Andere*]" announced with the "mindfulness of the truth of being [*Besinnung der Wahrheit des Seyns*]" is not the entirely new. In several reprises, Heidegger opposes change to the production of "novelty," if novelty is understood as meaning what has "not yet been," what has not, that is, happened. With the other change, with the passage from one beginning to the other, "it is not as if man simply enters a 'period' that has not yet been, but it is rather that man enters a totally different domain of history [*in eine noch nicht gewesene 'Periode,' sondern in einen ganz anderen Bereich der Geschichte*]."[21] This wholly other domain is not a new domain, but the very metamorphosis of the concept of domain and, as a consequence, of the concept of novelty as well. Heidegger even says that "the playing forth of . . . history . . . is not a historical addendum to and a portending of a 'new' 'system' but rather is in itself essentially a transformation-initiating preparation for the other beginning [*die wesentliche, Verwandlung anstoßende Vorbereitung des anderen Anfangs*]."[22]

For Heidegger, confounding change with the simple production of novelty comes down to believing naïvely in the power of inverting or overturning a state of things. *W, W, & V*, as we saw in the preceding chapter, never indicate an "inversion [*Umkehrung*]."[23] The *Wandlung* of one commencement into the other cannot be understood as a "great inversion [*große Umkehrung*]" insofar as it "requires a higher strength for creating and questioning [*eine höhere Kraft des Schaffens und Fragens*]" that is inherent to "transmutation." Veritable transformation involves "a *complete* transformation of relations to beings and to be-ing [*völliger Wandel der Bezuge zum Seienden und zum Seyn*]."[24]

It is in this way that the "turning" (*Kehre*) should be rigorously distinguished from inversion (*Umkehrung*). The power of a turning is in fact always measured by its power of metamorphosis (*Verwandlung*) or essential transformation (*Wesenwandlung, wesentliche Wandlung*). Its route, far from either following the mechanical movement of a rotation around an inflection point (*Wendungspunkt*) or being a formal reversal, should be organized according to a "transformed necessity [*gewandelte Notwendigkeit*]."[25] "What is entirely other in the other beginning, in comparison to the first beginning, can be clarified by a saying that seems only to play with a turning around [or inversion] whereas in truth everything is transformed."[26]

The coming of the other thought should, admittedly, "be awaited as a thrust [*Stoß*]."[27] However, this thrust, as we have seen, is not a "countermovement [*Gegenbewegung*]," as "a countermovement never suffices for an essential transformation of history [*genügt eine Gegen-Bewegung niemals für eine wesentliche Wandlung der Geschichte*]."[28] And "the other beginning is not the counter-direction of the first. Rather, *as the other*, it stands outside the counter and outside immediate comparability [*der andere Anfang ist nicht die Gegenrichtung zum ersten, sondern steht als anderes außerhalb des 'gegen' und der unmittelbaren Vergleichbarkeit*]."[29] The countermovement is always caught in comparability, that is, in a sense, in the logic of the *of value for*. It is this *equivalence* that must be metamorphosed and displaced.

So the movement of the triad of change recalls in certain respects the process of Hegelian sublation, *Aufhebung*. Moreover, Heidegger also stresses, in *Hebel: Friend of the House*, the proximity between sublation and metamorphosis: Johann Peter Hebel's "German poems are gathered [*aufgehoben*] in the triple meaning this word carries in the thinking of one of the poet's the great contemporaries, Georg Wilhelm Friedrich Hegel . . . *Aufheben* first means: to collect from the earth what lags. This type of *aufheben*, however, remains external as long as it is not specified in an *aufheben* that means to conserve. But this *aufheben* in turn only receives strength and endurance by provenance of a still more originary *aufheben* whose meaning is: elevation, transfiguration, ennobling—and consequently metamorphosis [*hinaufheben, verklären, veredeln, und dadurch: verwandeln*]."[30] Metamorphosis always signifies for Heidegger *raising, transfiguration, holding aloft*: "What is decisive is not productive in the sense of manufacturing but taking up [*das Hinaufbringen*] and transforming [*das Verwandeln*]."[31] It is only by virtue of this power of elevation and transfiguration that what is saved and upheld can be fundamentally transformed.

PASSING, ERRING

What has to be acknowledged, however, is that change at the same time dislocates its own power of sublation. In effect, the *continuist schema* sees itself endlessly contradicted by the thought of an *erratic displacement* made of irreparable ruptures, gaps, and caesuras.

One is struck, when reading *Contributions* for example, by the profusion of verbs conveying aimless movement and displacement, roaming, wandering, turning back around, circling, and, above all, *indecision between advance and retreat*. Attesting to this is the whole play Heidegger opens around the word *Rückung*, which designates, depending on the context, both retreat movement, retrogression, and progression or advance. The verb *rücken* effectively means "move," "push along," "displace," "put something back or ahead." Insisting on the significations of "back [*Rücken*]," "return [*Rückkehrt*]," and "retreat [*Rückgang*]," Heidegger discovers a type of mobility that consists of *advancing in retreat* or *withdrawing in the advance*.[32]

This advance that is withdrawn or detoured from what it goes toward, is always a wandering [*errance*] or *Verrückung*, the latter being a neologism most often translated into English as *errancy*. It should be recalled that if the verb *verrücken* signifies being displaced, the adjective *verrückt* signifies mad. This strange movement of an aimless wandering, of a displacement that hesitates between coming and going, precisely corresponds to the uncoiling of the metamorphosis of *Dasein*. *Contributions* announces "a transformation of humanness in the sense of dis-placing its site among beings [*eine Verwandlung des Menschseins im Sinne einer Ver-rückung seiner Stellung im Seienden*]."[33]

Now this errant, erratic displacement, this crazed *Wanderung* by which man changes place and form exactly contradicts the dynamic of saving, of continuity, proximity to the past, and, finally, ennobling replacement. In *Contributions*, "the change of soil" and "change of ground" needed for crossing to the other beginning appears as a *swaying between two banks*, a crisis concerning the proximity of the past that causes an abyssal distance to arise and puts *Dasein* before the necessity of working with *an improvised replacement.*

One would have to examine patiently the entire movement of the *Einspringen* insofar as it is precisely opposed to that of the *Aufhebung*. *Einspringen* signifies, in effect, *leaping into the breach, jumping in to substitute, improvising a replacement, and making do with what is at hand—however one can, and without elevation, transfiguration, or nobility.* Now it is *also* in this manner that the passage to the other beginning is accomplished: "Leaping . . . into the other beginning is returning into the first beginning, and vice versa. But returning into the first beginning ('the retrieval') is not displacement into what has passed, as if this could be made 'actual' again in the usual sense. Returning to the first beginning is rather and precisely distancing [*Entfernung*] from it, is taking up that distance-positioning which is necessary in order to experience what began in and as that beginning."[34] In the same manner, it is by following the movement of this *makeshift sublation* that the metamorphosis of being (*Sein*) into be-ing (*Seyn*) is achieved: "The other beginning is the leaping into be-ing's more originary truth, which transforms be-ing [*der andere Anfang ist der das Seyns verwandelnde Einsprung in seine ursprünglichere Warheit*]."[35] The replacement leap is thus less a saving of the "more originary" than something improvised—a *last-minute relief.*

Envisaged from this point of view, *migration* is not directed toward any goal. *We do not migrate as migrating birds do.* Heidegger tells us this in *What Is Called Thinking?*: "What must be thought about, turns away from man [*das zu-denkende wendet sich von Menschen ab*]. It withdraws [*entzieht*] from him. . . . But—withdrawing is not nothing. Withdrawal is an event [*Entzug ist Ereignis*]. In fact, what withdraws may even concern and claim man more essentially than anything present that strikes and touches him. . . . What withdraws from us, draws [*zieht*] us along by its very withdrawal, whether or not we become aware of it immediately, or at all. Once we are drawn into the withdrawal, we are—but completely differently than are migrating birds [*nur ganz anders als die Zugvögel*]—drawing toward what draws, [which] attracts us by its withdrawal. And once we, being so attracted, are drawing toward what draws us, our essential nature already bears the stamp of 'drawing toward.' As we are drawing toward what withdraws, we ourselves are pointers pointing toward it. . . . To say 'drawing toward' is to say 'pointing toward what withdraws ['*Auf dem Zuge . . . 'sagt schon: zeigend auf das Sichentziehende*]."[36]

We can even ask ourselves apropos this passage if *Wandel, Wandlung,* and *Verwandlung* are still even movements. Movement, indeed, remains forever tributary to a relation to immutable presence. Heidegger, elsewhere: "passing, *Ereignis* and history can never be thought as kinds of 'movements' [*niemals als Arten von 'Bewegungen' gedacht werden*] because movement (even when thought as μεταβολή) always relates to the ὄν as οὐσια—to which relationship δύναμις and ἐνέργεια and their later progeny belong."[37]

So if migration is not comparable to the travels of flocking birds, replacement ensures no preservation, advance and retreat confused, and every movement made of false starts, then just what do *W, W, & V* mean?

Contributions provides on this point a disconcerting response. Regarding the thinking to come, which is a thinking of "*be-ing*" (*Seyn*), Heidegger writes: "This thinking should never seek refuge in the figure of a being and in that form experience all the light of what is simple out of the gathered richness of its enjoined darkness. This thinking can also never follow the dissolution into what is figureless. In the abground of the figuring ground—this side of figure and figurelessness (which is, of course, only in a being)—this thinking must seize the resonating throw of its thrownness and carry it into the open."[38]

Neither the figure nor the figureless, this very difficult passage evokes the possibility that emerges between them of *a figure of the origin or of the very ground of the figure*, a ground not exhausted in any particular figure, emblem, or idol. *A figure that could no longer be sublated. A figure that would precisely figure the emergency replacement of sublation.* Taking shape, between the figured and figureless, is the possibility of a simple *outline of the figural*, a moving image of the birthplace of form caught in midflight, and thrown like a ball.

In this way, henceforth, our own figure runs before us, dashing in full stride. It no longer grips the ground supposed to be our identity. Transformable, it flies ahead, us running in pursuit, an aim that never finishes withdrawing. Metamorphosis from here out consists in the fact of succeeding at provisionally catching a face, in getting it settled for a bit in an aspect.

The Two Turns (of Phrase) of the Heideggerian Cineplastic

But how, once again, ought we understand the two essential modalities of the articulation of the migratory and metamorphic—of *the replacement*—at the interior of each change? How can we at the same time *change form and chase after form, see the form that changes us?* We will pause more patiently over the regime of mobility proper to the two changes.

THE POEM AND BIOLOGY IN SERVICE TO THE ONTOLOGICAL FANTASTIC

OVID'S PASSAGE

On the one hand, then, the Heideggerian determination of metamorphosis and migration incontestably presupposes a continuity of forms and a contiguity of thresholds. Moreover, how can one, in considering the history of metaphysics as Heidegger describes it, think of anything but the architecture of Ovid's *Metamorphoses*, of which, however, he never speaks? These *Metamorphoses*—"changes of shape, new forms"[39]—are portrayed both as *passages from one form to another* and *voyages from one end to the other* of *one and the same form.* A man, a god, or a demigod exchanges its essence for that of an animal or plant (the first metamorphosis encountered in the text is the nymph Daphne's).[40] Either animated beings take the form of inanimate beings—a titan becomes a mountain, a goddess becomes a spring, constellation, or echo—or, conversely, inanimate beings come to life, as with Pygmalion's statue.[41] These passages, which seem so extraordinary to us, always take place in the course of a *displacement*. Most often a flight, promenade, or voyage in the air.[42] This solidarity between advancing and transformation reveals, precisely, the perfect exchangeability of essences, their absolute convertibility.

Ovid made the body the place of a trial of crossing limits. Every character must go the full length of this trial, experimenting with each degree; metamorphosis is always progressive, despite its apparent instantaneity. The body's change takes place as a new growth, the growing within a body of another body, with its different rhythms, the slow putting in place of its motor schemes, its suffering its own pushing out.

If you go look at the statue of Apollo and Daphne in the Galleria Borghese in Rome, circle around it, and you will notice that each detail—Daphne's leaf-hands and foot-stalks, the foliage that had been her hair, the folding bark where her skin should be—marks a different stage in a metamorphic progression that follows its own course, as if transformation first had to explore the form that it itself is, embracing therein every turn, degree of intensity, and age. *An infinite reversion in a space of finite reversion.*

What Ovid already accomplishes is *the stripping bare of the exchangeability of beings, which is terribly violent, lacking cause, intention, and author. Metamorphosis and trailcutting, that is, come into view as the originary ontological condition.* Don't metamorphic passages, without philosophy being aware of it, figure the ontological send-off in the course of which the nudity of being gets clothed in the forms of its chronicle and dressed with epochal changes? Isn't metamorphosis always necessarily hidden in the folds of metaphysics, as its unconscious?

How can one not, in effect, think of the Metamorphoses *when witnessing in Heidegger the morphological and topological mise en scène of metaphysics as perpetual* Umformung, *each epoch reforming the preceding, displacing and conserving it at the same time? How can the call of being not be heard as the weeping of the mother nymph is? How can a certain contiguity of ontological space not be evoked, one which, from the one change to the other and in the leap from one form to the other, always allows us to tread the same soil?*

BEING AND PLANT

Continuity of forms, contiguity of thresholds . . . The triad of change also allows a complicity with nature to be discerned in Heidegger's philosophy, one with the tempo of the growth of living beings. Granted, Heidegger explicitly opposes his thinking of φύσις to the philosophy of nature "in the Goethean sense [*Goetheschen Sinne*]."[43] But if it is true that *Dasein* lives "amidst the changing [*Wandel*] . . . of the seasons, amidst the alternating [*Weschel*] of day and night, amidst the wandering [*Wandern*] of the stars," he also lives amidst the metamorphosis of plants and animals.[44]

Isn't there a secret kinship between *ontogenesis* and *ontology*? Couldn't the occlusion of the meaning of being emerge as the primordial form of philosophy, in the sense in which Goethe speaks of the "primal form [*Urform*]" of the plant?[45]

The continuity at work in the history of philosophy as Heidegger envisages it, the re-formation
that unites being's epochs and renders possible their
succession, the structural whole which forms the
tradition . . . don't these basically evoke ontogenetic
temporality? Doesn't metaphysics, like an organism
in metamorphosis, see its equilibrium constantly
adjusted?[46]

*I like imagining that being and beings form,
on account of their exchangeability, an interregnum
whose fate quite closely resembles that of the insects
known as metaboles. Isn't it precisely something like a
metabolic constitution of metaphysics that Heidegger is
seeking to bring out, an animal or arborescent essence
of philosophy?*

HISTORICAL MOOD SWINGS

Yet there are *ruptures* and *gaps*. The Heideggerian
cineplastic is far from being limited to these progressive slidings, which evoke, as do the fable and
biological growth, the movement of the continuous
formation of an individual. Unceasingly, the slow and
gradual *Umformung* reveals that it is not the mutation
of one *Urform*. Unceasingly, the metamorphic crisis
that transforms the individual so as to best confirm
the species sees itself transformed, displaced toward
a model of *growth bearing no fruit*. Unceasingly, the
passage from one form or side to another is threatened with sudden collapse, like pins a ball might
strike. *There is no Heideggerian invariant.*

The four principle motifs of passage and transition—*crossing, throwing, growth,* and *maturation*—
reveal it. Change, for Heidegger, certainly always
involves crossing, throwing, and maturing; the bridge

(*Brück*), the leap (*Sprung*), the pass (*Zuspiel*), ripeness or maturity (*Reife*) and incubation (*Inkubation*) are all for him, as is known, rich figures. These motifs, however, are ambivalent inasmuch as they invalidate the course or advance they nevertheless permit, and prohibit that way every *continuous* transformation. Hence the bridge does not always lead "beyond," the leap holds itself back, the ripening does not inevitably follow the picking, nor the hatching the incubation.

"THERE ARE NO BRIDGES"

Even if the other (ex)change, the passage to the other beginning, implies the crossing of a river, how the bank is to be gained remains unknown. Heidegger affirms this from the edges of *Contributions*: "there are no bridges [*die Brücken fehlen*]."[47] *What enables the crossing to take place remains metamorphosis, but this metamorphosis crosses ontological space without seeing the form it transforms. Dasein*, declares Heidegger, "overcomes the χωρισμός, not, as it were, by building a bridge between be-ing and beings—as if there were two riverbanks needing to be bridged [*nicht indem es zwischen dem Seyn (der Seiendheit) und dem Seienden als gleichsam vorhandenen Ufern eine Brücke schlägt*]—but by simultaneously transforming be-ing and beings in their simultaneity."[48] There is a precise kinship between the figure of the broken or absent bridge and the in-between of metamorphosis. The latter no longer evokes the transformation of a natural being or the fabulous passage going from one essence to another, but instead creates *an absolutely novel hybrid of being and beings*. No one knows what the simultaneity or contemporarity of being and beings could resemble, and nonetheless it takes place, and nonetheless it happens, crossing the limit.

Migration responds precisely to the urgency of the crossing but resembles at times a leap into the void. "In contrast," Heidegger in fact writes, "to a steady progress [*stetigen Fortgang*], where we move unawares from one thing to the next and everything remains alike [*alles sich gleich bleibt*], the leap takes us abruptly to where everything is different [*wo alles anders ist*], so different that it strikes us as strange [*befremdet*]. Abrupt means the sudden sheet descent or rise that marks the chasm's edge. Though we may not founder in such a leap, what the leap takes us to will confound us."[49] The point of arrival does not preexist the leap. It materializes from and with the latter. It is, in effect, thrown, and catches itself mid-leap.

THE LEAP HELD BACK

But is to leap or jump to move forward, stay in place, or go backward? The lexical movement at work in *Contributions* around the verbs *springen* (to leap), *vorspringen* (to leap forward), *einspringen* (to stand in for or to step into the breach), and *abspringen* (to jump off or bail out) clearly indicates that all forward momentum is at the same time held back, every throwing a recoiling, all progress a manner of remaining in retreat. The path is *discontinuous, discrete, ateleological*. The reason why is that it only ever leads us back to the place from which, paradoxically, it took us away. "Where have we leapt?," Heidegger asks. "Perhaps into an abyss? No! Rather, onto some firm soil. Some? No! But on that soil upon which we live and die, if we are honest with ourselves. A curious, indeed unearthly thing that we must first leap onto the soil on which we really stand. When anything so uncanny [*unheimlich*] as this leap becomes necessary, something must have happened that gives food for thought."[50] Why should we henceforth irrupt into the place we already are?

Because it is neither the soil nor the place, but the manner of investing or inhabiting them, that has changed. This metamorphosis and migration resemble a change of tonality or key. In *The Principle of Reason,* Heidegger endeavors to say precisely what such a change can be. It is, in effect, *a change of tonality (Wechsel der Tonart) that metamorphoses (verwandelt) the meaning of the principle of reason.* Heidegger writes that this change is heard when "[i]nstead of '*Nothing* is without *reason*' [the principle] sounds like 'Nothing *is* without *reason.*'"[51] Henceforth, the principle of sufficient reason can no longer be understood in accordance with its metaphysical signification, as a principle, that is, concerning beings and establishing that for every being, a reason can be furnished; the principle is instead a principle concerning being: being, itself without reason, is "reason that grounds."[52]

The transition from one understanding to the other "requires nothing less than that the manner of our thinking transform [metamorphose—*Verwandlung*] itself such that it responds to the state of affairs that the principle of reason means when speaking as a principle of being. We arrive at this transformation of thinking [*Verwandlung das Denkens*] neither through an exacting theory, nor through some sort of sorcery, but only by setting out on a path, by building a path that leads into the vicinity of the state of affairs we have mentioned. In so doing, it becomes clear that such paths themselves belong to the state of affairs."[53]

The path is not marked in advance. Migration and metamorphosis meet and are articulated together in the very place of the urgency of change, that is and first of all, the place of *the absolute break with the metaphysical understandings of metamorphosis and migration as continuous progression, derivation, wearing away, and elevation.* Heidegger insists on the fact that the principle of reason's "second tonality is not derived from the first." In effect, "[t]he second tonality rings out on its own without having any support in the first tonality [*klingt für sich und aus sich*]. The change of tonality is sudden [*ein jäher*]. Behind the change in tonality is concealed a leap in thinking. Without a bridge [*ohne Brücke*], that is, without the steadiness of a progression [*ohne die Stetigkeit eines Fortschreitens*], the leap brings thinking into another realm and into another manner of speaking [*in einem anderen Bereich und in eine andere Weise des Sagens*]. Therefore, we admit that the course of the previous sessions did not chart a transition from the realm of the principle of reason into the realm of being."[54] If a leap is necessary, it is, Heidegger once again says, owing to "this 'between' [*dieses Zwischen*] . . . that in some sense we leap over in the leap or, more correctly, that we leap through as through a flame [*wie eine Flamme*]."[55] *The urgency of passing through this ring of fire: when we go from one side to the other, we are left no longer the same. Nonetheless, the enigma of this in-between remains absolute.*

AN INCUBATION WITH NO OUTCOME

Movement of impeded incubation, exhausted genealogy. To be sure, if the change of tonality is possible today, if the time of the other (ex)change has arrived, this is because metaphysics is now consummated and has, as a result, reached *maturity* (*die Reife*). In *Contributions*, Heidegger precisely characterizes maturity as the midpoint between the "not yet" and the "no longer."[56] "[B]e-ing itself comes to its *maturity*. Maturity is preparedness for becoming a fruit and gifting [*die Bereitschaft, eine Frucht zu werden und eine Verschenkung*]. . . . In the fullness, in the vigor for the fruit and the greatness of gifting, there lies at the same time the most hidden . . . not: as not-yet and no longer."[57] So if change is possible—a change of tone and a convertibility of regimes of thought—it is because being is ripe for it. Yet at the same time, *this maturity never truly reaches maturity.*

We will take the example of the long period of the incubation of the principle of reason, which had to wait for Leibniz's genius in order to be finally brought out: "measured historiographically, two thousand three hundred years were needed until the principle of reason came to light and let itself be set up as a fundamental principle."[58] What is nonetheless astonishing is that *when the incubation comes to a close, what emerges is not what had been awaited. The egg is an egg no more, the butterfly no longer the future of the caterpillar.*

"Now if the incubation of the principle of reason," Heidegger writes on this point, "finds its end with the setting up of the principle of reason as one of the supreme fundamental principles, then this ending of the incubation must be due to the fact that, in the meantime, the *Geschick* of being has taken a turn, presumably in the sense that being as such has awakened and come to the fore. *But it is precisely at this point that the end of the incubation period of the principle of reason does not come to an end* [*doch gerade kommt es am Ende der Inkubationszeit des Satzes von Grund nicht*]. Indeed, something in the *Geschick* of being has taken a turn [*gewendet*], but in a totally different sense [*in einem ganz anderen Sinne*]."[59] In fact, when the principle hatches after its time of incubation, it hatches occluded. *It hatches without opening.* For Leibniz, in effect, it marks the domination of all beings and the foundation of the "objectivity of objects," not the truth of being. In this sense, the principle "has been, so to speak, pushed back into a still deeper sleep, into a still more decisive withdrawal of being as such."[60]

So it can very well be said that the history of metaphysics corresponds to a time of incubation, but since the other thinking profoundly detours the very idea of wait and development, the gestation of the meaning of being is an immature maturation. *The thinking of the truth of being only matures through its hatching being detoured.*

There are therefore two paired migrations and metamorphoses, and they separate without being disjoined. This is what makes for all the difficulty and profundity of the Heideggerian cineplastic.

Halfway between Ovidean mutability—for which there is an absolute equivalence of essences—and chance transformability, halfway between continuity and sudden crisis, *Dasein*, god, language, and philosophy can be seen crossing thresholds, leaping through the ring of fire . . . and *changing*. Between the adventure of a *refiguration* (the continuous route going from one figure to another) and that of a *dangerous morphing, their forms take an unforeseen direction.*

Part II

The New
Ontological Exchange

The least [*das Gering*] that may perhaps remain
is . . . the only question.

—Heidegger, *Mindfulness*

There is another (ex)change—an other (ex)change.
This is inconstestable, and Heidegger never stops
announcing it.

*An other—nonmetaphysical—(ex)change. An
other—non-capitalist—(ex)change. An other (ex)change
that owes nothing to the* Geltung, *which no longer
involves* "quick and fleeting circulation [*schnellen, augenblicken, Verkher*]," *and where the terms
exchanged [*ausgetauscht*] are "true equivalents [*wahre
Äquivalente*]."*[1]

Nonetheless, a change—W, W, & V.

*One that finally allows being to be in the way it
is—changing. A change that finally changes essence
into what it is—a place of exchange.*

*In its own way, then, the other (ex)change
continues to give change and throw off the trail.
This peculiar "way" will completely occupy us
here.*

It has to be repeated: the passage to the other
thinking and the conquest of another way of being

does not mark the suspension of conversion and transformation. Beings—whether men, god(s), animals, or things—continue to change. *Being and beings persist after their exchanges.* Original, structural, and destinal mutability and exchangeability *endure.* And as long as they endure, there will be change. They only endure, in fact, because there is change. As long as there is essence, metamorphosis "never rests."[2]

But despite all of this, ontological mutability does not play the role of an immutable instance. We have already said it: *there is no Heideggerian invariant.*

In effect, *mutability itself changes.* Heidegger affirms until the end that it all begins with a change, and that this is how we ourselves started. But in the end, this phrase *changes meaning. At the end, the beginning no longer changes in the same way.* And it is precisely from the end that we are going to start; it is through reading the "late" texts that we will be able to envisage the other (ex)change, *at the moment when it stops simply following after the first.*

How Is There Change from the Beginning?

Which means what? I could have and perhaps should have here broached what the analyses of the preceding chapter seem to announce: the passage to the other (ex)change that *Contributions* presents as a passage to *the other thinking* and *the other beginning.* I could and perhaps should have broached the other change by way of the famous "turning" that led Heidegger to elaborate the thought of *Ereignis.* I could and perhaps should have examined "the transformation [*Wandel*]" of Heidegger's thought via "the Saying of Appropriation [*Ereignis*]" and by asking "what happens in this movement [*was geschieht in dieser Bewegung*]? What does the transformation of questioning and answering [*wie sieht der Wandel des Fragens und Antwortens*]"[3] that comes with the turning looks like?

I have nonetheless confided to you that insisting on this type of change comes down, for me, to *identifying* Heidegger's thinking—an approach that can only end up freezing it. The passage from one epoch of Heidegger's thought to the other is as wholly mysterious—as continuous and discontinuous—as the passage from one epoch of the history of being to another, or as that from the guiding question to the fundamental question. *The Heidegger Change should itself also obey the double cineplastic regime that governs the mobility of metamorphosis and migration: the continuity and contiguity of constantly reformed forms as well as the emergency leap through the ring of fire.* The other (ex)change is of course explicitly bound up with *Ereignis*. But instead of attempting to envisage how things have *turned* in the sense of *Ereignis*, I would like to show you how *Ereignis* itself *was turned back against its first turn—how* Ereignis *was changed from the start.*

If a change in Heidegger's thought must be accounted for, then it alone, in my view, can be what leads the philosopher to go back on his conception of an originary mutation (a *Wandel* or *Wandlung*) of the essence of truth. Now it is precisely in his mature writings—those that come well after the *Kehre*—that Heidegger *changes mutability.* Texts like "Time and Being," "The End of Philosophy and the Task of Thinking," "The Turning," and "The Question Concerning Technology" are motivated by *an understanding of (ex)change that no longer presupposes an originary "change of essence." At the end, the thinking of fundamental mutation that is* Ereignis *(advent and coming) no longer presupposes the* Ereignis *(or event) of a first mutation.*

Recall that in *The End of Philosophy and The Task of Thinking*, Heidegger very clearly accounts for this change of perspective. "In the scope of this question," he writes, "we must acknowledge the fact that ἀλήθεια, unconcealment in the sense of the opening of presence, was originally only experienced as ὀρθότης, as the correctness of representations and statements. But then the assertion about the essential transformation of truth, that is, from unconcealment to correctness, is also untenable. Instead, we must say: ἀλήθεια, as opening of presence and presencing in thinking and saying, originally comes under the perspective of ὁμοίωσις and *adaequatio*, that is, the perspective [*Hinblick*] of adequation in the sense of the correspondence of representing with what is present."[4]

There is thus not or no longer a first (ex)change properly speaking. Change comes about by being put into play*, meaning as soon as being is given*—as soon as it "holds itself back and withdraws [*zurückhält und entzieht*]."[5] The structural bond uniting giving and withdrawal henceforth allows *change at the beginning to be thought, but without our climbing back to the beginning of change*. Thought cannot go back to the origin of the withdrawal, as though it had occurred after a first mutation. Short of withdrawal, there is nothing to think. "In the most extreme withdrawal of being [*im äußerten Entzug des Seins*]," as *The Principle of Reason* affirms, "thinking first brings the essence of being into view."[6]

Yet what I want to convince you of is that *the thinking of originary withdrawal does not dismiss that of an originary (ex)change but instead economizes it differently*. Starting with an analysis of the occurrences of *W, W, & V* in "Time and Being," I will be concerned in what follows to bring to light the intimate bond uniting giving, retreat, and change so as to show that giving is a *structure of substitution*, a *giving of change* at the origin that metamorphoses giving itself by transforming the ordinary understanding of it. It is impossible to think what giving change might mean without changing the gift.

It seems pertinent to me, then, to approach *Ereignis* in the flesh of its power of exchange, right where it is a question of its innate complicity with withdrawal and giving—which is to say in the circulation of a new exchange from which nothing escapes. *Nothing: not even—especially not—giving.*

Ereignis as Interchange

My proposal is that *Ereignis*, when cast in and clarified by the light of the late Heidegger's interpretation of himself, must be envisaged as an *interchange* in which the elements that circulate or "play" stop seeking to exercise mastery *on* each other and being of value *for* each other. At bottom, *Ereignis* is only the name given the possibility of an exchange *without violence* between the elements that it appropriates: *Dasein*, God, world, earth.[7] The possibility of such an exchange constitutes for me the *ethical* dimension of Heidegger's thought. This "exchange" leaves no room for *identification*: the instances present in it are neither identical nor identifiable with each other. What is at stake is an exchange, in the triple sense of a *contemporaneousness*, a *mutability*, and a *passage* into the other. At once "neither this nor that" and "everything at once."

Metaphysical "of value for" is the result of the substitution of the beingness of beings for being, and is a *compensating* exchange: essence *for* being.[8] The other (ex)change is, on the contrary, an exchange through *address*. At stake in *Ereignis* is a structure of address and reception, the instances at work in it remaining unique and mysteriously incomparable.

Gestell: The Essential Mechanism

The other (ex)change also reveals, then, a *new exchangeability between being and beings.*

Once again, abandoning the idea of an originary mutation of truth does not lead Heidegger to rule out a change of the origin. If there is not an originary change, change is at the origin. There is change.

The new ontological convertibility (being-beings, being-essence, man-God-animals-things), which must also borrow from *W, W, & V* in order to speak itself, in turn presupposes the double articulation of change—its being at once both migratory and metamorphic. The new ontological exchange proceeds both by displacement, and through a change of form. But which displacement(s)? And which form(s)?

In order to provide a response to these questions, we will watch the turning, changing *Gestell* in its metamorphoses and displacements—the Janus-headed essence-apparatus of technology that stands *between metaphysics and its other.* We will eventually see that *Gestell* is not only a fabrication of dominant forms and figures but that it also enables the emergence of the jagged trajectories and displaced, undone forms that give the last god, *Dasein*, beings, and being their new visibility (*Sichtbarkeit*).

Changing the Gift

*Envisage the other (ex)change, for itself, as if it pro-
ceeded from nothing. From nothing other than itself.
A brusque, emergency leap, no bridge below, an
improvised stand-in—here goes. As if it leapt from the
withdrawal of its own provenance, making visible the
originary withdrawal of all provenance.*

Together, we will read the lecture Time and Being,
*which lets appear in its own way—through the fan-
tastic phenomenality we will henceforth be contend-
ing with—this improbable place where donation and
change are confused; where the gift and change (W,
W, & V) are intimately interlaced.*

*Despite so much having been written on the gift
at the end of the twentieth century and the many
interpretations of the "there is, it gives"* (es gibt), *there
is not one single analysis of the central role* Wandel,
Wandlung, *and* Verwandlung *play in this 1962 text.*

You can see, then, what we are going to have to
do, which is to demonstrate how one of the essential
significations of change concerns the simultaneity of
withdrawal and of the gift, while also locating the
triad of change in the trace of the gift. "Being metamorphoses [*wird verwandelt*]," says Heidegger. *Being
is exchanged*, substituted for to the point of not keeping its name, so that it is possible to say: *Ereignis*.

But in what sense, this time, should we understand this "metamorphosis of being?" Recall this

proposition from the Summary of the seminar on *Time and Being*: "We must sharply distinguish from this meaning of transformation [*Wandlung*], which refers to metaphysics, the meaning which is intended when we say that Being is transformed—to *Ereignis* [*das Sein verwandelt wird—nämlich in das Ereignis*]."[1]

So then in just what sense does being metamorphose? We will only find out at the cost of a migration and a displacement, by proceeding with a new gait, the cadence Heidegger would have liked to impress upon the entirety of our Dasein *through the lecture's sole "step".*[2]

We will follow his step, letting ourselves be taken by the rhythm of the substitution presiding over the new ontological exchange.

The Appearances of W, W, & V in *Time and Being*

The motif of change constitutes the nuclear matter of *Time and Being*, its point of departure being a *metamorphosis*: that of being envisaged by way of its "wealth and abundance of transformation" (*Reichtum der Wandlung, Wandlungfülle*). This metabolic density or deployment of the mutability of being is what ensures, from its start to its finish, the consistency of the text's project.

At the same time, this density matures, draws tight, and then sprays out, forming a star. From the star's core to its points and from each of the points to the others, change projects out, *throwing itself*. What we are witnessing is the vertiginous *pass* of being, which loses its name so as to take another, which is lost anew to another, and yet again to another, until the *Ereignis*. At the center of the stars' points and from each one to the other circulates the mystery of a changing hold, a bond or gathering that is *changing. The mutability of being is the nuclear reaction of thought—the modification of its nucleus.*

We will now analyze together the *substitutive structure* of this explosive lecture, moving as close as we can to its incredible migratory and metamorphic power.

THE METAMORPHOSIS OF BEING

The declaration that opens the lecture is irrevocable: "Being, presencing, is metamorphosed [*Sein, Anwesen wird verwandelt*]."[3]

This metamorphosis draws all its resources from a "without" (*ohne*). Being "without beings" is the necessary and decisive *Verwandlung*—"the attempt to think being without beings becomes necessary."[4] "To think being itself," Heidegger specifies, "explicitly requires disregarding being to the extent that it is only grounded and interpreted in terms of beings and for beings as their ground, as in all metaphysics."[5]

The metamorphosis of being puts an end to the metamorphosis of being, the long and ancient history of its (metaphysical) exchange with beingness. *Yet the "without beings" which will henceforth furnish the meaning of being is not "without exchange."* Although barely metamorphosed and scarcely distinguished from beings, being will once again be exchanged. *Being without beings can no longer "be" since it can only "be given."* Being's deployment in presence no longer takes place as being, and therefore has no place being called "being" but only "*es gibt*," "there is, it gives": thinking being in its own right comes down, then, to thinking "the giving" of being, which is to say the "there is being."[6] *Being gets exchanged for its very gift.*

Heidegger then insists that the pass from being to the gift is not only a manner of speaking. "For the moment," he writes, "we have only changed the idiom [*den Sprachgebrauch geandert*] with this expression. Instead of [*statt*] saying 'it is' [*es ist*], we say 'there is,' 'It gives' [*es gibt*]."[7] In reality, a veritable exchange and transformation is accomplished with this shift from "it is" [*es ist*] to this "there is, It gives [*es gibt Sein*]." This swerve or *Wendung* in the idiom marks an authentic transformation of being itself, whose "proper" is not to be, but to (be) give(n).

THE "WEALTH" AND "ABUNDANCE" OF CHANGE

We now come back to the center or nucleus: since the " 'there is' can be experienced [*erfarhen*] and seen [*erblicken*],"[8] *we must first pay heed "to the wealth of transformation of being."* "This 'It gives, there is being,'" Heidegger writes, "might emerge somewhat more clearly once we think out more decisively the giving we have in mind here. We can succeed by paying heed to the wealth of the transformation [*den Reichtum der Wandlung*] of what, indeterminately enough, is called being, and at the same time is misunderstood in its core as long as it is taken for the emptiest of all empty concepts."[9]

Why are we again returning to the mutability of being? Why does shifting our attention to the wealth of the transformations of being allow us to see in clearer outline the point of the "there is, it gives?"

THE CONNECTION BETWEEN THE "THERE IS, IT GIVES" AND "THE TRANSFORMATIONS OF BEING"—A SIMPLE HISTORY?

Because being conceived without beings appears both as a metamorphic and migratory instance and as a wealth of change, there is something in it that points toward giving. Change is what puts thought on the road to *es gibt*, and allows for the radicalization of what *Being and Time* was already announcing, which is that the phenomenality of being is indissociable from a giving, from a "there is" or originary "It gives."

Being thought without beings—metamorphosed being—turns out to be, Heidegger now tells us, presencing, *Anwesen*. What the phrase "there is" indicates is precisely this presencing: what is born, comes, shows itself, appears, arrives . . . this is the moment of the analysis at which the motif of the *transformations* of being intervenes: "An attempt to think upon the abundance of being's transformations [*Wandlungsfülle*] secures its first foothold—which also shows the way—when we think being in the sense of presencing [*Anwesen*]."[10] What is the profound bond uniting presencing and the "abundance of transformation?"

We could immediately respond that the understanding of being as *Anwesen* corresponds to a historical [*geschichtlich*] change of its meaning. We could affirm that the "abundance of being's transformations" is just another name for its history, which corresponds to a sequence of metamorphoses and displacements of one and the same understanding of presence.

This argument is obviously not erroneous, but it is nonetheless incomplete, as it allows one to think that metamorphosed being—being thought as *Anwesen*—opens a new epoch of history that would be inscribed, just like that, after the others. But Heidegger categorically refuses this interpretation. "Here," he writes, "it is not a matter of [a] manifestation of being comparable to the metaphysical formations [*Gestalten*] of being and following them as a new manifestation."[11] It is not a matter of making the 'there is, it gives' of presencing appear a supplementary change that would come to enrich the metabolic plenitude of being. *The metamorphosis of being that comes when it is thought without beings is not a change like the others.*

"We can also note historically [*historisch*]," Heidegger says in a very clear affirmation of this, "the abundance of transformations of presencing [*Wandlungsfülle des Anwesens*] by pointing out that presencing shows itself as the ἕν, the unique and unifying One, as the λόγος, the gathering that perceives the All, as ιδέα, as οὐσία, as ἐνέργεια, *substantia, actualitas, perceptio,* monad, as objectivity, as will to power. . . . The development of the abundance of transformations of being looks at first like a history of being. But being does not have a history in the way in which a city or people have their history. What is history-like in the history of being is obviously determined by the way in which being takes place and by this alone. After what has just been explained, this means in the way in which It gives being."[12] Yet "the way in which 'it' gives being" does not mark the commencement of some new epoch. *There is no epoch of the it gives; upon the metamorphosis of being, epochs are no more.*

The relation, therefore, must be inverted, and presencing itself must be understood as change. To presence is to change. To come to be is to change, and it is because of this that there is history. That the originary substitutability of presence for itself can only take place in history and as historicity reveals that the structure of presence is an (ex)change.

You've already shown us this, you tell me impatiently. Ever since we began, you have not stopped affirming that being is nothing but its mutability. You keep saying that it all starts with a mutation.

I agree that what you say is true. But it was important to Heidegger to say, in a way that became more and more clear, *that mutation nowhere begins.* What constitutes presence is (ex)change, and this, perhaps, will allow us to explain why he abandoned his claim about an initial mutation of the essence of truth.

In its truth, according to what it in its own right is, being is from the outset changeable and changed. It substitutes for itself and is exchanged—in exchange for nothing; it loses its name. In fact, presencing can be defined, if you will, as pure substitution.

This pure substitution is given a particular name by Heidegger: "withdrawal [Entzug]."

ON SUBSTITUTION

If Heidegger returns to the abundance of the transformations of being so as to clarify the meaning of the "there is, it gives," it is in order to show that this pass—from being to the gift—is not unilateral. He is not at all affirming that the "there is, it gives" henceforth substitutes, violently and without reason, for being. This substitution is only possible inversely or in reverse, which is to say through another. *In effect, being has at all times substituted for the 'it' that gives it.* As early as Parmenides, Heidegger points out, presencing is called "there is," "it is being"—"For being is [*es ist Sein*]"[13]—so that from the onset, this 'it' was covered over and eclipsed: "In the beginning of Western thinking, being is thought, but not the 'It gives' as such."[14]

This occlusion of the "there is, it gives" indeed corresponds to the beginning of metaphysics. But the occlusion cannot occur, once again, as the mutation of an essence would; for as soon as being shows itself in its truth, it reveals its essence as a substitute—its substituting essence. *One authentically*

*substituting. Being has at all times been the substitute
for its presencing, for the "it" that lets it be. This is
why it can today let the "it" substitute for it . . . but
without ceasing to be—the replacing, the convertible.*

All presencing is thus the manifestation of a
withdrawal: one instance withdraws in exchange for
another, which takes its place. Being is, in its very
truth, the withdrawal of and from its own giving, and
giving is the structure of substitution, the possible
and necessary exchange of a gift (that gives) and a
(given) gift.

"Each of These Transformations Remained Destined in This Manner"

ANOTHER DIFFERENCE

Heidegger can now uncover the veritable historicity
of the "wealth of transformation" of being by showing that the unity of the change of being is at once
a *structure*—"pure" substitution or the withdrawal
of everything proper in its manifestation—and a
sequence of epochs.

Being is originally changing, as a change is
given with it to the very extent that what it properly
is—giving and given—is a fission of the proper (there
is/being).[15] *Opened therein, between being and itself,
is the play of a difference that is not the one that dif-
ferentiates it from beings.*

*This difference is that of being from its essence:
from its modes of coming and presencing themselves.
My proposal is that we name this difference the incision of the other in being.* This difference marks the
suspension or halt presiding over the fission and
sequencing of giving. The "it" contains and retains

its own manifestation. "Being given" contains and retains itself in giving.

Yet are you really entitled, you rightly object, to bring to light an originary economy of substitution ("pure substitution") in Heidegger, which would risk constituting the mutability of being into a transcendental authority [instance]?

What should be understood here is that in reality, *this mutability is itself only given in its changes*; that, to put it precisely, it "epochalizes" itself. "Withdrawal" and "holding back" are terms that take us back to the basic meaning of the word "epoch." "To hold back," as Heidegger says here, "is, in Greek, ἐποχή. Hence we speak of the epochs of the destiny of being."[16] He then adds: "Always retained in the withdrawing sending, being is unconcealed for thinking with its epochal abundance of transformations [*mit seiner epochalen Wandlungsfülle*]."[17] *There is no changing being, just each of the changes of being.* "Each of its transformations remains destined in this manner [*dergestalt geschickt bleibt jede seiner Wandlungen*]."[18] Being changes each time in a singular way. The play of the withdrawal of manifestation in manifestation involves not only originary (ex)change *qua* structure—a structure that could very well be provisionally qualified, if you wish, as "transcendental"—but also the epochal taking place of this (ex)change. "Being itself receives its own appropriation."[19] Being is, each time, shown in a completely unique fashion.

THE BALL TO TIME

The nucleus that is the abundance of the transformations of being only reveals, then, its fission and noncoincidence with itself. Proof of this is that *the*

pass goes to time. Isn't the self-difference of being—
its nuclear fission—isn't this difference time? This
is what Heidegger next asks, from the last point of
the star. Isn't every substitution—the originary gift of
change—a *Zeitigung*, a word the French translators
quite felicitously render as "*saisonnement*," passing of
the seasons? Isn't presencing quite simply originary
temporality?

Heidegger's response is to say that time itself, as
being, in fact undergoes a profound metamorphosis.

"Presence," he recalls, is in Greek παρουσία—
"being-present"—whose original meaning is "to
endure."[20] A secret kinship thus ties substitution
together with duration. *To endure is to change*: what
endures only lasts for a time, and is, as such, destined to lose its place. Essence (*Wesen*), moreover,
manifests a proximity with *währen*—to endure.
"What matter are we thinking when we say presencing? To presence, essence [*Wesen*], means to last
[*währen*]."[21] This enduring "requires that we perceive
biding and abiding in lasting as lasting in present
being [*Anwähren*]."[22] To endure means to remain for
a certain time.

Now what endures, moving into presence, enters
immediately into *tension* with the two other modes
of presencing: the past and the future. This *tension*
(*Reichen*) holds together the three ecstasies of time
while keeping them apart, and hence it emerges as
the fourth dimension of time. "True time is four-
dimensional. But the dimension we call fourth in
our count is, in the nature of the matter [*Sache*],
the first, that is, the giving that determines all [*das
alles bestimmende Reichen*]. In future, in past, in the
present, that giving brings about to each [*jeweils*] its
own presencing [*Anwesen*], holds them apart thus
opened and so holds them toward one another in

the nearness by which the three dimensions remain near one another."[23] This giving gathers together the three ecstasies while putting time outside itself.

At this point, you order me to stop, asking *"Haven't you been, from the very start, concerned with time, and not this originary mutability of being? Do* you really think you can speak this way of change without giving it some time, instead of devoting it a mere few lines?

Observe. At the moment time arrives (in the lecture bearing its name), it has already passed. Time can very well be named the incision of the other in being, but being is just as much the incision of the other in time. Look—time has already passed. It has been metamorphosed into what gives it, it too, in this tension: its "there is, it gives." Time is not the giving of being. In time, the gift of time has already been substituted for: "As extending is itself a giving, the giving of a giving [*das Geben eines Geben*] is concealed in true time."[24]

Time cannot be the name of originary change. Of what use would the triad be, if it only enabled one to say that time changes? "Does this reference show time to be the 'It' that gives Being? By no means. For time itself remains the gift of an 'It gives' [*die Gabe eines 'es gibt'*] whose giving preserves the realm in which presence is extended [*Anwesenheit*]. Thus the 'It' continues to be undetermined, and we ourselves continue to be puzzled."[25]

I understand the puzzle of this enigma as follows. The question is not only, who or what is this "it"?, but also: is the "it," the giving, itself definitively unchangeable and unexchangeable in its very withdrawal? Does it finally put a stop to the differential economy of change? *Is it the last word on time, being, and (ex)change?*

EREIGNIS IS NOT "A NEW DECLINATION IN THE
SERIES OF INTERPRETATIONS OF BEING"[26]

But this is where *Ereignis* comes in the lecture—
where the coming itself comes—and so we transfer
the question over to it: does *Ereignis* get the last
word on the enigma?

It is now appropriate, Heidegger at this point
says, to "think the 'It' in light of the kind [*Art*] of
giving that belongs to it: giving as destiny"—the
giving of being—"and giving as an opening up that
reaches out,"[27] meaning the giving of time. But
"what determines [*bestimmt*] both . . . in their own
[*in ihr Eigenes*], that is, in their belonging together
[*ihr Zusammengehören*], we shall call *das Ereignis*."[28]

Ereignis is indeed what "the 'It' that gives in
'It gives being,' 'It gives time,' proves to be [*bezeugt
sich*]."[29] The advent, or appropriating event, names
at once the incision of the other in being and the
incision of the other in time.

Is *Ereignis*, then, the star in definitive outline?
I pose the question once more: does Ereignis not
change, and exchange itself? *Where in it, in that
event, is the incision of the other?*

"But could it not be that we might suddenly be
relieved of all the difficulties, all these complicated
and seemingly fruitless discussions, by raising and
answering this simple and long-overdue question:
What is *Ereignis*?"[30] A return to the core? A return to
the abundance of the transformations of being? Not
in this case, for the nucleus has just lost its value
as ontological protoplasm; it too has *passed*: "if being
itself proves [*erweist*] to be such that it belongs to
Ereignis, then the question we have advanced takes us
back to what first of all demands its own determina-

tion."[31] *Ereignis*, the "Summary" states apropos this question, "is not a new imprint [*Prägung*] of being in the history of being" since "being belongs to *Ereignis* and is reabsorbed in it."[32] In other words, *Ereignis* is not a new destinal figure, and it marks, in this sense, a caesura in the midst of the abundance of the transformations of being. " 'Being as *Ereignis*': formerly philosophy thought being in terms of beings as ιδέα, *energeia*, *actualitas*, will—and now, one might believe, as *Ereignis*. Understood in this way, *Ereignis* means a transformed [*abgewandelte*] interpretation of being which, if correct, represents a continuation of metaphysics."[33] Nonetheless "the history of being is at an end for that thinking which enters into *Ereignis*—in that being, which lies in sending—is no longer what is to be thought explicitly. Thinking then stands in and before That which has sent the various forms [*Gestalten*] of epochal being. This, however, what sends as *Ereignis*, is itself unhistorical [*ungeschichtlich*], or more precisely without destiny [*geschicklos*]."[34]

No new point, *Ereignis* is the mode of being of the star as such: the coming to self of being and the coming to self of time—"time and being appropriated in Appropriation [*Zeit und Sein gereicht im Ereignen*]."[35] *Ereignis* expresses, then, the very movement of originary change, the mutual exchange of the instances gathered in it.

Can *Ereignis*, in that event, be considered what *fixes* this exchange? Heidegger certainly warns against it: "We can never place *Ereignis* in front of us, neither as something opposite us nor as something all-encompassing [*noch als das alles Umfassende*]." The question, however, remains: *does Ereignis put a stop to the "step" of the lecture?*

It is clear that the substitutive structure of the lecture that emerged during its declination of the occurrences of *W, W, & V* seems to get unequivocally suspended upon *Ereignis'* entry onto the scene. Indeed, "the step of the approach that shows" unceasingly executes leaps from one fundamental term to another, as if it could cross, by fording, the stream of change and then *end* with *Ereignis.* "The lecture," we now read, "goes from *Being and Time* past what is, peculiar to *Time and Being* to the It that gives, and from this to *Ereignis.*"[36] More exactly, the path goes from "being" to "time," then again to "being" as *Anwesen,*[37] then to the "there is, It gives,"[38] then to the structure of giving, to destining,[39] epochality, time, "tension [*Reichen*]," the giving of giving, to the "it" of the "It gives,"[40] and finally to *Ereignis.*

Heidegger affirms that there is no "gradation in the sense of an ever greater originality within the concepts named there"—they "do not present a gradation [*Stufung*], but rather stations [*Stationen*] on a way back which is opened and leads preliminarily into *Ereignis.*"[41] The question nonetheless rebounds. If all stations lead to *Ereignis*, what is *Ereignis*? A terminal? The finally immutable place where the metamorphoses of both being and time come to a stop? With *Ereignis*, doesn't the gift stop giving? Doesn't it receive its ultimate appellation, which suspends the substitution of names and the exchange of gifts?

And what if, at bottom, the metamorphosis of being has not taken place? And what if at bottom, whatever Heidegger might say, Ereignis, *on account of the very stability of its name—its stature as foundation and regime—leads us right back to the register of beingness* (Ereignis *as* summum ens)*, a register that we would in fact have never left?*

Ereignis and Donation

"THE VIOLATED ENIGMA"

These are the profound questions that Jean-Luc Marion addresses to Heidegger in *Being Given*.[42] Marion himself also insists on the economy of substitution that characterizes the itinerary of the lecture: being and time, he agrees, progressively disappear to the profit of giving, which is in turn abolished in *Ereignis*, which purely and simply takes its place.[43] But for him, this last substitution is a *violation*, a profanation of the enigma of the "there is, it gives," and consequently *a violation and profaning of the gift*. *Ereignis* would in its arrival take back everything that had been given, effacing the structure of giving that was otherwise so amply deployed in the lecture. By failing to maintain the anonymity of the "it," *Ereignis* invalidates the giving of giving. Heidegger insists on the importance of "capitalizing the 'It' of 'It gives,'" so that no proper name might lower the givenness that puts it into operation to the rank of a causation or effectuation by this or that being, privileged or not. The indeterminacy does not save just the enigma; it defends pure givenness."[44] Yet "contrary to his declared prudence," Marion continues, "Heidegger immediately lifts the anonymity of the 'it' and obfuscates the enigma. He violates his own interdiction as soon as he formulates it by baptizing the 'it' with the name *Ereignis*: the 'it' that gives in 'It gives being, It gives time,' proves to be *Ereignis*, that is, advent."[45]

In the end, Heidegger would supposedly not think the gift. He would evade the conceptual offering at the very moment when he pretends to confer upon

it an irreducible originarity. "At first glance" Marion
writes, "*Zeit und Sein* does indeed confirm and radicalize what *Sein und Zeit* put forth: the phenomenality
of being goes hand-in-hand with an originary *'cela
donne,'* to the point of passing into it."[46] But as the
lecture unfolds, the 'It gives' increasingly disappears,
to *Ereignis*' profit: "The first move [of the lecture]—
reducing presence (being) to a gift appropriate to
givenness—is completed and (also annulled) by a
second—abolishing givenness in the advent."[47] Even
if it is not a new interpretation of being, *Ereignis* is,
despite everything, *an interpretation of giving*, a surplus of understanding and identification that breaks
off the deployment of giving itself. *We would here be
taken back to the perspective of beingness*: *Ereignis*
covers or dissimulates the "it" in presentifying it.
In this sense, the "interpretation" that *Ereignis* is
would very much be, whatever Heidegger might say
about it, a new figure of metaphysics, an epochal
metamorphosis exactly like the others.

How could the initial aim of the lecture be
turned against itself this way? Marion starts with
the prefatory statement of the lecture, according to
which "being, presencing, is metamorphosed." He
shows that this metamorphosis corresponds to the
transposition of being into a regime of donation: "to
think that 'It gives' being (and time), therefore to
transpose being into the realm of givenness, does
not imply an arbitrary act of will . . . because it is
necessary to recognize the impossibility of holding
being within the horizon of being (only beings are,
being *is* not), therefore the obligation of assigning it
a new horizon."[48] So by ultimately christening *Ereignis* the "it" and thereby offending against the anonymity of giving, Heidegger *would have brought the
meaning of being back to its first horizon, annulling*

transposition. "Ereignis," by its very name, because it has and is a name, would still be "an ontic agent," and thus always capable of being made to indicate a referent.[49] *No metamorphosis or (ex)change, therefore, could take place.* "Givenness, to be sure, but only as a brief transition between being and *Ereignis*, a mere relay, provisional."[50]

The "Favor"

After an attentive reading of these analyses, and while admiring their power, we ask together: *what would an unexchangeable giving be? A giving that would always be what it is? If it were not exchanged, if it were not sequenced in its structure and distanced from itself, couldn't it be recuperated by the old pair of the ontic and the ontological? How, exactly, would the anonymity of the "it"—its being definitively fixed, and placed under house arrest from its very going-incognito— make it the guarantor of the veritable metamorphosis of being? What would a giving be that would have neither the possibility nor right to change names, to enter itself into exchange?* "A mere relay, provisional," *as Marion says, and thus changing indeed. So why not? Why not admit that the gift could be changing?*

That it could be named, for instance, Ereignis?

Like me, you know that the name *Ereignis* is perfectly interchangeable, that it does not mark any "stop." Quite often, *Ereignis* is assimilated to being, and being to *Ereignis*.[51] Yet *Ereignis* is itself changing. The *"Summary"* of the seminar devoted to *Time and Being* further specifies: "Thus the lack of destiny of *Ereignis* [*das Geschicklosigkeit des Ereignisses*] does not mean that it has no movement [*Bewegtheit*]. Rather, it means that the manner of movement most proper to *Ereignis* [is] turning toward us in withdrawal [*die Zuwendung im Entzug*]—first shows itself as what is to be thought."⁵² *Ereignis* turns, overturns, withdraws, shows itself to be changing. As soon as it is shown, it is immediately exchanged, "depropriated," "subtracts, down to its disenclosure, what is most proper to it." *In this sense, it designates nothing more, above all nothing other, than the "it" or the "that."*

What shocks a reader like Jean-Luc Marion is perhaps less the pretend nominative or substantive value of Ereignis *than a conception of giving as (ex) change, of self.* For what is indeed set up in the lecture, under the name of the *Verwandlung* of being and presence, *is the economy of an originary ontological substitutability that at once institutes and "destitutes" donation by offending against it with the names of its neighbors.*

In *Time and Being*, the question for Heidegger is not simply that of "the transposition of being into a regime of donation," to resume with the formula employed in *Being Given*. We concede that the term "transposition" (change of place, permutation, metathesis) adequately translates *Verwandlung*. But what better way is there not to accord this transposition any importance, to relegate it to the rank of a simple *passage* so as to stop at its result, than not to see, as we have said, that *W, W, & V* constitute the *core* of the lecture, the element through which it is deployed, and not to recognize that *the transposition necessarily affects the instances it transposes? The "transposition" of being "into a regime of giving" necessarily involves a transposition—a displacement and metamorphosis—of giving itself.*

In *Time and Being*, Heidegger no longer thinks change or the giving of originary (ex)change according to a genetic perspective (provided that he ever did);

rather, he presents them as horizons—structures at once horizontal and epochal—of transformation. The terms of the origin are turned into each other by virtue of *the absolute exchangeability of the originary gift.*

Giving, it is true, loses its position of favor. But so as to be better given to "the favor."

The new ontological convertibility is, in effect, an *economy of the favor* (*Gunst*). It is no longer beings that are *of value for* being; instead, giving, then the "it," and then *Ereignis itself* withdraw *in favor* of each other.

"To think being explicitly requires us to relinquish being as the ground of beings in favor of the giving which prevails concealed in unconcealment, that is, in favor of the It gives."[53]

This "favor" marks the coming of an exchange without privilege, in which no instance, rightly, receives *favorable treatment.* The "it gives" loses favor in favor of *Ereignis*, which loses favor by in turn entering exchange. The star forms a circle (*Ring*). The circle of all metamorphoses.

Second Incision

Gunst

There is an originary exchange of presence with itself that does not profit (from itself) or capitalize (on itself); an exchange, not of being for beingness, but of being for its essence. Reigning over the first exchange is the law of the "of value for" (gelten), while freely at play within the second is "the favor" (Gunst). Gunst *can mean favor, benevolence, good grace, privilege, gift, and opportunity, while "günstig" is what one calls an opportune, interesting, or propitious thing. The difference between* Geltung *and* Gunst *may seem slight, but it is nonetheless decisive. The first change is exchange through usurpation and enslavement; the other change is an exchange involving neither mastery nor violation, exchange through letting be. We said this before: exchange through compensation/exchange by address.*

The first exchange owes its possibility to the second. The substitution of beingness for being proceeds, though secretly, from the origin of a favor or grace. "In the beginning of Western thinking, being is thought, but not the 'it gives' as such. The latter withdraws in favor of the gift [*dieses entzieht sich zugunsten der Gabe*] which it gives. The gift is thought and conceptualized from then on exclusively as being with regards to beings."[1] *This is how it is with everything that comes to pass, epochality and history themselves:* "Epoch does not mean a span of time in occurrence, but rather the fundamental characteristic of sending, the actual holding-back of itself in favor [*zugunsten*] of the discernibility of the gift, that is, in favor [*zugunsten*] of beings with regard to the grounding of beings."[2]

No withdrawal, then, that does not withdraw "in favor of." This alone accounts for why every withdrawal is at the same time a dispensation: "Metaphysics is the history of the imprints of being [*Seinsprägung*], that is, viewed from *Ereignis,* the history of the self-withdrawal of what is sending in favor [*zugunsten*] of the destinies."[3] *The first change—the first apparatus of exchange—is that of profit, the second that of sharing, which is to say co-belonging* (Zugehörigkeit). *There are two distinct modalities of appropriation in appropriation. Appropriation through compensation is appropriation of the other, whereas appropriation "by address" is being appropriated by and to the other, a way of offering oneself to it. One of the senses of the word* Zueignung *is "dedication." Being appropriated by the other is like dedicating oneself to it, as though one was making or writing a dedication: this is what, privilege without privilege, the favor means.*

The favor of "the incalculable [das Unberechenbare]," *the favor of an "offering" through which* "there occurs [*ereignet sich*] . . . the grace that being has bestowed on the human essence, so that human beings may, in their relation to being, assume the guardianship of being."[4] *The favor of poverty.* "How else would a particular humankind," Heidegger further asks, "ever find its way into an originary thanking unless the favor of being [*die Gunst des Seins*], through an open relation to such favor, granted human beings the nobility of a poverty [*den Adel der Armut*] in which the freedom of offering conceals the treasure of its essence [*den Schatz ihres Wesen verbirgt*]."[5]

Perhaps, however, there is indeed no "authentic" thinking of giving in Heidegger. Perhaps the Heideggerian vow of poverty remains just short of a generosity that consists in "giving what one doesn't have." I will admit to you, though, that none of this matters to me—not at all.

What concerns me, on the contrary, is that we see that the favor does not, for Heidegger, interrupt change but instead appears qua *a new ontological exchange. The instances appropriated by each other continue to pass to and into each other—their essences are exchanged. They are mutually transformed, migrating in each other's direction and disappearing into each other. This means, for example, that when you give me something, you are, in a certain fashion, metamorphosed into me. You cannot, moreover, really give me anything unless it is through the favor of this transformability. This is what renders the gift possible as an act that, at bottom and in a particular fashion, consists foremost of knowing how to put oneself in the place of the other. Alterity is certainly not outside exchange. Don't you think it's time to remember this, and to start unsettling the understanding of alterity as pure transcendence and dissymmetry? Isn't it high time we consider the other, and finally relieve it of the burden of its alterity? A burden that is basically preventing us from doing what could be* for *it?*

Heidegger tells us that we number at least "four" in perpetually exchanging ourselves this way. The favor, it too, is a molt. There cannot be a gift without the passing or circulating of essences into each other, which happens by grace of a sort of quasi-animal mimesis.

I can only love and look after this, that, or those who allow me, in one way or another, to change (change myself) in them: "Thus Meister Eckhart says, adopting an expression from Dionysius the Areopagite: *diu minne ist der natur, daz sie den menschen wandelt in die dinc, die er minnet*—love is of such a nature that it changes man into the things he loves."[6]

This transformation, I will doubtlessly be told, is a reduction of the alterity of the other, of he or she who is loved and their foreignness. I believe, however, that there is nothing to this: the alterity of the other is perhaps just what announces itself in and for me, and as this very strange capacity I have to metamorphose, displace myself, and to be born beyond myself so as to become akin to the other—a capacity whose existence the other reveals to me. In tales, metamorphosis is always at once an effect of the other (of its kiss, for instance) and something addressed to it (I await it, like a prince; I am not at all available for it, like Gregor Samsa). What sense would there be to undergoing metamorphosis all alone and in the absence of witnesses? Heidegger recalls on this point a saying of Nietzsche's: "Only whoever transforms himself is related to me [*nur wer sich wandelt, ist mir verwandt*]."[7]

Pure gifts there are not, if by this one understands gifts that are not in play, never circulate themselves, and that neither want to lose their names nor enter the economic as remainders. Moving from the "of value for" to the favor does not at all signify the end of the circuit—economy never ends. The end of metaphysics does not put a stop to circulation. Mutability is all there is.

This is to say that Heidegger would not, in my sense, share Derrida's view that the gift "must not circulate, it must not be exchanged, it must not in any case be exhausted, as a gift, by the process of exchange, by the movement of circulation of the circle. . . . If the figure of the circle is essential to economics, the gift must remain aneconomic. *Not that it remains foreign to the circle, but it must remain a relationship of foreignness to the circle.*"[8]

The conception of the gift that I have been attempting to describe with and for you necessarily involves, on the contrary, ontological mixing, meaning that it is at once the giving of economy and an economized instance. Never will the gift abolish the mutability of being—or of the gift.

The phrase "economy of the gift," it is quite true, can simply and brutally signify the activity of subjects exchanging objects. This is not, however, what Heidegger means by gift. Nevertheless, he could very well offend against the gift if the latter is authentic only when it has no object. "The gift," as Marion says, "is given . . . even and especially if it loses all ontic and objective support."[9] But this, again, also is not true. Giving is first of all the giving of things. Except for them, nothing could be given, nor could "it" give something—anything. The thing, indeed, is exactly what can be given in the object. Heidegger never forgets this when he speaks of the gift as a new exchange between being and beings. He does not forget things.

The time has come to change the other—to speak of some other thing.

6

Surplus Essence

Gestell and Automatic Conversion

Thinking being in its own right does not, then, come down to serving notice to all exchangeability between being and beings. Indeed, the other thinking does stop taking beingness as its foundation. But the possibility of suspending the exchange of being and beingness— of giving the change that governs the entire history of metaphysics—only serves to liberate the play of a new ontological substitution: the "favor," the structure of a mutual (ex)change involving neither hierarchy nor domination between being and beings.

We have come back to the metamorphoses and migrations (W, W, & V) announced in Contributions *when the "other beginning" is. The new ontological exchangeability, we recall, is often called the "simultaneity [Gleichzigkeit] of being and beings." Dasein, writes Heidegger, "transforms [verwandelt] be-ing and beings in their simultaneity [das Seyn und das Seiende zugleich in ihre Gleichzeitigkeit verwandelt]."[1] This metamorphosis is not at all an occlusion of their difference but respects, on the contrary, their "separation" (χωρισμός).*

Could some other power than the one that proves to be the mutability of being and beings be revealed in this metamorphosis? Another power than this power enabling them to grant favors to each other, exchange themselves, and pass (in)to each other while not, for that, becoming confused?

"Just what are you getting at?" you ask impatiently.

What I am saying is that beings are not only *given(s)* [*étant donné*] but also something *giving* [*étant donateur*].

Metamorphosed beings give being its visibility. Returning to §32 of *Contributions*, we find Heidegger writing that "being itself, *Ereignis* as such, will be visible for the first time [*das Sein selbst, das Ereignis als solches, erstmals sichtbar wird*]."[2] And in what sense should "visible" be understood here? The response is clear: visible means figured, to be given in a figure: "The onset of be-ing [*Anfall des Seyns*] is posed and preserved for the first time in a figure [*in einer Gestalt . . . ertsmal verwahrt wird*]."[3]

What I dub "fantastic" is precisely this new figure of being, which, liberating the image of being as originary molting, reveals in the same instant the mutability of the figural, the ontic mutability, that is, which responds to ontological mutability as though it were the latter's echo or shadow—as the narcissism of a new era and time.

If certain readers of Heidegger are made uneasy by the fact that *Ereignis*, as a result of naming the "there is/it gives," could be a new intrusion of beingness into the very heart of the originary gift, if they venture only the least risk of ontico-ontological confusion or bastardization, it is because they are behind on *the metamorphosis of beings*. They remain quite deaf to Heidegger's affirmation that *beings, they too, have changed*.

It is surprising to notice that the majority of Heidegger's commentators think beings do not change. Being, yes, because it is transposable from one his-

torical regime to another, but not beings. Although the possibility of novel beings is everywhere acknowledged—technical beings, for instance, like clones, the internet, or novel social arrangements like pactes civils de solidarité (PACS)[4]*—that ontic structure itself might also be mutable is not.*

Nevertheless, the beings giving being its figure today are no longer the same. The good old beings of metaphysics are no more. And the figure is certainly no longer the old, reliable figure of metaphysics, no longer the imprint or body and sensible translation of being. No: the whole of beings is henceforth something else entirely. Being can only show itself "in altered figures of beings [*in den veränderten Gestalten des Seienden*],"[5] in figures, that is, become other than the figure. *The metamorphosis of beings renders the metamorphosis of being visible.* "[B]eings as such also [*auch das* Seiende *als solches*] undergo a transformed interpretation [*verwandelte Auslegung*],"[6] and this interpretation accompanies, even while it at the same time precedes, the metamorphosed interpretation of being.

Asking after, with regard to both of the changes, the migrations and metamorphoses of being also necessarily involves asking after the migrations and metamorphoses of the beings contemporary with them—an interrogation that aims at the point of a new convertibility of being and beings.

There is an exchange between being and beings that is not an incarceration of the ontological difference, but its liberation.

So then why does it go habitually unseen? Why do philosophers, you yet wonder, remain blind to this new visibility? *Because it is hiding.* Just as there is a withdrawal of being, so too is there a screening of beings: "*das bergende Seiendes*," says Heidegger:

"sheltering beings."[7] Beings, they too, are withdrawn. Now what was it you believed to be the case?

A secret simultaneity at all times governs the relation between the withdrawal of being and the withholding of beings.

If being as understood by metaphysics is not in its truth being, then beings as metaphysics understands them are not anymore in their truth beings. The new visibility of being—the metamorphosis of being confirmed in the metamorphosed figure of beings—is (in) the image of a double withdrawal that exits the forgetting. Another ontico-ontological convertibility can thus be deployed.

What reveals the Gestell *is this: the essence of modern technics.*

In effect, what Heidegger calls the Gestell, *or enframing, the "Janus-head" between the two (ex) changes, is an ontological hybrid; neither being nor beings, it is both at once. Everything in it changes, and everything in it is exchanged. Migrations are born from each other there, metamorphoses effacing the traces of each other.*

*And all of this happens by grace of a convertibility inscribed in its very name—*Gestell.

"A Change in Being—That is, Now, in the Essence of *Gestell*—Comes to Pass . . ."[8]

BETWEEN TWO CHANGES

The *Gestell* clearly appears as a currency exchange located between two changes. Heidegger, we recall, in fact characterizes it as an intermediary, a "Janus-head" between two understandings of change. "Between the epochal formations of being and the transformation of being into *Ereignis*," one can read in the "Summary of a Seminar on the Lecture *Time and Being*." "stands enframing. Enframing is an in-between stage, so to speak. It offers a double aspect, one might say, a Janus-head. It can be understood as a kind of continuation of the will to will, thus as an extreme formation [*Ausprägung*] of being. At the same time, it is a first form [*Vorform*] of *Ereignis* itself."[9]

Gestell itself appears, then, as an instance undergoing a mutation, a process enabling an exchange between the two fundamental modalities of mutability—the metaphysical and the ultrametaphysical. It is, first, a new "imprint" or *Prägung* of being, and opens, on account of that, a new epoch that will be inscribed in the tradition's long succession of figures. "Continuation of the will to will," *Gestell* is the consummation of the logic of domination governing metaphysics in its entirety: beingness that commands (as ground of being), man that commands, God that commands.[10] Modern technology bears in its achievement of itself the very concept of will, authorizing the absolute mastery of energies that are as much natural (mineral, hydraulic, and atomic resources) as intellectual (cybernetic domination) and as much economic (industrial agriculture and industry itself) as social (the exploitation of "human resources").[11]

The *Gestell* is also, secondly, the "first form" (*Vorform*), the prefiguration and annunciatory form of *Ereignis*, of a gathering involving neither violence nor domination. The *Gestell* is therefore not only the terminal form of the unleashing of the will. In itself, it is *a mode of unveiling*, which is to say *a mode of advent, of "eventness"* in whose midst "is shown what is." This mode indeed "unveils the real as [a] fund," a reserve (or "standing reserve"—*Bestand*) of available and masterable energy.[12] But it at the same time reveals the properly ontological texture of this fund. Technology is always, originally, a *mode* of *being*.

Between Two Modalities of the Metamorphic and Migratory

Janus-headed, the *Gestell* not only lies between an *epochal change* (one epoch more) and *the change of epochality itself* but is also the midpoint, one could even again say the turning point or hinge, *between two manners of changing, between, that is, the intra- and extra-metaphysical modalities of migration and metamorphosis.*

Metamorphosis has here been characterized, following its metaphysical understanding, as the re-formation or re-formulation (*Umformung*) of one and the same form. As to migration, it appeared, in accordance with its metaphysical definition, as a trajectory, a displacement (*Verlagerung*) that, while being erratic, no less follows the route set at departure. Now it is true that when understood in this sense, re-formation (*Umformung*) and displacement (*Verlagerung*) correspond to the kinetic regimes privileged by the essence of modern technology: "unlocking, transforming [*umformen*], storing, distributing, and switching about."[13] Enframing presides, on the one hand, over a *constant metamorphic enchainment*: "what is transformed [*das Umgeformte*] is stored up, what is stored up is distributed, and what is distributed is switched about."[14] And these transformations also trigger, on the other, a series of *displacements*. The flow of water is diverted, carbon extracted, stored and exported, and energies as such are directed to follow *one direction and one alone*: "This setting-upon [*das Stellen*] that challenges forth [*herausfordet*] the energies of nature is an expediting [*Fordern*]" and "it expedites in that . . . it is always directed from the beginning toward furthering something else, i.e. toward driving on to the maximum yield at the minimum expense [*bei geringstem*]."[15]

But it can just as much as be seen that a type of metamorphosis emerges with the *Gestell* that is not the disguised prolongation of this one same form, but rather a type of coursing that is no longer of the order of a simple phoronomy. These new modalities of change can be characterized as *the form of the estrangement of form, and the course of the estrangement of teleological coursing*. The *Gestell* therefore renders visible, right on the world itself, the two aspects of the cineplastic constituting the Heideggerian imaginary. Visible in it, on the one hand, are organic growths, energetic transformations, morphogenetic orientations, limit crossings, figurations of accumulation, bodies emerging from other bodies, maturation, clear directions, signposted routes, regulated and oriented displacements. These are *cineplastic* equivalences—a form by displacement, and a displacement by form—and cineplastic *equivalences*: every form and displacement are of value. "The *Gestell* lets the ground command, lets the absence of ground exercise its mastery. Everything is of value."[16] Also seen there, on the other hand, are abandoned, incipient forms, alien traffic, supple growths, and unmanaged exchanges—*cineplastic favors*. "When we once open ourselves expressly to the essence of technology, we find ourselves unexpectedly taken into a freeing claim [*in einen befreienden Anspruch*]."[17]

What is "ambiguous [*zweideutig*]" here is the *essence* of technology. It is this that is the *intermediary*, or *relay*, between the two changes.

BEING-BEINGS-ESSENCE: THE GESTELL "CHANGES" (IT ALL)

Essence, das Wesen, is indeed the nerve center of the Heideggerian thinking of *Gestell*. Everything I just recalled on the subject of the median character of *Gestell*, the Janus-head between two manners of changing, can now be brought back and reduced to its source: *the metabolism of the essential*.

The *Gestell*, we have seen, remains an imprint or epoch of being. It is, in this sense, a form of the essence of being: the reign of the "triggering" that is deployed today. The essence of technology and the essence of being are from a historical point of view the same thing. In *The Turning*, Heidegger writes that "[i]f Enframing is a destining of essence of being itself, then we may venture to suppose [*vermuten*] that the enframing, as one of the modes of being's essence, changes [*wandelt*]."[18] A new epoch of being comes forth. Being changes destinies, and *Gestell* is the name of this (ex)change. However, the meaning of the verb "to change" in the phrase "enframing . . . changes" is more difficult to apprehend than it would seem. In fact, it is quite equivocal, authorizing two readings.

AN INCOMPARABLE DESTINY

First reading. "*Gestell* . . . as one of the modes of being's essence, changes." In a certain way, the veritable subject of the verb "to change" (*wandeln*) here can be regarded not as *Gestell* but rather as—philosophical, not grammatical—being. "Being ever comes to presence as a destiny, and, accordingly, changes in the manner of a destiny [*sich geschichtlich wandelt*]."[19] The *Gestell* simply corresponds, then, to an epochal change of being. What Heidegger "ventures to suppose [*vermuten*]" in saying that "the *Gestell* changes" is that the reign of modern technology is but one of the figures of the destining of being, and that, contrary to what is too often believed, the deployment of modern technology signifies neither the interruption nor annihilation nor liquidation of being's sending but rather its *accomplishment*. A risky presumption, the *Gestell* as *ontological* change.

Yet Heidegger does not for that minimize the specificity of the enframing. "[W]hat gives destining its character as destining," he elaborates, "is that it takes place so as suitably to adapt itself to the ordaining that is ever one."[20] The singularity of *Gestell* is irreducible, since it has become today the foundation of our relation to being. "If a change in being—i.e. now, in the coming-to-presence of the *Gestell*," Heidegger affirms, "comes to pass [*wenn ein Wandel im Sein sich . . . ereignet*], then this in no way means that technology, whose essences lies in *Gestell*, will be done away with [*werde beiseitigt*]. Technology will not be struck down; and it most certainly will not be destroyed."[21]

Despite this, it can be asked if the role of the *Gestell* is limited to being only an *ontological aggravation*, a severe consummation of the forgetting of being and the first (ex)change. Many of Heidegger's statements lean in this direction, such as this one: "The *Gestell* is the essence of modern technology. The essence of *Gestell* is the being of beings itself; not in general nor of each being but rather as that which accomplishes the oblivion of the essence of being. The event of this accomplishment of the oblivion of being determines in a primordial way the epoch in which, today, being is in the mode of *Gestell*."[22] What is dangerous, Heidegger repeats, is not technology in itself but the forgetting of being revealed

164   The Heidegger Change

by it. *Being is what is dangerous, due to its being mutable, originally withdrawn, subtracted, and ready to give change (through its throwing off the trail) to the point that it forgets itself amid its metamorphoses, and indifferently turns its back on its possible capitalizations and history; to the point, also, that it no longer recognizes itself in any way, so that it becomes afraid (of itself).* "Gestell as the essence of being," writes Heidegger, "exposes being on the basis of the truth of its essence."[23] Yet being "is horrified [*entsetzt*] by its own truth."[24] "Being in its essence is the danger of itself [*Das Seyn ist in seinem Wesen die Gefahr seiner Selbst*]."[25] *The mutability of being is its horrible truth*: "Being turns away from its own essence into the oblivion of this essence, and in that way simultaneously turns counter to the preservation of its essence."[26] Being "denies its own essence."[27] *Ontological mutability is completely indifferent to itself.* Which is to say that *it makes no sense.*

Isn't the *Gestell*, then, merely the epochal and phenomenal servant of this forgetting and indifference of being?

AN ESSENCE-TRANSFORMER

Second reading. We return to the claim that "*Gestell* . . . as one of being's modes of essence, changes ([*wandelt*]," while considering this time the possibility that *Gestell* is the veritable—now both philosophical *and* grammatical—subject of the verb *wandeln.*

The Gestell *itself changes.* So that rather than being just one of the changes of being, *it changes this very change; it changes (the essence of) being.* "Something astounding strikes us," writes Heidegger. "It is technology itself that makes the demand on us to think in another way what is usually understood by 'essence.'"[28]

"But in what way?" we must ask with him.[29] *The Gestell is an essence-transformer* affecting not just its own essence (with the *Gestell*, Heidegger writes, "the essence of technology [is] led into the change of its destining [*in den Wandel seines Geschickes geleitet werden*]"[30]) but all essence, essence in general.

Why? We broach here what for me constitutes the decisive point of Heidegger's thinking of technology: *the Gestell is in itself, right down to its very name, a transformation. "Gestell" can name ontological convertibility because its very name has been converted.*

Which means what? In several reprises, Heidegger declares that he always twists *Gestell*'s ordinary sense when employing it: "According to ordinary usage, the word *Gestell* [frame] means some kind of apparatus [*ein Gerät*], e.g. a bookrack. *Gestell* is also the name for a skeleton."[31] Yet in philosophical language, *Gestell* no longer designates a technological object but rather *the essence of technology. And such a signification, says Heidegger,* is a "transformed meaning *(gewandelte Bedeutung)*."[32]

That a being, a "technological" object or Gestell *in the ordinary sense, would be in this way capable of letting its essence speak instead of and for it, and could immediately cede its place, without further ado: this is the sign that something in technology is originally ready for ontological conversion. The* Gestell *is a being that lets its essence be given for it. But what sort of being could do this? If this substitutability attests to a metamorphosis and migration of essence, it at the same time reveals a metamorphosis and migration of beings themselves.*

THE OTHER BEINGS

Gestell is the *mode of being by which the withdrawal of being appears*. The truth of the essence of technology is the phenomenon of the withdrawal of being. In the lecture entitled *The Turning*, Heidegger clarifies this point, which is of capital importance. On one side, as we saw, "as the danger, being turns about into the oblivion of its essence, turns away from this essence, and in that way turns counter to the truth of its essence."[33] And on the other, "in the essence of the danger there conceals itself, therefore, the possibility of a turning in which the oblivion belonging to the essence of being will so turn itself that, with this turning, the truth of the essence of being will turn in—into whatever is [*in das Seiende eigens einkehrt*]."[34] If the truth of being shows itself in the *Gestell*, then the oblivion, inasmuch as it is phenomenalized, is no longer an oblivion. If the oblivion "expressly comes to pass [*ereignet*]," then "oblivion as such turns in and abides [*einkehrt*]"[35] so that it is "is no longer the oblivion."[36] In an appendix to the 1949 lecture "Das Ding," "The Thing," Heidegger writes that the oblivion "remains all the same a forgetting [*bleibt auch eine Vergessenheit*]," but one that is "transformed [*gewandelt*]."[37]

Yet it is not only the oblivion that is transformed, but also beings, which are what let it appear. With the Gestell, it should be repeated, the truth of being makes its entrance into beings: "with this turning, . . . the essence of being will turn . . . into whatever is [*in das Seiende eigens einkehrt*]."[38] *Beings are then no longer the same. Ontological mutability, which is given with the* Gestell—*revealed and unveiled with it*—*provokes a displacement of the difference between being and beings.*

Technological beings are no longer the beings of beingness. Beings have become porous, essentially porous, and this lets the truth of being pass across them without this rendering it present *(vorhanden).*

This is why a technological being is never simply a program. It is always at the same time a promise, automatically opening the door to the essential. What the Gestell *bespeaks is precisely this point of indistinction between program—automatism—and promise, the essential.*

When I hold a technological object in my hands, I am never holding it alone, but the precipitate of an ontological mutation as well. An essence lies between my fingers, an essence about which I cannot form an idea; the sequential blinking of a being and its essence, their circulating and passing into each other. An entire history, which is also grounding and solidifying, sitting in the palm of one's hand, like Dali's soft watches. This is the new (ontological) state of things.

"Because we no longer encounter what is called the Enframing within the purview of representation [*nicht mehr im Gesichtkreis des Vorstellens*] which lets us think the being of beings as presence . . . , the Enframing no longer concerns us as something that is present [*als An-wesende*]" and "therefore seems at first strange [*befremdich*]."[39]

THE OTHER ESSENCE

This estrangement is also, of course, what of essence metamorphosed beings let pass *into* them, let pass *for* them. "It is technology itself," recall, "that makes the demand on us to think in another way what is usually understood by essence."[40]

The essence of technology might be nothing technological, but it also is not at all, in a certain fashion, of (an) essence anymore. "The essence of modern technology" no longer corresponds to the traditional definition of essence as a trait that is *generic* or *common* to several beings, which would belong as a result under its jurisdiction. "Enframing," writes Heidegger, is not "the common genus [*gemeinsame Gattung*] for everything technological."[41] The latter do not "fall" under the law of the "concept" of *Gestell*. *The* Gestell *is certainly a "gathering," but it does not constitute the beingness—or quiddity—of technological beings.* "Thus Enframing, as a destining of revealing, is indeed the essence of technology, but never in the sense of genus and *essentia*."[42]

Consequently, technological objects are no longer particular cases, not children of the same family. If "the word *Gestell* does not mean here a tool or any kind of apparatus," then reciprocally, "machines and apparatuses are no more cases and kinds of *Gestell* than are the man at the switchboard and the engineer in the drafting room. Each of these in its own way indeed belongs . . . within Enframing; but Enframing is never the essence of technology in the sense of a genus."[43] *The* Gestell *is neither a law nor a case of its own law.*

Essence, this time understood as *Wesung*, the metamorphosis and displacement of *Wesen*, is a sameness (*Selbigkeit*) that is not equality (*Gleichheit*), a co-belonging (*Zugehörigkeit*) that is not plurivalidity. This mobile gathering is precisely the one Heidegger calls the *Gleichzeitigkeit*, or *simultaneity, of being and beings.*

What appears in the Gestell is the sameness of being, beings, and essence. "The world and *Gestell* are the same [*Welt und Ge-stell sind das Selbe*]. They are, in a different way, the essence of being [*sie sind unterschieden das Wesen des Seins*]."[44] So that the *Gestell* (the essence of technology), being, essence, the essence of being, and beings (of the world) are all *differently the same.*

The sameness, once again, of these ontological instances is not their equality but the revelation of

*their interchangeability and simultaneity, their ability
to be metamorphosed and displaced into each other.
This sameness is the "meaning" of the new metamorphosis and the new migration, the meaning of the
other (ex)change.*

This mutual convertibility, which is precisely an
attempt to locate (in the fantastic spiral of a *mise en
abyme*) the Heidegger change, shows several faces:

*Being is dislodged from its meaning as the "ground
of beings"*[45] *so that the being of beings stops being
"of value for" being.*

*Essence stops being "of value for" beingness and
becomes, instead, what it is* (Wesung): *the metabolic
identity of being.*

Beings are transformed. They stop being "*of value
for*" particular cases rationally grounded in beingness. *The essence of the whole of beings dismisses,
precisely, its beingness;* it is no longer being present, or present-at-hand. The world and the *Gestell*
are not there in the manner "two present objects
[*vorhandenen Gegenständen*]"[46] would be.

As an ontological mutant, the Gestell *reveals the
originary mutability of ontology. The* Gestell *is the revelation of the point where being, essence, and beings
are each susceptible to losing (or ceding) their position.*
Being, essence, and beings "lose those qualities with
which metaphysics has endowed them."[47]

What Is a Changing Alterity?

"THE SAME IS NOT THE EQUAL"

We should linger for a moment with the pair of the
same and the equal. "The same," Heidegger states,
"is in no way the equal [*aber widerum: das Selbe
ist niemals das Gleiche*]. The same is even less the

coincidence without difference of the identical [*das Selbe ist ebensowenig nur der unterschiedlose Zusammenfall des Identischen*]. The same is rather the relation of the different [*das Selbe ist vielmehr das Verhältnis des Unterscheides*]."[48]

Being the same does not mean being *the same as the other*, which is exactly what *equality* conveys. The same (το αὐτό) does not presuppose the equality of "two terms."[49] The same is always the same of some other, but this other is first of all itself, or self-same. The same, in effect, is a gift of self. The same is *dative—for* (für) *itself and with* (mit) *itself—in relation to itself, and therefore of a different self-relation.* In *Identity and Difference*, Heidegger writes that "we are reminded of an old word by which Plato makes the identical perceptible, a word that points back to a still older word. In the dialogue *The Sophist*, 254d, Plato speaks of στάσις and κίνησις, rest and motion. Plato has the stranger say at this point 'Each one of them is different from the (other) two, but the same for itself. Plato doesn't just say 'each itself the same,' [*jedes selber dasselbe*] but says 'each the same for itself' [*jedes selber ihm selbst dasselbe*]. The dative ἑαυτω means: each thing itself is returned to itself, each itself is the same for itself with itself [*für es selbst mit ihm selbst*]."[50] In sameness, there is thus difference—opposition (*Entgegensetzung*) to self. "Opposition appropriates itself. It appropriates itself in the same as the essential of being [*die Entgegensetzung ereignet sich. Sie ereignet sich im Selben als das Wesende des Seins*]."[51] This "opposition" is *the incision of the other in the same*, an incision that remains occluded within relationships of equality. So in this sense *the same is the metamorphosis of the equal.*

At play in the *Gestell* are both the equal and the same. Held together in it are the two regimes of change and exchange: on the one hand, the reign of equality—*all things being equal, everything equivalent (alles gilt gleich)*—that also fundamentally governs the metaphysical conception of essence; on the other, *sameness*, the relation of exchangeability between instances that are nonetheless *unique* and *incomparable*, and that have no equivalent but are *metamorphosable* and *displaceable* by each other, in a sense that I will have to elucidate before we are finished.

The new convertibility at work in *Gestell*'s core (which prefigures the circulation of essences in *Ereignis*'s core) is difficult to apprehend since being is *incomparable* and does not, at first glance, seem capable of entering the circle of any exchange. Being, Heidegger affirms in several reprises, is *the alien, the unique, the one and only, the surprising*.[52] "However one being might surpass another," he writes in *Basic Concepts*, "*as* a being it remains equal to the other, hence it has in the other its own equivalent [*und hat so am anderen das Gleiche seiner selbst*]. Every being has in every being, insofar as it a being, its *equal* [*seinesgleichen*]. The tree in front of the house is a different being than the house, but a being; the house is other than the man, but a being. . . . How does it stand, however, with being? *Being has its equal nowhere and nohow. Being is, over and against all beings, unique* [*einzig*]. . . . The uniqueness of being has incomparability [*Unvergleichbarkeit*] as a consequence. However, being is never merely what is equivalent in the manifold beings stone, plant, animal, man, God. For to be what is equivalent it would have to be multiple. Being, by contrast, is everywhere *the same* [*das Selbe*], namely itself [*es selbst*]. . . . Being is distinguished by uniqueness in a unique way, incomparable with any other distinction. Being in its *uniqueness*—and in addition to this, beings in their *multiplicity.*"[53]

If being is incomparable (to beings), it cannot designate even the slightest characteristic common to beings, nor be *of value for* some reference situated beyond or outside the sphere of exchange so as to fix the latter's terms. Being, because incomparable, is not the standard, rule, or norm of either equivalence or comparison. *Giving circulates.* The sameness of being, its incomparability, does not make it a fetish. So that it will always be in the play of circulation and exchange and not in the distant horizon of an inaccessible transcendence that being "is" or could be called "incomparable."

If *being the same* originally means *being self-(ex)change* (the withdrawal of oneself in self-giving—the play of the dative) and letting the other be in the self, and if, originally, identity is a metamorphosis, then the incomparable character of being simply designates the impossibility, for everything that is, of being equal to itself. A being could be just like another being, but it cannot be just like itself in that it originally differs from itself. The being of beings is what inscribes in beings the difference of beings from themselves. Στάσις and κίνησις very well are the first words of presence.

This indentation or incision opened in that which is, this mark of being (which it itself bears in the difference it maintains with its own essence) is a mark of the other. The complicity between being, essence, and beings revealed by the other (ex)change stems from this "trademark," this suture and rupture of identity that makes each thing simultaneously an essence, a being, and the difference between the two; a dative self-difference that prevents every self-enclosure. When I encounter you, when we start becoming attached to each other, I move into you, exploring your difference, the singular play opened in you between your essence and itself. It is exactly there, at that place, that you welcome me. What Heidegger calls *Ereignis* is also the place where this can happen, there where there is some room—room for the way of the other.

This welcome and arrival or passage into the other neither is pure transcendence, nor does it form a transcendental hospitality; it provokes, it should be recalled, migrations and metamorphoses. There is no alterity without change. The other changes me because I change myself in it. There are, as you know, strange resemblances between people who live together without being kin; between lovers, friends, and children. *Alterity is transformation—fashioning of and by the other.*

Yet the metamorphosis and migration of *Dasein*, God, the relation to being, beings, etc., announced by Heidegger corresponds neither to the sudden appearance of new monsters nor to what are ordinarily called fantastic creatures. The new metamorphosis and migration results from the way in which all things, from here out, breathe the same air, and live the same novel ontological condition: being-essence, being-beings, and being the difference between the two. In the midst, again, of this gift form mobile, nomad assemblies, groups of resemblances and "resemblants," and clusters of metamorphoses that all have such-and-such an aspect.

Identity itself, its "principle," receives a new meaning. "What would have become the title of our lecture?" Heidegger asks. "*The Principle of Identity* would have undergone a transformation [*gewandelt*]."[54] "On its way," that is, "from the principle as a statement about identity to the principle as a leap into the essential origin of identity, thinking has undergone a transformation [*hat sich das Denken gewandelt*]."⁵⁵

THE ACCORD

Identity and the thinking of identity are changed to the extent that essence, as the *Gestell* shows, is not the closed circle of generic community or commonality but a *gathering* that precisely does not *generalize*. *Essence is henceforth a remaining open, the revolving door of the house of being through which the exchange of the favor passes.* The essential is fluid and moving.

"If we speak of *Hauswesen* [household affairs/ essence of the house] and *Staatwesen* [affairs of state/ essence of the state]," Heidegger writes in *The Question Concerning Technology*, "we do not speak of a generic type; rather, we mean the ways in which house and state hold sway, administer themselves, develop and decay—the way in which they 'essence' [*wie sie wesen*]. Johann Peter Hebel, in a poem, 'Ghost on Kanderer Street' [*Gespenst an der Kanderer Straße*], for which Goethe had a special fondness, uses the old word *die Weserei*. It means the city hall inasmuch as there the life of the community gathers and village existence is constantly in play, i.e. comes to presence [*west*]."⁵⁶

Entering and exiting, identity is destined to traverse, circulate, and form itself in passing, to occur, in effect, by unwinding.

"ESSENCE IN ITSELF IS CHANGEABLE"

Do you remember this decisive phrase from the first volume of Nietzsche, *the one that set our book in motion?*

The traditional understanding of essence as generality or plurivalidity is not originary but *derived*. §110 of *Contributions* affirms the "retroactive [*nachträglich*]" character of the idea understood as beingness and community or commonality. Generality is a *subsequent determination (Folgebestimmung)*, not a first or principal definition of essence. Yet "strangely," says Heidegger, "this after the fact [*nachträglich*], subsequent determination of ἰδέα as beingness, the κοίνον, then becomes the first and last determination of beingness (of being); this is the 'most general!'"⁵⁷

This *identifying of essence*, he continues, "would of itself not have been so fatal had it not for centuries barred the way to a decisive question."⁵⁸ The decisive question is that of a *"unifying unity" having neither a unifying character nor the power to generalize or assimilate.* Originary unifying unity can only unify the multiple and the changing through remaining itself *multiple and changing in its very (same) unity—through only lasting for a while.* "The essence in which the many dovetail must be one and the same thing for them. But from that it by no means follows that the essence in itself cannot be changeable [*aber daraus folgt keineswegs, daß das Wesen in sich nicht wandelbar sin könne*]. For, supposing that the essence of truth did change, that which changes could still be a 'one' that holds for 'many,' that relationship not disturbing the transformation [*denn gesetzt, das Wesen der Wahrheit wandelt sich, dann kann das Gewandelte immer wieder, unbeschadet der Wandlung, das Eine werden, was für vielen gilt*]."⁵⁹

"Real unity does not disturb the transformation" since the one in it is not (the) immutable.

It will be said in response, Heidegger elaborates, that "the notion of a change of essence leads to relativism."[60] But "the right to such an objection to the change of essence of truth stands and falls with the appropriateness of the representation of the 'one' and the 'same' therein presupposed, which is called the absolute, and with the right to define the essentiality of essence as manifold validity. The objection that the change of essence leads to relativism is possible only on the basis of deception [*Verkennung*] concerning the essence of the absolute and essentiality of essence."[61] The latter appears as ipseity (*Selbstheit*) and self-sameness (*Selbigkeit*), which have nothing at all to do with empty identity and uniformity, the indifferent inequality pertaining to the understanding of the unity of essence as generality (*Einerlei*). The transformed definition of essence, which is to say the *unicity* (*Einzigkeit*) affirmed against *genus* and *genre* (*Gattung*), corresponds to a "metamorphosed interpretation (*verwandlete Auslegung*)" of community.

The identical is no longer the common. The unity of the same is a different unity, that of a face that is exchangeable and divisible without being general, and that gathers without enclosing, giving change—that is, alterity. Although this unity sometimes still happens to be called "genre," this word (which in French, again, also conveys what "gender" does in English) henceforth designates precisely the transformation of genre, what no longer, that is, has a genre, but only lives through displacements and metamorphoses of generic, traditional essence.

When Heidegger characterizes the *Gestell* as the locus of another exchange, when he thinks *Ereignis* as the gift and circulation of *sameness*—simultaneity and co-belonging—he has in mind the *metabolic unity* of a *holding together* that is not a rigid framing but a changing bond and supple relation. *A plastic, phenomenal crossing of things.*

The conversion of metaphysics into its other condenses itself into every technological object (into everything, as will be seen a little later). The Gestell can be said, on that account, to be *the real of the ontological difference,* an expression that can be understood in a double sense: as an *objectivation,* on the one hand, of ontological difference, which is to say as the latter's occlusion—being made the object of beings in the enframing; but also, on the other, as a *liberation* of the ontological difference, *as its (fantastic) coming into print on things.* Ontological difference, from here out conceived as the sameness of being, essence, and beings, *is our world itself.*

The ontological reality of technology occurs to the extent its power of *derealizing traditional ontological divisions* does. This power overturns the old definitions of being, essence, and beings.

What the real is, is change.

7

The Fantastic Is Only Ever an Effect of the Real

Initially these questions concerning form and *Gestell* remain peculiar considerations [*zunächst bleiben diese Fragen nach Gestalt und Ge-stell absonderliche Überlegungen*]. They should not be imposed on anyone, especially since their very concern is of a precursory nature.[1]

Why speak of the "reality" of the ontological difference? What is the bond uniting change to the real, and why keep this old word "real," which Heidegger seems in Being and Time *to dismiss forever?*

Does my understanding of the "real" have something to do with the figure of being, with the collection [recueil] of its visibility? Does it pertain, somehow, to the fantastic, which is to say to a certain way of imagining or imaging change—the two changes at once—in a place where every concept comes up lacking?

At this point, you tell me, I must, if I am to address these questions, attempt to interpret what Heidegger announces under the title of the metamorphosis and migration of Dasein, *the gods, language, the relation to being, and philosophy. What is the μορφή proper to these metamorphoses? What is it that the shape of the pathway of these transformations resembles?*

*Off we go again. But before we do, we'll make
ourselves as little [petit(e)] as can be. What should be
elucidated, in the final analysis, is indeed this: ultrametaphysical thought is coming to grips with the little.*

The Crossing of Essences

THE LETTING PASS OF THINGS

The *Gestell*, we saw, is a being that lets its essence
be given for, pass into, and (attempt to) pass for it.
It is clear that this ontological porosity is not, for
Heidegger, solely the privilege of technological beings.
What takes place with such beings, in an immediate manner and as a primary fact of our everyday
experience with them, reveals what arises in the
midst of beingness in general in the epoch of the
consummation of metaphysics. Beingness henceforth
characterizes itself as *essential ductility*. Beings,
when inside the economy of the other change, are
constantly *changing in(to) their essence*. This capacity
for ontico-ontological conduction characterizes, for
Heidegger, thingness—*Dingheit*—in general: things
are the mirrors of being.

　　When I speak of "reality," I am referring to this
thingness, its conductive body. I am after the fashion
in which the ontological difference becomes visible
right on things. What Heidegger describes under the
rubric of thingness—which is itself a metamorphosis of objectivity (*Objektivität*)—is less "the being of
things" (the essence of the thing in the traditional
sense: *wassein, wie sein*) than the thing of being, the
movement of being in things. The thing, Heidegger
tells us, gathers. It holds the fourfold together:
"Thinging, the thing stays the united four, earth and

sky, divinities and mortals, in the simple onefold of their self-united fourfold."[2] What the thing gathers and shelters this way is a *circulation*—that, quite precisely, of essences. The thing is their crossing, or place of exchange. The term "fourfold" designates nothing else but the dimension of the new convertibility. The thing lets the essential pass through gathering. Nothing in it checks the evidence of its own essence, which appears with it; and from this very fact, its essence shows itself to be an exchangeable instance, a movement toward the other. Essence comes out of things. The presence of things reveals the (ex)change of presence.

All this, you are right to say, is obscure. So understanding it will require returning to the issue of schematism. I have tried from the start to show that *essence is the imaginary place of convergence (or focus point) of ontology.* In this place, *two images* meet and are exchanged: the metaphysical image (the visibility) and the ultrametaphysical image of being. The meeting between these two images, their point of convergence, which is therefore a meeting and exchange between two regimes of visibility, *is itself visible.* There is, then, a visibility of the suture, of the point of convertibility between metaphysics and its other. I also insisted that this point of convergence is depatriated, stateless in relation to concepts, on the fact that it could only be invested with images. I affirmed that, for me, the entirety of the Heideggerian thinking of imagination was motivated by this *focus imaginarius* that is the suturing of the two changes. This new visibility results, on one essential side, from metaphysics' irrepressible and structural drive to represent itself to itself, to cross back through itself, to schematize itself in such a way that the schema ends by entering into presence, the visible slough of visibility. Yet the new visibility also results, on the other side, from the movement of the other (ex) change, which reveals the structure of the favor, which in turn appropriates being, essence, and beings to each other such that each stands down on behalf of the other, lets the other be shown in and for it—the schematism of another era and time.

I have from the start dubbed *fantastic* the meeting point of these two imaging processes. Philosophy is henceforth and necessarily *fantastic thinking* insofar as, because it is itself included in the crossing that it must think (the crossing of the two (ex)changes and the circulation of the two modalities of the triad of change) *it can only imagine what it thinks.* Not in the sense that what it thinks would not exist, but in the sense that *the reality of what it thinks is divided, as if through the middle and in its body, by an imaginary line, an image-line lying between two histories.* Heidegger never stopped insisting on the paradoxical reality of the imagination as power of "nihilation" (*Nichtung*).[3] The suture between the two changes "is" not—this is why it is (ontologically) imaginary—*but it is not for that any less real, which is to say visible on and among things.* The fantastic, far from designating a simple logic of the phantasm or an intrusion of the phantasm into the real, characterizes precisely the real of the phantasm. Ontological difference, the convertibility between the two (ex)changes, the new ontological gift, and the new exchangeability are not pure abstractions. They constitute our real, the way the real registers the impact of its deconstruction and change: it renders itself visible in a different way. *The fantastic is another dimension, that of the real image of thingness.*[4]

The two (ex)changes, then, encounter each other in this real image and intersect in each and every thing—in everything. All things let the fantastic suture of metaphysics and its other be seen in them. Everything has a double face: metaphysical and nonmetaphysical. A sort of improbable line (like the ages of a shell, we could again say, as these are inscribed directly into it) separates them—a line of transformation, an improbable tipping point. *Everything has two presences.* Everything is in itself both metaphysical and destructuredly-deconstructedly metaphysical. Everything—you and me as well (of course). It is up to the philosopher to discriminate between and think together these two sorts of being and these two images, these two images of being. *This double physiognomy is presented to the gaze at the moment when the favor of the other exchange lifts the thick screen the first change hung over the essential.* We have seen how the *Gestell* loosens the metaphysical bolt by giving beings back their ontological porosity. "The play of the world" (which is precisely what makes things glimmer[5]) is the play, then, of a passage, an exchange between two changes that is rendered possible by the ontological ductility revealed with the new gift, the favor of *Ereignis.*

A "MODEST" DIFFERENCE

Although visible, the point of suture mostly goes unnoticed. This point of articulation—the soft point and living tissue of thought, so fantastically real—is typically abused and ignored. Who truly pays it any attention? It is so *small. There is, in effect, something entirely little in and for philosophy, an entirely little world within the world;* as Deleuze and Guattari say with such pertinence and lucidity, there is *a becoming minor of sense. Philosophy's thing, along with philosophy itself, is becoming imperceptible, without publicity and well off to the side. We, us philosophers, scarcely exist anymore; our reality is now imaginary. To migrate and be metamorphosed, is always, in a sense, to become the least.*[6] *We have become the very least.*

I said before that everything has two presences, that the improbable suture between metaphysics and its other is marked on all things. This mark corresponds to what we together characterized as *the incision of the other* in being, essence, and beings. Each thing, everything, has in it an incision, an opening through which it is exchanged with itself and with the other; being, in favor of beings, beings, in favor of their essence, and essence, in favor of being. *Essence is nothing but the mobility of the incision of the other in essence, beings, and being;* the tiny indentation through which each thing is crossed and exchanged with itself, and opened to the other. Essence, *"weserei,"* as we saw in the preceding chapter, is a play of doors, and the fourfold, in turn, is merely one possible name for this ontological circulation.

Recall the enigmatic declaration from *Contributions* according to which "the last god will show itself [*der letzte Gott sich zeigen wird*]. In its hinting, being itself, *Ereignis* as such, first becomes visible [*erstmals sichtbar*]; and this lighting-up [*dieses Leuchten*] needs the grounding of the essential sway of truth as clearing and sheltering . . . and their final sheltering in the *altered figures* of beings [*ihrer* letzmaligen Bergung in der veränderten Gestalten des Seienden]."[7]

The visibility of being found amid transformed beings is born precisely from the new ontological exchange, where god can be shown as *Dasein*, *Dasein* as god, being as a being, and a being as a god, but without any of these essences either gaining power over or trying to alienate each other. In this new exchange, the divine, the thing, man, and being from time to time show in each other, are installed in each other in passing. Essence—stand-in, double, halo, aureole—is the other name for what, in a thing, god, *Dasein*, or animal and in being itself (the essence of being, once more, is nothing but being's self-difference), is the most *exposed*, the most *fragile*. *The littlest*, Heidegger even says—*the modest, the least*. This point, where things are at once upright and capsized, reveals in each of them, in everything, the living tissue of a constant autotransformation: a thing's capacity to take leave of itself so as to be crossed and exchanged with another. There can be no "co-belonging" without this suppleness of gathered terms, a suppleness that permits them to fold into and substitute for each other while remaining what they are.

We saw together that "*Wesen* understood as a verb is the same as *währen*, to last or endure."[8] What endures, Heidegger further affirms, "accords [*ereignet*]" and lets itself approach "in little things,"[9] "*im Geringen*."[10] *Das Gering* is the substantive form of an adjective, *gering*, which signifies weak, small, and modest. Why, then, have the French translators chosen here to render *das Gering* with "*la souplesse de ce qui est petit*," "the suppleness of what is small"? What does this addition mean? Is it somehow legitimate? "Nestling, malleable, pliant, compliant, limber—in Old German," Heidegger says, "these are called *ring* and *gering* [*schmiegsam, schmiedbar, geschmeidig, fügsam, leicht heißt in unseren alten deutsche 'ring' und 'gering'*]."[11] *Das Gering* therefore designates the little, littleness as suppleness or *plasticity*. *This suppleness and plasticity constitutes what, in a thing, can change. The modulatable aspect, both migratory and metamorphic, of its aspect.* Apropos the fourfold of sky, earth, gods, and mortals, Heidegger writes that "in the ringing of the mirror-playing ring [*im Gering des spiegelnd-spielenden Rings*], the four nestle into their unifying presence, in which each one retains its own nature [*schmiegen sich die Vier in ihre einiges und dennoch je eigenes Wesen*]. So nestling, they join together, worlding the world [*also schmiegsam fügen sie fügsam weltend die Welt*]."[12] This round of essence is the living tissue of change and exchange. The round of essence is what makes (the) Heidegger change, enabling thereby *the ethical dimension of his philosophy* to be affirmed. Respect for the other is respect for this fragility, which maintains itself changing; a fragility that is only given modestly, in the poverty of a gaze. The fantastic is destitute.

Essential destitution results from what we previously characterized as the *indifference of being to its own mutability.* Being, we now know, "denies its own essence."[13] *Ontological convertibility takes no interest in itself.* And no one, in turn, has any interest in exchange, since being itself pays it little regard. When all is said and done, there is nothing at all to be gained from it. So philosophy will henceforth have to be concerned with the essential's character as the least and the minor. Something else is begun with this disinterest or distinterestedness.

When there is nothing left to lose or gain, we can only be *watchful.* This is the sense of the metamorphosis and migration of *Dasein* that Heidegger conceives as its *becoming-shepherd*: "the 'subject' in man must transform itself into the founder and guardian of this abode [*Erbauer und Wächter das Subjekt des Menschen sich verwandeln muß*]."[14] Guarding is loving, and love, we have seen, is a power of transformation. Love for being, in its place; loving being, in its place. *It is necessary to look after and protect what is supple, without the least concern for oneself.*

A Form Whose Homeland Is No Longer Metaphysics

What is supple—in Greek, μεταβολικός—is the crossing of change in a being.[15] Essence, then, is the *form of suppleness.*

THE RUNNING OF THE FOX

But how, you ask, can one still speak of form? Heidegger distinguishes between two understandings of form that are already, by his account, at work in the heart of Aristotle's thinking of change (μεταβολή) and movement (κίνησις), in the blinking of the four regimes of mobility of αὔζησις and φθίσις, ἀλλοίωσις, φορά. Observe, Heidegger says, a running fox. It is engaged in change, since it changes direction (φορά). However, "the fox is at rest in that it keeps the same color [*dieselbe Farbung behält*]."[16] Its running is displacement, but not alteration (ἀλλοίωσις, *Veränderung*); the fox changes place but remains the same, "as it was constituted."[17] It can be said, then, that what does not change in the fox appears thanks to a change. *The fox only is what it is in changing.* Just as rest, Heidegger recalls, is itself only ever a modality (and the most accomplished) of movement, so can the fox be said to conserve its form (μορφή)—continue having the face and air of a fox—only to the extent that it is *in itself* a change that never stops changing meaning and direction. Μεταβολή, declares Heidegger, is a trait that binds together, without completely congealing, several modalities of being-moved: "If we perceive all these overlapping 'appearances' [*durchkreuzenden 'Erscheinungen'*] as types of movedness, we gain an insight into their fundamental character, which Aristotle fixes in the word and concept of μεταβολή."[18] The identity of the fox-form is born from the incessant U-turns of metabolic routes of identity. The essence of the fox is what streaks the animal, *right on its run*, with flashes of being. Ontomorphic velocity.

So the air of a fox, its ειδος or μορφή, owes its essence solely to a perpetual metamorphosis. In Aristotle, then, there is a *metamorphic understanding of form* bound up with the vision of *coming to presence*. Heidegger proposes, moreover, translating μορφη no longer as "form" but with "*Gestellung*," "installation," or, more precisely, "installation in the aspect [*Gestellung in das Aussehen*]."[19] Μεταβολή, Heidegger again says, is the unity of a movement of throwing in which something shoots out, a flash that makes a face visible. Form, in this case, would designate not only the results of an installation, but the very constitution of the face, the movement that consists in coming to be lodged in an aspect the way one settles in a nest.

To install or to install oneself is to find a place, but a kind of place that invents what there is to install in it. What form designates is precisely the emergence of what is installed—a face or aspect—in the very act of its localization. "Aristotle," Heidegger further writes, "demands that we see that the individual beings in any given instance (this house here and that mountain there) are not at all nonbeings, but indeed beings insofar as they install themselves into the aspect of the house and mountain and so first place this appearance into presencing. In other words, ειδος is genuinely understood as ειδος only

when it appears within the horizon of one's immediate addressing of a being."[20] Form is a "composi-
tion," one that installs the essence and the particular
thing that lodges in it *for awhile*: the face "installs
itself into a given thing that is 'there for awhile' (the
'appearance' 'table,' for example, that puts itself forth
into this table here). We call an individual thing *das
Jeweilige*, 'that which is there for awhile,' because
as an individual thing 'it stays for awhile' in its
aspect and preserves the 'while' (the presencing) of
this appearance, stands forth in and out of it—which
means that it 'is.'"[21]

Heidegger shows that there is a conflict at the
heart of Aristotle's thought between this *mobile-form*
and the *idea-form*, which is always already installed.
Aristotle also at the same understands the ειδος, in
Plato's fashion, "as something independently present
and therefore as something common (κοίνον) to the
individual beings that 'stand in such an appearance.'"[22] Form, when understood this way, is a seal
that imprints its mark onto movement and stops it
in order to render it thinkable. Moreover, Heidegger
recognizes that the German word *Form*, the most
recent translation of Greek μορφή, has completely
devolved into meaning this logic of impression and
thus does no justice to the movement of installation,
to the fragility of the essential. In translating μορφή
not by Form but *by Gestellung in das Aussehen*
(again, "installation in the aspect"), Heidegger wants
first of all to express two meanings, both of equal
value, "that are thoroughly lacking in our word 'form.'
First, installing into the aspect is a mode of presencing, οὐσία. Μορφή is not an *ontic* property present
in matter, but a way of *being*. Second, 'installing in
the aspect' is movedness, κίνησις, which 'moment' is
radically lacking in the concept of form."[23]

FORM'S DIVORCE

SUFFERING

Heidegger's address to Jünger in "On the Question of Being" largely bears on the possibility of renewing this sense of form from right at its traditional understanding. Heidegger shows how Jünger's work itself attests, though unwittingly, to this remodeling. On the one hand, Heidegger says of the latter's oeuvre, "it remains housed in metaphysics [*in der Metaphysik beheimatet bleibt*]" precisely for not having perceived "the way in which *Gestalt*, ἰδέα and being belong together [*die Zusammengehörigkeit*]" and for remaining, thereby, at the same time dependent on this.[24] On the other hand, Heidegger recognizes Jünger's oeuvre for causing a metamorphosed sense of form to emerge from within this very conception of the figure. "When in your work *The Book of the Sandclock* (1954)," he writes, "you say, '*Gestalt* is confirmed in pain [*im Schmerz bewährt sich die Gestalt*],' then, so far as I can see, you retain the fundamental configuration of your thinking, but let the fundamental words 'pain' and '*Gestalt*' speak in a transformed sense [*in einem gewandelten Sinne*]."[25]

What next follows enables the significance of this "change" to be specified. "This would be the place to go into your treatise *On Pain* [*Über den Schmerz*]," continues Heidegger, "and to bring to light the intrinsic connection between 'work' and 'pain.' . . . [T]he Greek word for pain, namely, ἄλγος, would first come to speak for us. Presumably ἄλγος is related to ἀλέγω, which as the *intensivum* of λέγω means intimate gathering. In that case, pain would be that which gathers most intimately."[26] This passage is fundamental. It effectively enables us to understand that pain and suffering maintain a natal tie with the *logos*, meaning with gathering, or even co-belonging (*Zugehörigkeit*). *An essential bond would in this way unite suffering and gathering.* "Pain would be that which gathers most intimately," in the *littlest*, most *fragile*, and *exposed fashion*. The supple, precisely, which is to say *the changing gathering*, would be thought's thing—*logoalgia*, the resource of every system and synthesis, *the pathetic minimum* given, in the end, for itself and outside of every system and synthesis. A brute given, a gift, [*donné(e) brut(e)*] that is at the same time the new meaning of form.

The coming to presence of this *minimum*, this suffering *miniature* and its strange and difficult phenomenality, effectively requires a *bringing into form*, a *figure* whose concept relinks with the Aristotelian determination of "installation." The least is installed in gathering, appearing in what it holds together. Corresponding to the metamorphosis of suffering (this emergence of the originary complicity of *logos* and *pathos*) is a metamorphosis of μορφή itself, a transformed sense of form, which we are reconnecting to its essentially metabolic meaning. Now the validity of this transformed sense—its future, if you will—this proof for an ultrametaphysical viability of form, depends on an essential alternative quite clearly distinguished by Heidegger. The traditional synonymy between form and ἰδέα might be *derived*, in which case there would be an originary non-ideal resource of form, which would henceforth request only to live and show itself. Or, alternatively, this synonymy could be first, having no past, and form would be unable to outlive its idea—essence, immutability, community, generality—and forever remain, in that case, the form of metaphysics. Heidegger develops the alternative in these terms: is "ἰδέα a *terminus ad quem* for us" or "a terminus *a quo*"?[27] In other terms (you understand), is form an endpoint—a derivation—or an origin, from which all particular "forms" proceed? We saw that the definition of form as ἰδέα resulted from the first (ex)change, and that it would for that reason be, already and originally, the migration and metamorphosis of *another form*. Yet it remains to be seen whether form can find or rediscover this sense at the moment when the first change changes, when the idea ceases to be what it is.

Heidegger specifies: if idea is a "terminus *ad quem* for us and a terminus *a quo* in itself [*als Letztes für uns und als Erstes an sich*] . . . , what paths can this question concerning the essential provenance of ἰδέα and *Gestalt* take? To put it in a formulaic manner, does the essence of *Gestalt* spring in its origin from the realm of what I call *Gestell*? Does the essential provenance of the ἰδέα accordingly belong to the same realm from which the related essence of *Gestalt* stems? Or is *Gestell* only a function of the *Gestalt* of a particular humankind? If the latter were the case, then the essencing of being and above all of the being of beings would be a product of human representation. The era in which European thinking came to this opinion continues to cast its shadow on us."[28]

IS THERE AN ALTERNATIVE TO "ONTOTYPOLOGY"?

We encounter, again, the alternative uncovered in the conclusion to our chapter on Nietzsche. This alternative takes on some particularly grave accents, which are in fact political. There is a way in which everything hangs in its balance: not just the fate of the book you have in your hands, but also, well beyond it, that of both the entirety of Heidegger's philosophy and even the philosophical, political, social, and economic future of originary ontological mutability. *Everything, that is, depends on the fate of form.* Of this, I have long been persuaded—hence my attachment to the concept of plasticity.

(1) *Perhaps form remains form* (the form of metaphysics), exhausting and failing to exceed its (traditional) form. So that the coming forth in the epoch of the *Gestell* (as its fundamental effect) of originary ontological mutability, of the evidence, that is, for the transformability of being (for being as nothing other than its transformability), would overtly mark the start of a new bricolage, a manipulation, an endless *Umformung*, the action of man putting his stamp on everything (on himself foremost), a series of metamorphoses throughout which one and the same form is reformed, types typed, kinds fashioned, and essences fabricated. So that the revelation of ontological transformability (which indicates the accomplishment of metaphysics) would not, at bottom, break metaphysics' hold, and would still be within the limits of the categories of metaphysics— the categories of form—that would accomplish this transformation, and with which one would then have to think, meaning not think. If this is the case, then Philippe Lacoue-Labarthe is right to diagnose form as Heidegger's *ontotypological symptom*, what in him leads to the worst, and makes us believe that it is possible to form, or more exactly, type and stamp out an essence.[29] If, once more, all this is the case, then metamorphosis and migration, even when decked in the beautiful hues in which I have tried here to clothe them, leads to the *unnameable, to the fabrication of a new* Dasein, *a new god, a new language—to a bricolaged ontology.*

(2) *Perhaps form can cross the line.* In that event, everything would be different—and Heidegger knew it. I am indeed quite certain he knew that everything

depends on this possibility that *form exceeds presence* by going beyond *its* presence. Lacoue-Labarthe even seems to concede this when he recognizes that "in the letter to Jünger . . . Heidegger in fact denounced ontotypology and came to impugn . . . the whole ontotypological thematics of the figure or statue (*Gestalt*), of the stamping and the imprint (*Prägung, Geprägung*), which had nonetheless been his from 1933 on."[30] But what Lacoue-Labarthe apparently does not acknowledge is that this "impugnment" (a word, moreover, that does not seem to me particularly suitable here) is undertaken in the name of *another thinking of form*, a metamorphosis of form that has its source in an ancient, unperceived link between *Gestell* and *Gestalt*, a source so archaic that ἰδέα itself, along with all the typological metaphors—brand, stamp, imprint, wax seal—result from it.

Perhaps form can cross the line, in which event everything is different. I do not believe that Heidegger had to wait until his letter to Jünger to have an intimation of it: we have seen from the start that this other form has at all times been, in multiple fashions and according to multiple senses, Heidegger's fellow traveler. If form "springs out in its origin from the domain of the *Gestell*," then this means that form can rightly designate, as we saw before, *the nontypological schematic mode of being of things*, their nonreferential ontological porosity, a letting-through without mimeticism, illustration, incarnation, or symbol. Form and figure can be for Heidegger the form and figure not of nothing, but of a nothing of form and figure—the mode of appearing of the fragile round of exchanges, of a minimal suffering, this grievous gathering of the small and the least. This suffering is without form, if one understands by form the beautiful pattern of an imprint. Suffering is form itself if form is understood to be the momentary metabolic arrangement of the exchange of essences in the smallest possible gathering.

The other form, then, is finite presence, what we previously dubbed the outline: a little presence—the least presence—and its changing modesty.

What Heidegger calls the metamorphosis and migration of *Dasein* (and of the relation to being, beings, god, and the rest) can only be understood when juxtaposed with the run of the fox, by inventing a *kinetic* and *metabolic* approach from mutant instances. Their transformations, remember, can only be grasped in flight; they are only made in passing, and installed just for a time. The metamorphosis of *Dasein* is a *swaying* (as *Wesung* has been translated into English) between *Dasein* (being-there) and *Wegsein* (being-away); the last god is a *swaying* between arrival (*Ankunft*) and flight (*Flucht*); being, a *swaying* between the closest (*Nähe*) and the farthest (*Ferne*), and beings, both a *swaying* and *fluttering* of the doors of their essence. One or many?[31] Each thing is the fox of itself, an installation of self in the animal simultaneity of movement and rest. Each thing, in other words, is the installation of self in the other, a passage into the other: god-*Dasein*-beings-being-animal-thing. They pass into each other because they are passers-by seen only in passing, sliding toward the other and over it, and signing through that its body—dedicating it.

An ontological transformability there is, a porosity of limits having nothing to do with the possibility of fabricating or "ontotyping" an essence. This transformability or permanent convertibility of related things constitutes the suffering heart of gathering, the kernel of the mobile, supple, and changing favor of the essential—*the plasticity of an incomparable exchange.*

If form crosses the line, then serenity is possible. *Gelassenheit,* or serenity, is conceived by Heidegger as a *Wandlung,* a transformation of thought that molds in its movement the transformation occurring in the *Gestell.* Nonmetamorphosed philosophical thought sees in the *Gestell* only a simple menace, the calculation of possibilities of destruction. Although it is true that "the rootedness [*Bodenständigkeit*] of man is threatened today in its core," serenity nonetheless involves "the possibility of dwelling in the world in a totally different way [*eine ganz andere Weise in der Welt aufzuhalten*]."[32]

The transformation brought on by serenity is located precisely at the articulation of the migratory and metamorphic. As much as does the *W, W, & V* of thought, serenity opens "a new path that leads to a new earth"[33] and whose shape is in the figure of a new rooting: "Serenity toward things and openness to the mystery give us a vision of a new rootedness, which someday even might be fit to recapture the old and now rapidly disappearing rootedness in changed form [*in einer gewandelten Gestalt*]."[34]

A novel form and pathway, metamorphosis and migration lead "to the last bridge [*zur letzten Brücke*]" *and enjoin us to contemplate* "the way mortals carry out on earth and under the vault of the sky their migration [*Wanderung*] from birth to death."[35]

This migration is precisely "multiform [*vielgestaltig*] and rich in transformations [*reich an Wandlungen*]."[36] *So many things pass through it.*

Third Incision
Changing the Symbolic

We come back, again, to the triad of change: W, W, & V. *Nothing can be done without it. Of this, you are now convinced. First change or other change, the three terms touch everything: the essential,* Dasein, *being, god, thought,* Gestell, *the origin . . . They touch everything because they are of such little consistency. We have not stopped emphasizing their hybridity, neutrality, and (owing to these facts) their capacity to plug the holes in history and seal together epochs or, on the contrary and because they themselves have no history, to break up all continuity.*

No doubt these figureless words, *which say every-thing in their very simplicity, are living proof of what Heidegger announced about philosophy and poetry: the end of* the sensibilization of the concept *as the essential poetico-schematic resource of discourse. The end, that is, of imagistic language, the end of meta-phor as noetic clothing and vehicle.* The end of the symbolic in general *and the emergence, from that fact, of a new form of the real.*

As we saw at the beginning, Hölderlin says in the hymn "The Ister" that a river is a peregrination, a Wanderung. *Heidegger remarks that this claim is neither a comparison nor a metaphor and neither a symbol nor an image.* "We are not saying that it is an 'image' of peregrination [*wir sagen nicht, er sei*

197

ein 'Bild' der Wanderung]" or peregrination an "image of humans journeying on their path from birth to death."[1] Hölderlin is no longer mobilizing the "Christian image" of "a passage through the earthly realm [*Durchgang durch das Irdische*]."[2] No, "the river itself is this peregrination [*der Ström selbst ist diese Wanderung*]."[3] In the same way, rivers "are not gods. They are not humans. . . . Nor indeed are they 'symbolic images' of the earthly journey of human beings."[4]

Rivers "are" peregrinations, sojourns, transformations, and time. They really are so. But what would "reality" mean here? Saying "rivers really are what they are" is to say they are not possible sensible translations of a concept, and that in being what they are, they do not refer to anything other than themselves, which is to say they refer to the other in themselves.

A symbol is by definition always torn from the living flesh of what it symbolizes; it is always detachable from its referent and, because of that, interiorizable and assimilatable. The symbolic is the energy of ideality. Affirming that the river is not a symbol entails that there is nothing for it to take into itself, nothing either to interiorize or idealize. Unless an entirely different idea of the river comes together—a real idea. Heidegger is the thinker of the destitution of the symbolic understood as what ideally resists in the real.

There is, then, no relief; no way to get rid of the triad of change's presence in Heidegger's texts by saying that its meaning is metaphoric or symbolic. The Verwandlung *of* Dasein, *the* Verwandlung *of god, the* Wandlung *of the relation to being . . . all these cannot in any event be considered "metaphors" or ways of speaking.* Wandel, Wandlung, *and* Verwandlung *are not, as we said, concepts, but neither are they images anymore. They are really what they are and form a device for change, which changes the way we image, symbolize, and translate. W, W, & V are the intrusion of the real into philosophical language. The "transformed saying" Heidegger several times announces does not entail, it should be remembered, the emergence of another language. It takes place, instead, right on language, the metamorphosis of language within language. W, W, & V is the testament to this, what inscribes this mutation of language in language. What neither introduces nor forges anything but which changes everything.*

The real does not allow anything to unmoor from it, as it permits neither our taking it into ourselves nor mourning and saying goodbye to it this way.[5]

When I spoke before of the ontological power of reverberation of things—their letting their essences pass through them—I did not mean to say that things are sensible representations, metaphors, or images of an intelligible reality transcending them. In letting their essences be given for them, things refer to nothing— to nothing else but themselves. This strange coming into print is very well, if you will, the emergence of an image, but a real image whose essence surfaces right from what is.

> *The symbol—is what is.*
> *Metamorphosis—is what is.*
> *Migration—is what is.*

Ereignis, *Heidegger tells us in* Contributions, *is the imagination itself. A real imagination, what we together dubbed the fantastic. A metabolism of gaze and thought that alone enables mutants and mutations (metamorphoses, migrations, and transfigurations) to be perceived.*

"*Dasein* . . . is the highest actuality in the domain of imagination [*die höchste Wirlichkeit im Bereich der Einbildung*], granted that by this term we understand not only a faculty of the soul and not only something transcendental (cf. *Kant and the Problem of Metaphysics*) but rather *Ereignis* itself, wherein all *transfiguration* [*Verklärung*] reverberates. 'Imagination' as occurrence of the *clearing* itself. Only 'imagination,' *imaginatio*, is the name that names from within the [metaphysical] perspective of the direct receiving of ὄν, a be-ing [*Seyn*]. Reckoned from this perspective, all being and its opening is a *product* added to what is supposedly stable. But everything here is the other way around: What is 'imagined' in the usual sense is the so-called actually extant—imagined-into [*herein-bildet*], brought into the clearing to shine, into the there."[6]

    The symbol—is what is.
    Metamorphosis—is what is.
    Migration—is what is.

From Fourtanier's commentary on Ovid's Meta-morphoses: *"Comparison rests on an explicit parallel indexed by comparative terms—"like" or "such as." Metaphor is an implicit parallel that can go so far as to identify two elements with each other. Metamorphosis is in some way a realized metaphor, which completely confuses relation and being."*[7]

The regime of the favor is a regime of real substitution. Giving is no longer symbolic economy. The metamorphosis of being and beings real-izes imagination.

Part III

At Last, Modification

I've gone through a bad patch, but I'll get out of
it again

—Kafka, *The Metamorphosis*

The best thing, no doubt, would be . . . to relive in
the mode of reading this crucial episode of your
adventure, the movement that was produced in
your mind accompanying your body's displacement
from station to station and through the intermediary countries, toward this future and necessary
book whose form you hold in your hands.

—Michel Butor, *La Modification*

In each thing, which is to say in everything, there is
a line of demarcation between two modes of being:
the metaphysical and the ultrametaphysical. This
line in each thing, which is to say in everything, is
like a parting of the historical waters. Everything
is at once united and sundered on account of this
incision that, like a joint, assembles and braces it
between two modes of presence.

On one side, each thing, which is to say everything, continues to present itself, and will never be
finished doing so, in the ever-renewed actuality of
a durable now. Each thing, through an essential
aspect of itself, maintains through its presence its
appetite for the value of presence—for the metaphysics of presence.

Look around you. First and foremost at people: at those whom you like and at those you don't, as well as at those you only like from afar. They all indicate, in ways entirely their own, a limitless attachment to the presence of the present, a high resistance to destruction (Destruktion, Abbau)—*a fear of what strikes, distances, destroys, displaces, replaces, and reforms.*

On the other side, each thing, through an equally essential aspect of itself, is always beforehand carried beyond itself, as a presence that promises—to be different. *Each thing is always another beginning of itself. Look around you. First and foremost at people: at those whom you like and at those you don't, as well as at those you only like from afar. All things indicate, in ways entirely their own, an ontological improvisation that interrupts their presence to themselves and allows them to invent the style of their de(con)struction.*

Each thing, which is to say everything, is opened to and by this mutability. Objects as well, and the least being. Even being and language; reading, understanding—everything.

Everything henceforth draws its resources from this double mode of being, from this real coexistence—meaning in the real—of metaphysics and its deconstruction.

Heidegger is the thinker of this line of demarcation. He never stops both describing and making it appear, and elaborating through that the conditions of its visibility. The name I have proposed giving the ensemble of these conditions is the fantastic, since my desire is to characterize the philosophical gaze required for perceiving this line—for discriminating between what it divides, and for making out the new ontological critique—and for perceiving as well the "existence" of this line itself.

Everything plays out through this line, which doubtlessly shares a deep kinship with Jünger's: *the meaning of ontological difference as ontological change and exchange*, as the circulation of essences within the two metabolic regimes that the line really, fantastically, gathers and separates.

But is "line" really the appropriate word here? I have spoken so far of a mark, an incision, a place of tension, and a crossing. In truth, however, line, mark, and incision remain inadequate terms. Still too graphically determined, they might lead us to think that the division I am after is just a trait of writing, a trace lacking in thickness—in form. Place, though, is too vague; crossing would be better, except that it is still too indeterminate, far too *open* in some way. We are aiming, you and me, at a kind of metabolic intimacy that is *never formless*, a sort of fragile and, as I said before, suffering gathering, a tender point in a thing where the two modes of its being are exchanged.

The modes of being, which is also to say the modes of exchange, are two, since it will from here out be clear to us that every presence is a change—the living tissue of exchange in each thing. The originary metamorphic and migratory condition of everything that is, the exchange of changing instances in each one of the (ex)changes, the metaphysical and non-metaphysical: *Dasein,* god, beings, being, essence, and language are unceasingly converting and passing into each other, and changing their regimes of change so that philosophy is finally made capable of thinking "endless metamorphosis." *Between the "of value for" and the favor, between power and poverty and the gigantic and the least, how can we name the living tissue of exchanges, and what name will be given the reality of its inscription? What could this point of cineplastic convertibility in the end be called, this point between two metabolisms that will never entirely separate, even if they issue in opposite directions?*

What Cannot Be Left Must Be Returned To

In an attempt to respond, we will change change one last time. In closing, we will turn our gaze toward *Being and Time* and return, at last, to the beginning.

We come back, then, to Being and Time, *that great book from which the triad of change is noticeably absent and where change goes by another name:* modification. *The 1927 work is effectively the book of modification,* Modifikation. *Modification made book.*

From Wandel, Wandlung, and Verwandlung to Modifikation

The concept of modification, which Heidegger borrowed directly from the phenomenological lexicon, enabled him to articulate his "first" thought of change.[1] But faithful to himself, Heidegger started out by modifying this change—by modifying modification. He diverted it from the signification it received in Husserl and very quickly assigned it to a new sphere of deployment, *the passage of* Dasein *from one mode of being to another, from a "proper" or "authentic"* (eigentlich) *mode of being to an "improper" or "inauthentic"* (uneigentlich) *mode of being and back.* If *Being and Time* is, as I am hazarding the following formula in order to say, "modification made book," it is not only because over forty-six occurrences of the words *Modifikation,* *Modifizierung* (modification), *Modifikationmöglichkeiten* (possibilities of modification), *modifizierbar* (modifiability), *modifizieren* (to modify), and *modifieziertes* (modified things) are to be found there, and only two instances of *Wandel,* one of *Wandlungen,* and none for *Verwandlung.*[2] The more profound reason is that the book can be regarded as the unfurling of the space of play of modification—the singular *exchange* that takes place unrelentingly, meaning as long as *Dasein* lasts, between authenticity, or the proper, and inauthenticity or the improper: the modifications of care into preoccupation, preoccupation into care, the "they" into the ownmost power to be, the latter into everydayness and fallenness, *Verfallenheit,* into resoluteness, *Entschlossenheit* . . .

What I am asking, here at the end, is that you consider how examining modification in all its turns will, through its illumining the past of the triad (which, again, first becomes noticeable in Heidegger's output in 1929 and 1930), enable us to respond to the questions that were just posed: how can the place, line, mark, and crossing of exchange—the *form and route* of the incision of the other in what is, meaning in being itself—how can these be approached in the most satisfactory way and, furthermore, named?

But you interrupt me here: *if modification so well illumines this point, then why not start with it?*

I have two responses:

First, because modification only derives its importance and value as a dominant motif *after the fact.* It has always seemed necessary to me, that is, to end with *Being and Time* instead of beginning from it: reading from its metamorphoses and displacements on, and primarily from the metamorphosis and displacement of modification itself. Envisaged from its posterity, modification loses the mechanical, routine, and flat look it has, as will be seen, in *Being and Time* and acquires, through a strange effect of retroactive reverberation, the *historical relief* it is lacking in 1927. In return, the triad of change itself gets casts in a new light when confronted with what was obviously for Heidegger the entirely first figure of change: the modification of *Dasein,* which is, significantly, the modification of a *Strukturganzen* or "structural whole." Only now, after having followed so many pathways and engaged in so many metamorphoses, can we ask ourselves if structure is really, at the end of the day, the most suitable term for bespeaking the line of division that from here out passes through the heart of things.

Second, in order to insist both that the new philosophical orientation that was freed by the turning, or *Kehre* (which itself consisted in the sublation of the weaknesses of the analytic of *Dasein*), ought not be interpreted as a *diktat* and that *Being and Time* was still too propaedeutic and anthropological.[3] "The reader who jumps from *Being and Time* to Heidegger's later philosophy," Jean Grondin rightfully states in *Le Tournant de la pensée de Martin Heidegger*, "has the feeling of having achieved what the Greeks called a μετάβασις εἰσ ἄλλο γένος, or passage into another universe of discourse. Everything seems to be transfigured in the writings that come after 1930: the form and content of Heidegger's philosophy appear to have undergone a profound metamorphosis."[4] But this metamorphosis is nonetheless only ever *the metamorphosis of another metamorphosis*, meaning *the metamorphosis of modification*. Would it be possible to affirm that every change in and of Heidegger's thought is always the change of a change, in which case rigidly separating out its so-called periods would be precluded? *The passage into another universe has always already begun,* and seeing this has enabled us to take stock of the sheer complexity of what changes of epoch, soil, form, and direction mean for Heidegger.

So this is the way Heidegger never stops, from one end of his oeuvre to the other (starting, that is, with *Being and Time*), characterizing *Dasein* as *the promise of metamorphosis*—as something else besides a subject, and as something other than man: "In philosophical knowing a transformation of the man who understands takes place with the very first step [*beginnt mit dem ersten Schritt eine Verwandlung des verstehenden Menschen*]—not in a moral, "existentiell" sense but rather with *Dasein* as measure [*nicht im moralisch-'existenziellen' Sinne, sondern da-seinmäßig*]."[5] From step one, *Dasein* has already started on the path of its transformation.

It would be difficult, then, to consider the *W, W, & V* of *Dasein* first announced in 1930 and soon after reaffirmed in *Contributions* without referring it back to *Being and Time*'s perspective concerning *the essential modifiability of existence*. If all the reservations Heidegger expressed about *Being and Time*[6] obviously must be accounted for, how could one miss that circulation and exchange—the first version of the exchange of the two changes—are already at work in this *essence* that is *Dasein*'s *existence*? An exchange whose idea Heidegger never stopped specifying, modifying, metamorphosing, and displacing, *without ever abandoning it?*

HYBRIDIZATIONS

We return to our first reason for not starting with modification, which is the schema that necessarily presupposes modification: *the structure of* Dasein qua *articulated totality.*

The description of the living tissue of all exchange, the point of convertibility between changes, and the intimacy of the crossing of essences is elaborated in Heidegger's work in the course of a constant reworking of the concept of structure—during the quest for a type of jointure (the structure of *Dasein,* then

Ereignis, then the fourfold . . .) equal to the event and that would know no rest.

Heidegger will never relent on this point: change is only possible through and in what he calls a "jointure," *Fügung. Change and gathering are, as we have seen, indissociable.* So that every change, it seems, would be a change in and of structure. In his thinking of modification, Heidegger brings to light this processuality of change that he will specify but not disavow: *every modification is the modification of a structure.* The structural whole or articulated totality, *gegliederte Ganzheit,* that is *Dasein* in the unity of various modes of being—of various possibilities of existence. The structure is differentiated into "moments" even as it remains one.[7] *The modifiability of structure never disarticulates it.* Modifications "each . . . concern their structural factors,"[8] but this differential concern does not call its originally unitary constitution into question. Modification could very well be envisaged as a passage from one place to another, yet Heidegger continually repeats that it requires *no outside*—no exteriority, overhang, or overview. The most striking example of this *transformation in place* comes in §38, which concerns the passage from fallenness to the ownmost power to be, and from there to everydayness. "In falling prey, nothing other than our potentiality for being-in-the-world is the issue, even if in the mode of inauthenticity. *Dasein can* fall prey *only* because it is concerned with understanding, attuned being-in-the-world. On the other hand, *authentic* existence is nothing which hovers over entangled everydayness, but is existentially only a modified grasp of everydayness [*sondern existenzial nur ein modifiziertes Ergreifen dieser*]."[9] There is no exteriority of the modes in relation to each other—only a sliding from one mode to the other that it is *right at*; a folding and unfolding of finitude that does not, curiously, carve up existence. *This schema of a modification that has neither inside nor outside, and that is characteristic precisely of the modification of structure, never stops governing Heidegger's imaginary.*

Because of this, we can now see the kinship between the concepts belonging to the different "periods" of Heidegger—between, for instance, the articulated totality of Dasein *and the cross of the fourfold.*

At the same time, we can also at this point see that Heidegger always kept the structural paradigm at a distance. Wandel, Wandlung, and *Verwandlung* are largely a neutralization. Much more vague, making not even an implicit reference to what would today be called self-regulation, the terms of the triad enable us to open and emancipate the change that, although at first an existential phenomenon (modification within the mobile closure of structure), becomes the mode of the advent of being within which the metamorphosis and displacement of epochality is at the same time prepared.

It seems important to me, then, that both the proximity and distance Heidegger's thought maintains with the concept of structure now be examined. To do this, I will attempt in the pages that follow a *hybridization.* I propose that the triad be retrospectively clarified through an analysis of the notion of modification developed in *Being and Time.* Reciprocally, I will at the same time endeavor to show just how existential modification anticipates its own modification, announcing the definite, quasi-systematic adoption of the triad in Heidegger's oeuvre that begins in 1930.

The hybridization will consist in this: an attempt to interpret modification not only as *Dasein'*s passage from one possibility of its being to another but also as *the passage, right on* Dasein*, from metaphysics to the other thinking—the first inscription, right on* *existence, of the history of being. I will help a Dasein to appear that crosses times and lets, like a tattoo, the mark of this (ex)change be seen on it.*

What authorizes this approach is precisely the lexical hybridization of change in Heidegger: the simultaneous use of the concept of *Modifika-tion* and the triad in the texts coming immediately after *Being and Time*. The analyses of *Stimmung*, or affective attunement, in "What Is Metaphysics?" and *The Fundamental Concepts of Metaphysics* is where this mélange is produced; *Stimmung is the place of (Dasein's) analysis where modification and existence at the same time transform themselves.*

Initially structure, *existence becomes event.* And Heidegger explicitly presents this becoming as a "metamorphosis." All the attention meriting it must be granted this major claim from *The Fundamental Concepts of Metaphysics*: "We find ourselves forced to adopt another language because of a fundamental metamorphosis of existence [*wir sind zu einer anderen Sprache gezwungen aufgrund einer Verwandlung der Existenz*]."[10]

The triad of change makes its entry into Hei-degger's lexicon at the very moment existence reveals the full scale of its concept's historical mutation and therein ceases, quite simply, to be existence.

We must head without delay, then, for the place where modification encounters migration and metamorphosis.

We set out, one last time, in search of the mark, crossing, crossroads, and living tissue of all exchang-es: the line of division inscribed in each thing—in everything.

8

Metamorphosis to Modification

Kafka Reading Being and Time

One day he carried a sheet on his back to the sofa—it cost him four hours' labor—and arranged it there in such a way as to hide him completely [daß er nun gänzlich verdeckt war].[1]

So it is now, and only now, that I invite you to open *Being and Time*.

We have followed, since the beginning, the migration and metamorphosis of Heidegger's thought of originary change, which transforms the affirmation that everything proceeds from a mutation of essence of truth into the view that (ex)change is but the other name for the withdrawal of being. Out of these two affirmations emerges one and the same conclusion: the change, which is just as much an exchange, has already taken place. Change—exchange and change—has already begun.

Our taking up *Being and Time* only now, our keeping it, as we have, for last, precipitates these affirmations, conferring on them a new depth. In effect, the order of our inquiry, which turns back from the triad of change toward modification and thus accomplishes a temporal and logical inversion, implies that metamorphosis and migration also *have already taken place*, and even come prior to the modification they nevertheless follow; that they have already been accomplished, inscribing that way the undatable seniority of change into the trajectory of Heidegger's thought. Everything happens as if we have in the end become incapable of knowing if modification introduced the triad of (ex)change or instead marked its conclusion, and if everything we have been analyzing consequently does not, in the last reckoning, constitute a possible prelude to *Being and Time.*

Modification has already taken place, since it is only legible to us on the basis of its migratory and metamorphic modification, without which it has no future.

Let me suggest that you now follow with me the route and play of modification in *Being and Time*, by holding to this strange, circular movement, which recalls to some extent that of a certain beetle . . .

The hybridization (metamorphosis-migration-modification) has already begun.

Modification at the Beginning

HISTORICAL MODIFICATION, EXISTENTIAL MODIFICATION

In order to justify this introduction in the least enigmatic manner, I must first situate the concept of modification (*Modifikation*) in *Being and Time* and specify that it belongs to two distinct yet structurally linked registers of analysis: the *existential* and the *historical.*

Existential modification, as I mentioned before, concerns the circulation of the different modes of being of *Dasein* as well as the passage or mutation (*Umschlag*) from one mode to the other.[2] *Historical modification* characterizes the general movement of derivation (*Ableitung*) of meaning that was initiated by the history of metaphysics and confounded with it, a movement in whose course the significations of originary words—being, truth, logos—are unceasingly displaced, bastardized, and sedimented. "[T]he various modes and derivatives [*Modi und Derivate*] of being, in their modifications and derivations [*Modifikationen und Derivationen*], becomes intelligible through consideration of time."[3] Hence the originary meaning of the word λόγος—speech—has been modified to mean "statement,"[4] the "apophantical" emerges as the modification of the "hermeneutical,"[5] and "truth" understood as "correspondence or accordance [*Übereinstimmung*]" is the "modification" of "ἀλήθεια."[6]

Historical modification and existential modification are thus indissociable. Heidegger exposes, furthermore, the bond uniting the history of meaning with "the disclosedness" [*Entschlossenheit*] of *Dasein*, which is always susceptible to being modified through its potential not to be itself. Yet the fallenness [*Verfallenheit*] of *Dasein* emerges as an *existential derivation.* On the one hand, Heidegger writes that "understood as agreement, truth has its origin in disclosedness by way of a definite modification. . . . The kind of being of disclosedness itself leads to the fact that initially its derivative modification [*abkünftige Modifikation*] comes into view and guides the theoretical explication of the structure of truth."[7] Yet on the other, "truth in the most primordial sense is the disclosedness of *Dasein* to which belongs the discoveredness of inner-wordly beings. . . . *Dasein* is co-originally in truth and untruth."[8] So it is clear that in *Being and Time*, as Jean-Luc Nancy stresses, "the historical task [is] correlate with the existential analytic."[9]

Before describing more precisely the relation that supports the two types of modification, it should be noted that they share in common one constitutive trait: *they do not begin. They do not*, properly speaking, *arrive*. If Heidegger returns upstream to the Greek beginning, it is not, paradoxically enough, in order to constitute it into an originary instance, if one understands by this *a nonderived instance,* one *nonmodified* that is. *In effect, historical derivation has always begun insofar as the beginning is confused with the very possibility of its modification.* Heidegger declares on this point that "what remains concealed [*verborgen bleibt*] in an exceptional sense [*in einem ausnehmenden Sinne*], or what falls back and is covered up again, or what shows itself only 'in disguise' [*verstellt sich zeigt*] is not this or that being but rather, as we have shown in our foregoing observations, the *being* of beings."[10] *Being only shows itself in disguise: this is how it starts.* Being "is"—"is" but—an archimodification, which again raises the question of the interpretation of this *originary going-in-drag*: was there a mutation of the essence of truth (change of the origin), or was change given at the very outset (change at the origin)? These questions have accompanied us from the very beginning, with *Being and Time* now opening the road in a disturbing fashion.

Existential modification, it too, has already begun. The modifiability of *Dasein* is nothing but its *finitude*. This should not be taken as meaning that *Dasein* would undergo, as would a subject or a preconstituted agency, modifications or changes, that it would simply be transformed, for example, by aging or the accidents and circumstances of life.[11] What must instead be admitted is that owing to the fact of its existence, *Dasein* finds itself *originally modified* and *originally transformed. Dasein* changes form and route only because its "beginning" and "end" are themselves modifications.

Modification has already begun. Which means that modification has no beginning.

Man, as rational animal, is himself also and in the same stroke always already dismissed. The Dasein *of* Being and Time *somehow anticipates the metamorphosis of it announced in the later texts. Always already modified,* Dasein *is from the outset a metamorphosis of man, a migration of its definition; a "man" metamorphosed and displaced.* It is a matter, Heidegger declares apropos of the existential analytic, of "arriving at the appropriate ontological foundations of the being which we ourselves actually are and which we call 'human being.' For this purpose, it was necessary from the outset to change [*herausgedreht werden*] the direction of our analysis from the approach presented by the traditional definition of the human being."[12]

Does everything we have so far examined—the originary giving of change/throwing off the trail or ontological archidrag, the play of masks, and the modification-metamorphosis of man included—emerge, then, as the fantastic past of Being and Time, *as the illustration, even, of what a change at the origin or originary change is, of the impossibility of dating the origin of change, of our incapacity to pinpoint a beginning in Heidegger's thinking?*

In raising these questions, I am quite aware of having come back to the fundamental problem, the one already contended with several times over during the course of our progress: does (ex)change constitute the invariant (the eternal return of the identical) of Heidegger's thought? But this problem takes on, from here out, another inflection: *if modification, and with it metamorphosis and migration, has always already begun, can they still happen? Does Being and Time not announce the absolute saturation of the horizon of metamorphoses, even though it seems only to prepare and prefigure it? If it all starts with a change, who is it that can yet change? Can we change? Have we? Are W, W, & V a finished work, or one yet to come?*

Gregor Samsa—a Proper Name for *Dasein*?

How can the quicksand of originary mutability be escaped? How can the circle be exited without revealing a sort of alterity of the mutability of the origin to itself, without attempting to join together two broad perspectives on the mutability of the origin, two gazes that never exactly cross?

Let me propose that you keep in mind, as a discrete guidebook for the trek of this chapter, Kafka's *Metamorphosis*. Not that my intention here is to carry out some "comparison" of the *Dasein* of *Being and Time* and Gregor Samsa; rather, it is to provoke, surreptitiously, an unexpected encounter between them. I have always been struck by the strange likeness between the 1912 text and the 1927 work, one all the more improbable because Heidegger, in all likelihood, never read Kafka.[13] Moreover, it is perhaps for this very reason that this parallel has always fascinated me.

"As Gregor Samsa awoke one morning from uneasy dreams he found himself metamorphosed [*verwandelt*] in his bed into a gigantic insect."[14] The first sentence of the story, and everything has already happened; the metamorphosis of Samsa has already been produced, and, in this sense, can no longer be produced. The deployment of the operation itself—"*die Verwandlung*"—is occluded.

Isn't an occlusion of this sort, despite appearances (which suggest a deployment), what is at stake in *Being and Time*?

Aren't Dasein's *ownmost potential to be and its inauthentic potential to be confused in this locus of the impossible possibility of metamorphosis?* So that they have always arrived, having never arrived?

The Essential Characteristics of Modification

This hypothesis will be explored to the end, beginning, once more, with a morphological description.

AN INFRANGIBLE STRUCTURE

In *Being and Time*, modification characterizes the *specific mobility* and *differential richness* of a structural whole: the manner in which, in changing, this whole gets deployed *without ever losing its unity*. Modification can, in effect, intervene only *there* where there is a "whole" structure.

The structure that is *Dasein* is articulated (*gegliedert*), which is to say (precisely) mobile and differentiated. It is deployed according to the different modes of being that are the "existentials." These fundamental ontological characteristics—existentiality, facticity, and fallenness—are in turn declined in particular "modes," which form what Heidegger calls their "manners" (*Weisen*), in a few cases their "transformations" (*Abwandlungen*), or, further still, their "varieties."[15]

Modification can be radical and violent, transforming *Dasein* top to bottom, or, as Heidegger says, "upturning" it. But it always *remains whole*. Modification does not induce fragmentation. Although it can mark the worst dissensions and gravest conflicts a *Dasein* might have with itself, the latter never breaks up. All modes of dissociation are only possible on the basis of an originary unity. The structural unity or being-whole of *Dasein,* Heidegger declares, is "unrendable [*unzerreißbare*]."[16]

What modification describes, then, is precisely *the mobility characteristic of an infrangible structure.* One finite and absolutely exposed, but nonetheless ontologically whole. This is why the existential analytic deploys the reversions of modification only while at the same time seeking to bring out the always higher unity presiding over this very richness, via a "complete look through this whole [*Durchblick durch dieses Ganzes*]" that sees only "an originally unified phenomenon which already lies in the whole in such a way that it is the ontological basis for every structural moment [*Strukturmoment*] in its structural possibility."[17] On the basis, then, of being-in-the-world, Heidegger progressively draws out the phenomenal unity that *care* is,[18] which is itself shown to be related to an ultimate unity—temporality.[19] "In first establishing this articulated structure," he writes of care, "we referred to the fact that with regard to this articulation the ontological question had to be taken further to the exposition of the unity of the totality of the structural manifold. *The primordial unity of the structure of care lies in temporality.*"[20]

In ever bringing about the play of the unity, modification does not modify its own structure, which is to be the modification in the structure.

No Inside, No Outside

The structural unity also goes by another name: being-in-the-world.[21] Modification can only—this is its second trait—intervene *within the world*; where, that is, there is *neither inside nor outside*. "*Dasein*," declares Heidegger, "does not first go outside of the inner sphere in which it is initially encapsulated [*verkapselt*], but, rather, in its primary kind of being, it is always already 'outside' [*draußen*] together [*bei*] with some being in the world already discovered."[22] This "outside" obviously does not refer, as the quotation marks indicate, to an exteriority. There is neither interior nor exterior; there is just the world, which is more intimate than any inside and more alien than any outside. It is, properly speaking, neither entered into nor come out from. To exist is neither to enter nor exit but to *cross ontico-ontological thresholds*. Now what modification renders possible is precisely one such "crossing." All adventures, crossings, and experiences—*death itself included*, as we will see—"must be understood [*begriffen werden*] *as modifications of originary being-in* [*Modifikationen der ursprünglichen In-Seins*]."[23]

Hence disorientation, fallenness, and defeat, the feeling of having lost the world or being lost to it, are always already only modifications of being-in-the-world: "In falling-prey, nothing other [*nicht anderes*] than our potentiality for being-in-the-world is the issue, even if in the mode of inauthenticity. *Dasein can* fall prey *only* because it is concerned with authentic, attuned being-in-the-world [*das verstehend-befindliche In-der-Welt-sein geht*]. On the other hand, *authentic* existence is nothing that hovers over entangled everydayness but is existentially only a modified grasp of everydayness [*sondern existenzial nur ein modifiziertes Ergreifen dieser*]."[24] Neither inside nor outside nor high nor low, what comes and arrives is only surprising because of *modification* and *transformation*. A mode, then, arises only from the modification of another mode, whose *place it takes. This mutual substitutability of modes* governs resolution as much as it does *dissimulation.*

Modification-dissimulation is, in effect, what makes the world seem like what it is not, a milieu or sphere present in the manner of the things "in which," as an effect of the outside and inside at once, *Dasein* stands. The constitution of everyday being-in-the-world is "what initially misses itself and covers itself over [*sie selbst im ihrer alltäglichen Seinsart ist es, die sich zunächst verfehlt und verdeckt*]."[25] "Since the phenomenon of the world is," in effect, "passed over in this absorption in the world, it is replaced [*tritt an seine Stelle*] by objective presence in the world, by things."[26] So in one way or another, every effect of absolute alterity (whether inside or outside the world) is, *qua* modification, the result of the "covering up [*Verdeckung*]" of a "concealment [*Verborgenheit*]" of a "burying-over" [*Verschüttung*] of a "distortion [*Verstellung*]."[27] In the same way as well as reciprocally, the "call" or "interpellation" of moral conscience does not resonate in a locus of exteriority or absolute transcendence but instead makes itself heard on the basis of and as the modification of dissimulation or inauthentic potentiality-to-be. "[L]ostness [in the they]," Heidegger writes, "can be summoned [*angerufen*] by one's own *Dasein,* the summons can be understood in the mode of resoluteness. But *authentic* disclosedness then modifies [*modifiziert*] primordially the discoveredness of 'world' grounded in it and the disclosedness of being-with others. The 'world' at hand does not become indifferent as far as 'content,' the circle of the others is not exchanged for a new one, and yet the being toward things at hand which understands and takes care of things, and the concerned being-with with the others is now defined in terms of their ownmost potentiality-of-being-a-self."[28]

One can cross thresholds but not change soil . . . neither transgress nor enclose oneself in them but only dissimulate or discover oneself . . . take something's place but without a change of place . . . and undergo the experience of alterity (the call of moral conscience) on the basis of the failure of every alterity of pure transcendence (there is neither the possibility of exit nor of infinite distance): these are the conditions of existential itinerancy as ruled by the process of modification.

Parting Without Separating

The structural whole cannot deploy all its richness at the same time or in one single moment, *tota simul.* What modification rules is precisely the sequential and diachronic entering play of the different regimes, of the ontological gamut of structure. Hence *Dasein's* ownmost potential-to-be emerges at the same time as its inauthentic potentiality-to-be. Modification tempers the presencing of the modes, so that they take their turn. This is why the emergence of a mode is possible only through the modification of another that is not thereby torn or caused to burst. A mode does not "eliminate" what it replaces but *takes root* in it. A mode appears in some way *right on* the latter but without exceeding or destroying it. Heidegger affirms with respect to "understanding," for example, that it "is either authentic, originating from its own self as such, or inauthentic. . . . Turning to one of these fundamental possibilities of understanding, however,

222   The Heidegger Change

does not dispense with the other [*legt aber die andere nicht ab*]. Rather, because understanding always has to do with the complete disclosedness of *Dasein* as being-in-the-world, the involvement of understanding is an existential modification [*existenziale Modifikation*] of project as a whole."[29] One mode of understanding finds itself "invested" or "determined" without for that being separated from another, since this "investment" or "determination" completely modifies the situation, which is to say *the other mode itself*.

The constant passage from the proper to the improper, the unrelenting reversals of the modes, never transpires through exclusion or effacement. Modification renders possible an indentation where emptiness is absent, and this enables *the other to be let past, there where the other comes up lacking*. A mode never saturates the whole space and is never definitively installed; it always lets the other break through or "emerge" in or after it. Heidegger declares with respect to the they and its tranquillization that "tranquilized 'willing' does not signify that one's potentiality-for-being has been extinguished [*nicht ein Auslöchen*], but only that it has been modified [*nur ein Modifikation*]."[30] A mode is "born"—springs out—from its other, from which it never parts.[31]

Existence involves the coexistence of the modes, and is confounded with it.

The Other, the Other!

THE BAD INFINITY OF REVERSION

It is impossible to rend the structure; there is neither inside nor outside; alterity emerges without rupturing with the identical . . . could we somehow be deceived?

What must be recognized is that the immense fascination the existential analytic holds over us is *modified into lassitude* when *modification's route* through it is followed. After some time, modification ends up seeming merely *routine*, as if its movement constituted the *everydayness* and *banality* of the text. Whatever the diversity of the contexts of its appearance, modification functions mechanically . . . to the point that it seems to be confounded with the rhythm of this "montage" or assemblage that Heidegger nonetheless takes so much care to distinguish from structure and that consists of the two gearwheels of a binary logic: authentic/inauthentic, the "they"/being one's self, fallen temporality/originary temporality. Might this give us the impression that we are taking the train, like in Michel Butor's *Modification*?

The movement indeed seems forever the same. Nothing arises that would not be the modification of the preceding state of things, and this applies all the way to the end. The economy of modification can be seen with particular clarity in "Being-in as Such," the fifth chapter of the text's first section. Heidegger distinguishes there between two "levels" at which *Dasein* is its "there," which is to say its openness or disclosedness: that of its primordial existential constitution ("the existential constitution of the there"), and that of its everyday mode of being ("the everyday being of the there and the fallenness of *Dasein*"). The first level comprises the analysis of the three existentials or fundamental modes of being of *Dasein* qua its *disclosedness*: *attunement*, *understanding*, and *discourse*. The second level examines the inauthentic modes of discourse and understanding in *idle talk*, *curiosity*, and *ambiguity*. The routine aspect of modification truly leaps from the page in the reading of this chapter, since all these modes are tirelessly folded and refolded into each other until care is reached. And in the following chapter, care itself endlessly *crawls* through modification, and into its other ("preoccupation").

In the second division of *Being and Time* (which is devoted to temporality), the same rhythm seizes hold of the text.[32] So after affirming, for example, that "[t]he primary phenomenon of originary and authentic temporality is the future," Heidegger writes that "[t]he priority of the future will vary according to the modified temporalizing of inauthentic temporality, but it will still make its appearance in derivative 'time' [*der Vorrang der Zukunft wird sich entsprechend der modifizierten Zeitigung der uneigentlichen Zeitlichkeit selbst abwandeln, aber auch noch in der abkünftigen "Zeit" zum Vorschein kommen*]."[33]

From being-in-the-world to the analysis of temporality, every new step the analytic takes thus sees itself subjected to this same process of modification, which always functions in the same way. Each new stage seems to have been made only to develop or illustrate section 27's fundamental affirmation that "authentic being one's self . . . is an *existentiell* modification of the they as essential existential."[34]

But then how can *Dasein* be modified, emerge, submerge, tranquillize itself, open or close its eyes, go traveling, make small talk, or philosophize without either snapping or, conversely, *hardening* into one mode or another, without, that is, becoming *mad*, dissociated, or dislocated? How can it constantly support the wheel, motor, and mechanism of the two modes, the rhythmic emergence of their one-two, one-two without a *change of atmosphere*, without, again, modifying modification itself?

Must *Dasein* Go Without Metamorphosis?

About this "authentic being-a-self [as] *existentiell* modification of the they," Heidegger asks "what does this modification imply [*was liegt in deiser Modifikation*], and what are the conditions of its possibility?"[35] Now does he truly address this question, or does he instead send modification back into its bad infinity? Can *Dasein* abandon its status as the *rational animal* if modification does not abandon anything, which it to say itself? *Can modification truly change something if it does not modify itself?*

Kafka's *Metamorphosis* negatively supports my questions, since the insect-Samsa can be regarded as *a being that is incapable of being modified by dint of modification,* "the metamorphosis" paradoxically marking the impossibility of metamorphosis.

So demeaned would it be that it could not make the *other* mode of being emerge; so resolved to be modification, that it could no longer lower itself into *man.*

What Kafka's *Verwandlung* shows, in any case, is *the breakdown of modification,* something in it which seems to be out of service as a result of running well: *the authentic and inauthentic, that is, stop being compatible from their cohabiting.* And what if, at bottom, this is how it is with Heideggerian *Dasein*? Just what is modification, this sterile chrysalis, this mechanism that *resembles itself too much* and that brings about the emergence of the fantasmatic possibility of a being not or no longer capable of being modified for want of some rebellion against its rigid side (which is as implacable as the natural metamorphosis of insects) and its existential metabolism?

What would the metamorphosis of a being forever deprived of the possibility of metamorphosis be? Whatever could it say, and what could it understand? And how? Authentically or inauthentically? And who yet could understand it? And how, again: authentically or inauthentically?

Is existence, because archimetamorphic in its structure, metamorphosis in perpetuity?

The structure is articulated, *gegliedert*, and ringed, as though it were the shell and underbelly of an ontological beetle.

It has neither inside nor outside, like Gregor's *Verwandlung*, which became a *Wanderung* in a world that was nothing more than a room; a world-room, a claustrophobic world, a game of doors that only ever grants access to other rooms and more doors (leading to other rooms . . .) in the world.

The structure does not snap when modified. "His fall was broken to some extent by the carpet, his back, too, was more elastic [*elastischer*] than he thought."[36]

Everything was (completely un-)changed. "Did he really want his warm room, so comfortably fitted with old family furniture, to be turned into [*verwandelt*] a naked den in which he would certainly be able to crawl unhampered in all directions but at the price of shedding simultaneously all recollection of his human background? He had been so near the brink of forgetfulness that only the voice of his mother, which he had not heard for so long, had drawn him back from it. Nothing should be taken out of the room; *everything must stay as it was [alles mußte bleiben]*."[37]

So once more: does modification truly change things?

We again find here the disquieting leitmotif motivating us: so what if change was, at bottom, Heidegger's insidious invariant? And what if this archimodification or archimodifiability inscribes, into both existence and being, the worst sort of constancy? The mutation of essence, originary substitutability, the "of value for" or "the favor" would all be, in the last analysis and after the event, modifications of one and the same instance, modification itself. So that there would be an (immutable) fall of mutability.

CHANGE AND THE IMPOSSIBILITY OF IT

Clearing your head for a second of this confusion, you attempt to justify the monotony of modification by proposing a three-part response.

First argument. This feeling of routine, of reiteration, of the eternal return of the same, you say, can be nothing else besides the feeling of existence itself. Nothing else, because there is nothing else—apart from this *feeling of the incessant.* Blanchot could indeed say this of *Dasein* as much as Samsa: "Gregor's state," reads a passage in *De Kafka à Kafka,* "is the very state of the being who cannot depart from existence, for whom existing is to be forever condemned to fall again within existence. Having become vermin, he continues to live in the mode of falleness, he sinks into animal solitude, he approaches even closer to the absurdity and impossibility of life. But what happens to him? Precisely this: he continues to live."[38]

Perhaps modification is, after all, just a continuation.

Second argument. Is modification also not, in the end, just a manner of speaking? A reprise of Husserl, more or less? "*Dasein can* be itself," Françoise Dastur writes, "either authentically [*Eigentlichkeit*] or inauthentically [*Uneigentlichkeit*], because it *is* its possibility and must appropriate its own being."[39] Speaking in terms of modes, showing that the authentic is only a modification of the inauthentic, functions simply to "de-substantialize" the existentials, to show that they are not separate categories or immutable essences but possibilities.[40] Apropos of *Dasein*'s ownmost potential to be, "the existential modification of the they," Dastur further states that "to speak in terms of modification implies, to borrow again from Husserl's phenomenology, that there are not two substantially different 'subjects'—the 'they' and the 'authentic' self—but rather different ways of being the *same* subject (or, as Husserl would say, two different intentionalities toward the same object)."[41] There is nothing else to look for!

Third argument. Nothing, that is, apart from this impossibility of deciding that is not, for all that, to be confused with the undecidable. In the "Decision of Existence," Jean-Luc Nancy shows that these "[two different ways] of being the same subject" (proper/improper, authentic/inauthentic) effectively concern *decision* and *dissimulation* (a way of not deciding). Decision and resolution are thinkable and possible only as transitions from the one mode (*Eigentlichkeit*) to the other (*Uneigentlichkeit*). "Decision decides neither in favor of nor by virtue of any 'authenticity' whereby the world of existence would be surmounted or transfigured in any way whatsoever," he writes. "The decision is made (it grasps itself, is grasped by itself, surprises itself) *right at*"—my emphasis—"ontical experience, and it opens to ontical experience. In fact, there is no other experience, and only in illusion could our experience claim to decide for and 'within' another world (and yet even illusion is part of experience . . .). Ontical experience takes place *right at the 'they,'* and nowhere else. More-

over, there is no 'elsewhere': that is 'the meaning
of Being'. . . ."[2]

Being-in-the-world is the experience of an absence
of the outside. Everything that happens, then, only
can right in the world, and this mode of transpiring
"right in" brings us back to the heart of the movement
of modification. The true stakes of the problem of
modification concern the passage from the "they" to
resoluteness. Nancy proposes a commentary on §38,
which is entitled "Falling Prey and Thrownness" and
where Heidegger writes, it should be recalled, that
"*Dasein can* fall prey *only* because it is concerned
with understanding, attuned being-in-the-world. On
the other hand, *authentic* existence is nothing that
hovers over entangled everydayness but is existentially only a modified grasp of everydayness."[43] Nancy
recognizes this himself; Heidegger's text, he writes,
"teaches us nothing else" about the subject of "this
modification."[44] Yet according to him, *we have no
need to know more about it,* since we already know
the essentials. "This last sentence," he writes about
the close of §38, "is decisive for the understanding
of the analytic in its largest dimensions. This sentence plays out decision on the decision. Indeed, it
asserts that the *properness* of existence—its own
truth, its own sense—*does not distinguish itself in any
way* from what could be called *existentiell* existence
except insofar as the former is a 'modified grasp' of
the latter"[45] Speaking this way comes down, then,
to recognizing that modification, in a sense, *makes
a difference by not making it.*

But in that case, I ask quite simply in turn,
why and for what is there modification?

So as to make clear, you respond, that the
"change of mode: from the Modus of the 'floating'
to the Modus of the 'decision'" is not "a change of

ground."[46] One remains *"right in and on."* As Levi-nas indicates, *"Eigentlichkeit*—emergence from the 'they'—is gained by a shaking-up within the everyday existence of the 'they."[47]

What interior, I insist on asking, is at issue, since there is no interior? What is *Dasein right in? Right on* what does it fall? Just what is caught *right onto* again? *What disturbing mastery is concealed in this "right in," this "right on"?*

It always comes down to the same argument: modification is a strategy of fleeing right where there is no possibility of flight, while it is at the same time the possibility of not fleeing where there alone exists possibilities of flight. One disappears in place.[48] One is transported in place. One has nothing *to do*: "The they has always already taken [*immer schon abgenom-men*] the apprehension of these possibilities away from *Dasein*."[49] "What is discovered and disclosed [*das Entdeckte und Erschlossene*] stands in the mode in which it has been disguised and closed off [*steht im Modus der Verstelltheit und Verschlossen*] by idle talk, curiosity, and ambiguity. Being toward beings has not been extinguished [*ist nicht ausgelöscht*] but uprooted. Beings are not completely concealed [*völlig verborgen*], but precisely discovered, and at the same time distorted [*verstellt*]. They show themselves, but in the mode of illusion [*im Modus des Scheins*]."[50] Granted, *Dasein* should "bring itself back from itself [*zu ihm selbst zurückholen*] from its lostness in the they."[51] However, for that, a simple modification will suffice: "when *Dasein* thus brings itself back . . . the they-self is modified in an existential manner so that it becomes authentic being-one's-self."[52] And so I ask you: what is meant by this feeble transition, this miserable manner of reversing (its) sides?

I will continue to demand of Heidegger proof of the plastic power of modification, of something like a *form*. *Yes, a form: a form that attests from between the modes, and that bears scars from its transitions; a power of modifying modification itself and, consequently, a locus for the constitution of individual histories and adventures that could permit for an account of how it is that no* Dasein, *no modification, resembles another; a displacement of structure that decides the fate of structure.*

"The Thin Partition That Separates *Dasein* from Itself . . ."

> He began now to crawl to and fro, over everything, walls, furniture, and ceiling, and finally in his despair, when the whole room seemed to be reeling around him, fell down on the middle of the big table.[1]
>
> —Kafka, *The Metamorphosis*

This witness-form exists.

It is a question of a wall, or partition, of very little thickness. Of a quasi-imperceptible separation. Of an articulation even more intimate than the one forming the joint between the existentials. Of a limit without any analytic, ontological, or existential status and whose profile is only hastily drawn. In fact, this partition appears *only once* in *Being and Time*, as though covertly, even though the vitality of modification depends on it.

Take note, once more, of the hybrid, conceptually depatriated character of the places in Heidegger attesting to our metabolic reality.

The witness-form tightens, trembling, upon each cut taken from its transitions. It does not, curiously,

close the exits but instead renders a crossing possible and therein promises *Dasein* a different fate
than that of being an insect stuck crawling the walls.

Modification's Lot Is Fixed to the Wall

It is apropos of a flight, apropos of the very possibility of flight in general, that Heidegger intervenes with
this "wall." At issue is the "flight from conscience"
analyzed in §57.[2] What kind of flight is at stake?
How flight? What can the meaning of this verb be,
since the call of moral conscience proceeds from
nowhere, it being neither the work of a person nor
something occurring, again, where there is an inside
or outside? What calls, we know, is simply "*Dasein*
in its uncanniness."[3] The call comes neither from
"the heart" nor from "elsewhere" since "*Dasein* is at
the same time the caller and the one summoned."[56]
How, then, is there flight? The response again comes
readily: *Dasein* flees *through modification*. It flees *in
place* in letting itself slip or fall toward its "power
of being-improper"; it is modified, that is, into fallenness. Modification therefore appears (as usual) to
be the answer to the question of what evasion could
be in a space devoid of all interiority and exteriority. There would be nothing special about the flight
from conscience, as it would be just one modification
more. It would only serve to verify the hypothesis
envisaged in the preceding chapter: the bad infinity
of modification is what masks that every metamorphosis and migration become impossible in *Being
and Time*. Nothing would happen with modification;
Dasein, paradoxically, could not change.

But there is the "wall." The flight before conscience, says Heidegger, is "a way out [*Ausweg*] for

Dasein along which it slips away [*wegschleichen*] from the thin wall [*dünne Wand*] that separates the they, so to speak, from the uncanniness of its being [*die gleichsam das Man von der Unheimlichkeit seines Sein trennt*]."[5] *The wall is what* Dasein *flees*. What is at issue, then, is a flight that consists not in passing from one mode to another, but in this "slipping away" from the very division between the authentic and the inauthentic.

Something here is indeed *in between—between* Dasein *and itself; a third term* that *economizes the transitions*. Heidegger's writing "so to speak [*gleichsam*]" here ("the thin wall that separates the they, so to speak [*gleichsam*], from the uncanniness of its being") cannot diminish the decisive character of the sudden appearing of this separation. Insisting on the simple, "metaphoric" status of this wall would not lessen its importance. Whatever we might choose to call it, we can be certain that this mysterious frontier *mobilizes modification* and thus wrests it from the humdrum procedure and incessant repetition that sometimes seems to send *Being and Time* off in a direction Heidegger obviously neither chose nor envisaged, even if it constitutes the fabulous shadow of his book: *a metamorphosis deprived of possibles, of ethical possibles in particular*, and where error would consist in fleeing the division of the modes of being, and resolution, in knowing one can only flee if its unbearable, binary character is to be evaded.

The meanings of both *modification* and *resolution* depend, then, on the wall. This wall is not a rigid barrier that, fitted with a door, would authorize transitions from one mode of being to another without being itself modified. The wall instead has the appearance of a *locus of exchange* that does not just enable the mutual transformation of the modes of being, but also *modifies itself in proportion with its passages.* "Thin partition" thus makes for a more satisfactory translation of *dünne Wand* than does "thin wall" (it allows for more suppleness and mobility than do equivalents to *Wand* like "wall" or "barrier"), and will accordingly be used from here out. Jean-Luc Nancy quite rightly declares that the partition at once marks the "incommensurability" and possible "osmosis" of the instances it separates. *Dasein,* he writes, "remain[s] right at a wall, a wall whose presence indicates the incommensurability of the 'they' with its uncanniness of being, but whose thinness indicates the (quasi-osmotic) communicability of the one with the other. By not pulling away from the wall (or from difference), by remaining stuck to it and its thinness, *Dasein* occupies its space—the space of its nil and impenetrable thickness."[6] As much watertight as porous, *modification's lot is fixed to the wall.*

Unless one assumes the existence of *an ontico-ontological membrane* that transforms to the extent that the modes pass, the transit from one mode to another will basically just be an absurd mechanism. The modes of being are mutually modified. Nonetheless, *everything does not come back to the same.* The improper is not "of value for" the proper. The wall already introduces *the favor* into modifiability and exchange. The adjective *dünn* signifies "fine," "light," "lean," "slight." It also means "modest" (*gering*). The partition already inscribes in *Dasein* the possibility of a *modest difference*; a snip opening each exchange, passage, modification, and crossing. This "nothing-ness" or denseness without density of the partition spaces *Dasein,* distancing it from itself while also at the same time uniting it to itself and gathering it. The partition is *the living tissue of exchange.* This is why *Dasein* can desire "to slip away": so as not to *suffer.*

How could one think that modification modifies only the modes of being and not their profile nor their hinge or jointure, *the structure, that is, of their structure?* How could it be thought that *Dasein* would be able to resolve itself or make a choice, cross the boundaries between the existentials without some kind of *exchange* with itself occurring, without, that is, the weft of its history, the plastic destiny of its individual adventure, finite transformation, and choices about existence? How could one think that *Dasein is neither formed nor displaced (by itself) in its exchanging (with) itself?* I am not sketching here the broad strokes of some inner depth or psychological space where *Dasein* would negotiate, debate, and speculate on itself; rather, I am simply attempting to show that crossing from one mode to another is not a *depthless* operation but one that creates *furrows* and *reliefs* for the quite simple reason that it takes time, that it *pulls taut. Dasein* may not burst open, but it does *tighten* when it passes, its articulations bending, something that *intensifies* even as it *wears out*. Fatigue and suffering are constitutive of its existence. The partition appears, then, to be *an articulation in the articulation* that *renders the structure sensitive]—to itself.*

Minus this sensitivity, what meaning could resolution, flight, fallenness, and falling have? In *Francis Bacon: The Logic of Sensation*, Deleuze shows that the very "idea of the fall implies no context of misery, failure, or suffering" for "[t]he fall is what is most alive in sensation, that through which the sensation is experienced as living."[7] "In short," he says, "everything that develops is a fall. . . . The fall is precisely the active rhythm."[8] Or again: "the fall exists to affirm the difference in level as such. All *tension* is experienced in a fall."[9] *Can these statements really hold given that they make no reference to Heidegger and fallenness* (Verfallenheit) *as he specifically characterized it? Have we not noticed that the fall is neither a collapse nor a tumble insofar as existential space is without high or low? And that the fall instead involves a change of intensity?* Isn't all this contained in the idea that "*Dasein* plunges out of itself into itself [*aus ihm selbst in ihm selbst*]"?[10] And if it is true that "all tension is experienced in a fall," then it must be added that "all fall is experienced in a tension." The partition separating *Dasein* from itself is vibratile; it reacts as an instrument does, marking *differences of level in the midst of the modes of being.*

What interests me here is the affirmation of *differences in level*, the putting into relief of difference itself *qua* difference of thresholds. In striking the partition, modification puts the existential flesh on difference's uneven cobblestone; a flesh without which difference would effectively only be a mechanism, and resolution, a hollow term. For there to be leveling (*Nivellierung*), must there not first be levels? There is neither inside nor outside, just levels of intensity, which are rendered possible by the *existential resonance* of the wall. The absence of interior and exterior is simultaneously reflected and abolished in this intermediary zone between the modes, the zone of *Dasein*'s perpetual deconstitution and reconstitution, of the transit of identity which is the book where existence is (self-)written. A locus of tension, resistance, and contraction, of distancing and gaps, of pressure, differences of power, contraction, and concentration, of *stress*.[11] Beyond interior and exterior, in this flight that is the impossibility of flight, this fleeing in place that is my life, there is the mobility and suppleness of the partition—of *the sensitive string.*

Molding and Movement

The partition is the ontico-ontological articulation itself, the connecting link, the *affect* or *feeling of difference*. This trait, which never takes the same form twice, constitutes what I will call the existential fontanelle, the spot where the modes join; a tiny opening, which quickly closes up again, leaving forever its thin, modest, and slight mark. The fontanelle, where the beating of existence occurs, is not, however, made of bony membrane but of *clay* and *movement*. Of clay en route. *This mobile ontological materiality is what Heidegger dubs "care."*

It is necessary to relate the problematic of modification to "the fable of care" from §42 of *Being and Time*, the fable wherein it comes out that molding is in essence related to temporality. "Once when 'Care' was crossing a river"—a border—"she saw some clay [*tonhaltiges Erdreich*]; she thoughtfully took a piece and began to shape [*formen*] it."[12] You are familiar with the rest. Each of them wants to name the statue (*Gebilde*) after itself: Jupiter for having breathed spirit into it, the Earth for providing it with a part of its body, and Care for having sculpted it. Saturn (that is, Chronos), who is consulted in order to settle the dispute, "gave them the following decision, which seemed to be just: 'Since you Jupiter, have given rise to its spirit, you should receive that spirit at death; and since you, Earth, have given its body, you shall receive its body. But since 'Care' first shaped this creature, she shall possess it as long as it lives. And because there is a dispute among you as to its name, let it be called 'homo,' for it is made out of humus (earth)."[13]

The fable says in a preontological mode, to take up Heidegger's expression, that *man is a sculpture in movement*, working as much as enduring his existence via his very finitude, which *modifies the articulations,* the invisible joints—the thin partition of a fourfold come before its time. This molding in movement, this clay-rhythm and partitioned care, is nothing else but *change*; time, that is, as change—*temporal (ex)change.* A striking occurrence of *Wandel* in *Being and Time* occurs here: "The preontological characterization of the essence of human being expressed in this fable thus has envisaged from the very beginning *the* mode of being that rules its *temporal change in the world* [*seinen zeitlichen Wandel in der Welt*]."[14] *Dasein*'s temporality corresponds to "the turning of the seasons" of its modifications and exchanges, to the rhythm of the negotiations taking place in it between the authentic and inauthentic, and its attempts to "slip away" from this very division.

A naïve reading of the fable could allow one to think that existence molds *Dasein* like earthen clay. We have already insisted on Heidegger's mistrust of the concept of form when it is understood as a standard or seal applied to matter. Modification is not the alteration of a preexistent form. The hermeneutic sense the image of molding impresses onto the existential analytic is not that of self-sculpting. The form attesting to the passages—the zone, just evoked, that is the place and trace of change—is the point where the modes of being meet. For this reason, its profile is never fixed and it can itself appear only under such-and-such a mode, *as changing.* What is molded and, in reality, modulated "according to the mobile and projectile character of thrownness," is only the degree of relaxation or vibrational intensity of the partition. Care-ful molding is *the scar tissue of difference*—not its monument. The scar, itself neither being nor beings, of being and beings. This then is what, from one *Dasein* to another, is molded and modified.

The partition is the form within structure, and in being put into play this way, it at the same time confirms the notion that it already *threatens* the latter by *deforming* it. The partition marks, in effect, *structure's farewell to itself*. Modifying the thresholds of time or modes of being, it does not simply pass from room to room, opening and closing their doors. It is instead, as we saw, exchanging and self-exchanging, as though *Dasein*, in passing, bid each time both hello and farewell to and also intersected with itself—sometimes authentically, sometimes inauthentically—but without ever encountering itself; as though it were perpetually modified, perpetually displaced, and perpetually metamorphosed. How many times must we pass over the partition like smugglers, unrecognizable to ourselves and always covered, recovered, and discovered to the point of startling and no longer again finding ourselves? How many torsions do we, within a lifetime, imprint into this hidden, tense, sensitive, and sickly partition inside us? How many transformations and scars does it bear? Do these crossings not end by exceeding the "totality" of structure through always already breaching it, already tracing in filigree the characterization of existence as a simple movement between "being-there" and "being-away?"

Breakdown of Self

We have come back, again, to change. We have already indicated that Heidegger sometimes employed the word *Umschlag*, or mutation, as though it were synonymous with *Modifikation*, and therein brought the latter and Aristotelian μεταβολή together in some of their shared senses: thrown, turnaround, passage. Such a "mutation" is that which is produced, for instance, when the tool "falls damaged" and appears thereby in another, *surprising* light. "In its conspicuousness, obtrusiveness, and obstinacy [*Auffäligkeit*]," writes Heidegger, "what is at hand [*das Zuhandene*] loses its character of handiness. . . . It does not just disappear, but bids farewell, so to speak, in the conspicuousness of what is unusable. Handiness shows itself once again [*noch einmal*] and precisely in doing so the worldly character of what is at hand also shows itself, too."[15] And then, later: "The understanding of being guiding the heedful association with innerworldly beings *has been mutated* [*hat umgeschlagen*]."[16] Everything takes place as though the tool emitted a sign prior to its disappearance, signifying its mutation; as though its crossing the threshold of usability rendered visible its bidding itself farewell. As though the two ways of being of the tool intersected at some improbable point that marked the time of their exchange, this farewell also being an encounter. If the tool is indeed capable of surprising us, this is because it can break with its customary use and thereby obtrude for the first time.

All of these analyses in *Being and Time* secretly prepare *the last mutation of* Dasein, its "mutation [*Umschlag*] into no-longer-being-there [*Nur-noch-vorhandensein*]."[17] The final modification is death. This inscription in *Dasein*'s structure of the possibility of a farewell to itself (which is very much also, as will be seen, the possibility of an encounter with itself) is the possibility of a farewell of structure to itself. The secret insistence in *Being and Time* on the plasticity of the partition already displaces and metamorphoses the figure of the structural whole, cracking and introducing into it, against all expectation, a line of flight, which is to say the possibility of *breakdown* and *failure*. The partition inscribes onto *Dasein*'s brow the future of modification and through this the future of structure as its own breakdown and infirmity. What is clear is that the partition, whose presence nonetheless so very well "slips away" in the text, demands much fuller development because *it already exceeds the framework of the existential analytic*. Announcing itself here is what, in the texts immediately following *Being and Time*, will be bound up with the thinking of *Stimmung*. *Stimmung*, or affective tone, resolutely takes in those writings the partition's place. It takes shape as an intersection, a place of division and exchange at the heart of which *the existential and the historical are no longer distinguishable*, which further complicates the difference between the authentic and the inauthentic. Henceforth, as we will see, *passing over the parition means surpassing* metaphysics, an equivalence not yet drawn in *Being and Time*.

As the inscription of the fantastic in Being and Time*, the "partition" prefigures another dividing line: the one separating metaphysics from its other. It already impresses, right on* Dasein, *the improbable wrinkle of the difference of time.*

We do not at bottom know if derivation results in *Being and Time* from the same movement as falling prey, if what is at issue, that is, is *the same modification*. We do not know if the meaning of being is separated from itself by a "thin partition," if a parallel between the modification of the modes of being and those of the epochs "sedimented in tradition" can be established with certitude, if the plasticity of thresholds also concerns the nature of the crossing from metaphysics to the other thought.

This ontico-ontological fontanelle makes the emptiness of this question apparent, as the former already inscribes on *Dasein*'s body the temporal and historical articulation between the tradition and its destruction. It announces a crossing where not only the ecstasies will be exchanged, but all the epochs as well.

This is what remains to be examine through the becoming-*W, W, & V* of modification. What remains to be seen is how modification definitively escapes the fate of being an immutable routine, and how something like the *forming* of *Dasein* through modification can be outlined—a *formation* precisely corresponding to its *metamorphosis.*

10

Man and *Dasein,*
Boring Each Other

In the philosophical concept [*Begriff*], man, and
indeed man as a whole, is in the *grip of an attack*
[*Angriff*]—driven out of everydayness and driven
back into the ground of things. Yet the attacker is
not man, the dubious subject of the everyday and
of the bliss of knowledge. Rather, *in philosophizing
the* Dasein *in man launches the attack upon man.*
Thus man in the ground of his essence is someone in the grip of an attack, attacked by the fact
'that he is what he is,' and already caught up in
all comprehending questioning.

—Heidegger, *The Fundamental
Concepts of Metaphysics*[1]

Analyzing the meaning of the wall or partition in *Being
and Time* leads us, then, to consider another line
of division, secretly drawn in the route of the first,
which separates the two understandings of change
from each other. This separation is clearly marked
in Heidegger's work when the vocabulary of modification (*Modifikation*) starts to be abandoned for that
of change (*Wandel, Wandlung,* and *Verwandlung*) in
the texts immediately following the 1927 work. The
two lexicons will at this point intersect each other,
exchange, and pay regard to each other for the first

and last time as texts such as "What Is Metaphysics?" and *The Fundamental Concepts of Metaphysics: Word, Finitude, Solitude* attest. And then, after 1930, the vocabulary of modification will altogether disappear from Heidegger's oeuvre.

This disappearance can certainly be explained by invoking the necessity (which imposed itself on him with increasing clarity) Heidegger felt of no longer taking recourse either to properly phenomenological terminology or, more generally, to technical philosophical language and concepts. Yet considering what is at work in this change in the lexicon of change, such an account would be, quite obviously, insufficient. In this final moment of our journey, I would like to try to show that the abandonment of modification for the triad of change corresponds to a complete overturning (here again, a change . . .) of the understanding of what it is that changes. In 1929's "What Is Metaphysics?" and in the 1930 lecture course *The Fundamental Concepts of Metaphysics*, a discrete but nonetheless sure and definitive substitution is brought off: *the substitution of the* Dasein-*man pair for that of the authentic and the inauthentic.* When the process of *Dasein*'s modification is contrasted with that of its metamorphosis (*Verwandlung*) or transformation (*Wandlung*), one notices, in fact, that it is with the latter no longer a question of *Dasein*'s experience of unevenness, or differences of level, on the same existential soil or plinth but of its carving out the gap (through its also filling it in some way) between itself and what is not itself, what no longer at all moves on the same soil, what is its most intimate other: *man.* In "What Is Metaphysics?," Heidegger tells us that "This requires we actively complete the transformation [metamorphosis] of man into its *Dasein* [*die Verwandlung des Menschen in sein Dasein . . . nachvollziehen*]."[2]

Yet what separates man from *Dasein* is no longer the thin partition but rather . . . the history of philosophy in its entirety. Every *Dasein* bears man inside itself, and the historical and metaphysical thickness of this concept of man as *animal rationale* bores into each *Dasein*, into each of us, this distance from us (through our relation to ourselves) that destines every existence, even the most modest and least concerned with philosophy, to secretly undergo the experience of the accomplishment of metaphysics and what, beyond that, it promises.

We previously recalled the statement, in *Being and Time*, that with the existential analytic, "it was necessary from the outset to change the direction [*herausgedreht werden*] of our analysis from the approach presented by the traditional definition of the human being."[3] Evidently, the need to think in a more profound manner this "change of direction" and to constitute it into a constant, metabolic experience for *Dasein* imposed itself on Heidegger very quickly, since he will henceforth show that change is not, or no longer only, the transition from one mode of being to another, but the crossing from the one tradition to the other, *the everyday experience and test*, in other words, *of the impossible possibility of overcoming metaphysics*. Which also means, then, the experience, on the part of each *Dasein* (the least philosophical of them included), of *the impossible possibility of metamorphosing philosophy*.

The distance opened between man and *Dasein* stops being marked by the form attesting to the partition and now is, instead, by a tonality: *Stimmung*. *Stimmung*, or attunement, is the originary possibility of the migration and metamorphosis of man into its *Dasein*. "We attempted," Heidegger writes in the *The Fundamental Concepts of Metaphysics*, "without orienting ourselves toward any particular metaphysical question, by *awakening a fundamental attunement of our* Dasein, . . . to transform [metamorphose: *verwandeln*] the humanity of us human beings into the *Dasein* in ourselves."[4]

The deployment of the analysis of *Stimmung* that goes from *Being and Time* to *The Fundamental Concepts of Metaphysics* by way of "What Is Metaphysics?" accomplishes the metamorphosis and migration of modification, initiating this way a new union between the existential and the historical.

I now invite you to return to the affective, even musical, sources of what *The Fundamental Concepts* calls "the *possibility* of a completely new epoch of philosophy."[5]

Stimmung and Metaphysics

THE MIXED LEXICON OF CHANGE

The lexicon of modification and the triad of change still sometimes coexist in this period, as can be seen in the 1930 course collected under the title of *The Fundamental Concepts of Metaphysics: Word, Finitude, Solitude.* Boredom, the fundamental affective tone closely analyzed in this text, appears to be a modifiable and modified instance as much as a power of metamorphosis or transformation. Heidegger effectively conceives boredom, on the one hand, as *temporal modification:* "we are," in boredom, "cut off from our having-been and from our future. This *being cut-off* . . . does not mean that the latter are factically removed or taken away, but means a dissolution of the future and having-been into the mere present, a *modification* of having-been and future."[6] He also affirms, on the other, that "[t]his attunement to which we give expression in 'it is boring for one' has already transformed [*gewandelt*] *Dasein.*"[7] The two vocabularies join and intersect so often that the translator utilizes the terms "modification," "change," and "transformation" interchangeably. It is true that the analysis of boredom at first glance closely resembles the one of anxiety developed in *Being and Time,* as the latter mood is indeed characterized there as a modification. Although boredom is initially said to be, like all attunement, a "mode" of "availability [*Befindlichkeit*]," it soon emerges as "a modification of complete being-in-the-world" that belongs, on account of that, to care.[8]

So the mixing together of the concepts of change would itself appear to be quite unremarkable. An attentive reading, however, permits not the equivalence, but the *slippage* between the two vocabularies to become noticeable, since, as we are going to see, the lexicon of modification is only used to characterize *the modes of being of one and the same tone* (the different "forms" of boredom for example), while the triad intervenes each time it is a question of *the historical significance of modification.* "What Is Metaphysics?" shows this clearly, as anxiety is conceived there as what brings about the metamorphosis of man into his *Dasein* at the same time as it prefigures the overcoming of metaphysics. And the 1930 lectures confirm it: "the understanding of attunement ultimately demands of us a transformation [*Wandel*] in our fundamental conceptions of man."[9]

MODES AND MODALITIES

The question that must initially be posed here concerns the relationship *Stimmung* maintains with
modification. This "affective tone" emerges as a mode,
a "manner" or "way," of a particular type. In *The Fundamental Concepts of Metaphysics*, Heidegger declares
that "attunements are ways of the being-there of
Dasein. . . . An attunement is a way, not merely a
form [*Form*] or mode [*Modus*], but a way [*Weise*]—in
the sense of a melody that does not merely hover
[*schwebt*] over the so-called proper being at hand
of man, but that sets the tone for such being [*den
Tone angibt*], that is, attunes and determines [*stimmt
und bestimmt*] the manner and way of his being. . . .
[A]ttunement is a fundamental manner [*Grundart*], the
fundamental way [*die Grundweise*] in which *Dasein*
is as *Dasein*."[10]

These claims immediately raise a particular line
of questioning. What, in fact, is the precise status
of affective tonality in relation to the other modes?
Should it be considered, insofar as Heidegger dubs
it the "fundamental genre" or "fundamental modality," an archimode that, whatever else might be said
of it, would be destined to "hover" over the others?
An attentive reading of *The Fundamental Concepts
of Metaphysics* could allow for a positive response
to the question. Heidegger in fact writes there that
affective tonality is a manner of "binding [*binden*]
ourselves to our *Dasein*."[11] *Stimmung* emerges, then,
as *that which ties* Dasein *to itself*, a characteristic
that seems to confer upon it a privileged status.

But in reality, *Stimmung* enjoys no existential
priority. Affective tonality is not added to the modes
as one mode more but is, rather, *the mode of being*

of the partition itself. In effect, what turns up attuned as a result of an affective tone or a particular mood— anxiety or boredom, but also, as Heidegger says in "What Is Metaphysics?," "joy [*Freude*]"[12]—is the *community of* Dasein*'s modes of being.* Their milieu or "between," what Heidegger dubs their "fabric."[13] But this does not confer on *Stimmung* a position over them. Indeed, *Stimmung* is always changing. If the thin partition is always found to have such and such a temperament and if *Stimmung* is what lends the tone to these temperaments, it constantly itself changes atmospheres. Hence the transition from one mode of being to the other itself always takes place under a particular mode, a *particular* modality, of mood. Mood is, by definition, eminently variable.

The existential fontanelle or ontico-ontological articulation is always "tempered" in a certain way and for a certain time, since *Stimmung* is unstable on account of its ontologically hybrid character: though not ontic, neither is it ontological. This is what Heidegger affirms in *The Fundamental Concepts of Metaphysics* when he writes that "boredom—and thus ultimately every attunement—is a hybrid [*Zwitterwesen*]."[14] Attunement, again, is not a being, but a manner or way.

Philosophy in Exchange

Being in a mood is always being in the mood to change moods. In multiple reprises, Heidegger makes *Stimmung* seem less like a mood than the very possibility of a swing in mood. He declares in *Being and Time* that "both the undisturbed equanimity and the inhibited discontent of everyday heedfulness, the way we slide from one to another or slip into bad moods [*das Ausgleiten in Verstimmungen*], are by no means ontologically nothing. . . . Mood makes manifest 'how one is and is coming along."[15] Moods always "can be spoiled and change [*Umschlagen*]."[16] Moreover, when he comments, in "On the Essence and Concept of φύσις," on his decision to translate μεταβολή with *Umschlag*, Heidegger comments on what the "metabolic" is in relation to changes of mood, time, and the seasons, and even to the transit of goods and merchandise. "When we speak of a change in the weather [*schlägt um*] or a change of mood," he writes, "what we have in mind is an 'alteration' [*Änderung*]. We also speak of exchange points [*Umschlageplätzen*] where commercial goods change hands in business transactions [*im Verkehr*]."[17] Attunement emerges, then, as the inscription of μεταβολή *right on existence.* "*Dasein* as *Dasein* is always already attuned in its grounds. There is only ever a change of attunement [*es geschieht nur immer ein Wandel der Stimmungen*]."[18]

Changes of mood, which traditional philosophy never accorded any real attention, play a fundamental role at the core of *Dasein*'s being-constitution, or *Seinsverfassung*. As we just saw, attunement is what permits *Dasein* to be tied or bound to itself. Contrary, then, to what might at first be believed of it, "attunement is not something inconstant, fleeting, merely subjective. Rather, because attunement is the originary way in which *Dasein* is at it is, it is not what is most inconstant [*das Unbeständigste*], but that which gives *Dasein* consistence and possibility [*Bestand und Möglichkeit*]."[19] In effect, "[i]n attunement [*Befindlichkeit*], *Dasein* is always already brought before itself [*vor es selbt*]."[20] The analysis of *Stimmung*, then, reveals to *Dasein* the essential, which is, namely, that *the essential is changing.*

This revelation allows us to understand why *Stimmung* is presented in both "What Is Metaphysics?" and *The Fundamental Concepts* as a fundamental condition of philosophical questioning. Changes of mood, which grant *Dasein* its world, disclose the meaning of the mutability of existence as *freedom*, and, in this sense, *summon philosophy*. "Philosophy," writes Heidegger, "has meaning only as human activity. *Its truth is essentially that of human* Dasein. This *Dasein*, however, occurs in freedom. Possibility, change, and predicament are obscure [*Möglichkeit, Wandel, und Lage sind dunkel*]. *Dasein* stands before possibilities it does not foresee. It is subject to a change [*Wandel*] it does not know. It constantly moves in a predicament it does not have power over. Everything that belongs to the existence of *Dasein* belongs just as essentially to the truth of philosophy."[21] So if it is true that it is characteristic of metaphysical questioning for the questioner to be included in her question, their being outside themselves in relation to each other is also necessary. *Stimmung* alone renders this rapture possible.[22] *Dasein* can think only on the basis of the (ex)change (of who thinks) in it.

If *Stimmung* is susceptible to completing the metamorphosis of man into its *Dasein,* this is first of all because it reveals, through its power of rapture, *another foundation of philosophy*. The veritable root of philosophy is precisely this affective rapture. We could even go so far as to say that *the origin of philosophy is the affective rapture of change granted by the essentially changing character of affective rapture. The root of philosophy is, then, "the affect (of the) metamorphic" as such.* In changing, *Stimmung* announces not only the advent of another mode of being but also that of *another animal, one differ-*

ent than both the rational animal and man. It casts upon man "the shadow . . . of something quite other [*ganz anders*], of that which we call *Dasein*."[23] In the introduction appended to "What Is Metaphysics?" in 1949, Heidegger tells us that the analysis of anxiety that was developed in 1929 permitted "liberating [*herausnehmen*] the determination of the essence of the human from subjectivity, but also from the rational animal" and thus prepared "the metamorphosis of the human into its *Dasein*."[24]

This metamorphosis, as you by now understand, is not separable from a metamorphosis of philosophy. Heidegger clearly affirms this when he says that "if our thinking should succeed in its efforts to go back to the ground of metaphysics, it might well help to bring about a change in the human essence [*ein Wandel des Wesens des Menschen*], a change accompanied by a transformation [metamorphosis: *Verwandlung*] of metaphysics."[25] Why? "Anxiety," he continues, "grants an experience of being as the whole of beings." *More surely than would a lesson in philosophy,* Stimmung *enables* Dasein *to experience the ontological difference.*

The attunement "in which we 'are' in one way or another and which determines us through and through, lets us find ourselves among beings as a whole."[26] As with anxiety, during profound boredom, beings in their entirety "slip away" and "recede": "All things and we ourselves slip into indifference [*Gleichgültigkeit*]. This, however, is not in the sense of mere disappearance. Rather, in their very receding [*Wegrücken*], things turn toward us. The receding of beings as a whole, closing in on us in anxiety, oppresses us. We can get no hold on things. In the slipping away of beings only this 'no hold on things' comes over us and remains. Anxiety makes manifest the nothing [*die Angst offenbart das Nichts*]."[27] The nothing, which "is encountered at one [*in eins mit*] with beings as a whole," reveals "beings in their full . . . strangeness [*Befremdlichkeit*]," the whole of beings as "radically other" to being."[28]

"Anxiety," Heidegger continues, "is no kind of grasping of the nothing. All the same, the nothing becomes manifest in and through anxiety."[29] How ought this to be understood? In anxiety, beings and being are absolutely dissociated from each other. The being of beings no longer appears *qua* being-ness, *Seindheit*, but as *Unwesen* or nonessence, the nihilating of the nothing. "In the being of beings the nihilation of the nothing occurs [*in Sein des Seienden geschieht das Nichten des Nichts*]."[30] In the same stroke, *the mutual exchangeability of being and beings* is revealed. *The experience of the indifference* (*Gleichgültigkeit*) *of the whole of beings*, its "everything being equal,"[31] allows us to understand that beings can be of value for being and that this is precisely what happened in and as traditional metaphysics. *Stimmung is the affective revelation of the first change at the same as it is the sensible prefiguration of the other (ex)change.*

In the deepest intimacy of *Dasein* and the grip of affective rapture, there is an opening of this fissure that, because it makes a possible alterity of meta-physics appear, also frees the fantastic phenomenon of a possible alterity of man.

It can be granted that §40 of *Being and Time* had already brought to light the ontologico-pedagogical character, if it can be put that way, of anxiety, and the fact the expression "the ontological difference" does not yet fully figure in the 1927 work in no way prevents the reader from seeing that it is exactly the abyss between being and beings that anxiety, in an instant, opens before it. "Anxiety assumes in the existential analytic," Didier Franck writes, "a central methodological function analogous to the transcendental reduction in the intentional analytic of subjectivity: it reveals *Dasein* to itself in its being-in-the-world toward death."[32] However, in *Being and Time* the thematic of the metamorphosis and migration of the human into its *Dasein* is not developed. *These movements of transformation exceed, in effect, the framework of modification in which they are confined.* In *Being and Time*, the vocabulary of modification restrains the metamorphic force of anxiety. In the subsequent texts, though, the problem rapidly changes. "What is required," Heidegger declares in "What Is Metaphysics?," "is that we actively complete the transformation of man into that *Dasein* that every instance of anxiety occasions in us, in order to get a grip on the nothing announced there as it makes itself known."[33] From here on, the analysis of *Stimmung* applies less to *Dasein* than to the adventure of metaphysics affectively inscribed in its core. In "What Is Metaphysics?" it is less a matter of insisting on anxiety's power of modification as what enables *Dasein* to cross the wall than of following the strange turnaround through which *Stimmung* (in, again, the furthest intimacy of *Dasein*) *redoubles the originary turnaround to which metaphysics owes its name.*

During a discussion in *The Fundamental Concepts of Metaphysics* linking the term to an elucidation of the meaning and history of the word "metaphysics," Heidegger recalls that "in Greek, μετά means after [*nach*], behind [*hinterher*], as in . . . μέθοδος, method, i.e. the way in which I go after a matter."[34] But the prefix "μετά," he adds, "has a further meaning in Greek, however, which is connected with the first. If I go behind a matter and go after it, in so doing

I move away [*bewege*] from one matter and over to another, i.e. I turn myself 'around' [*umwenden*] in a certain respect. We have this meaning of μετά in the sense of 'away from something toward something else' [*von etwas weg zu etwas anderem*] in the Greek word μεταβολή [changeover, *Umschlag*]. In condensing the Greek title μετά τά φυσικά into the Latin expression *metaphysica*, the μετά has altered [*geändert*] its meaning. The meaning of changeover, of 'turning away from one matter toward another,' of 'going from one over to another,' came out of a purely positional meaning. τά μετά τά φυσικά now no longer means that which comes after the doctrines on physics, but that which deals with whatever *turns away* from the φυσικά and *turns toward* other beings, toward beings in general and toward that being which properly is."[35]

It is clear, then, that at the origin, metaphysics is nothing but a turnaround (*Umwendung*) or a changeover (*Umschlag*). It is the act of turning from one thing to another, and this original swerve decides its destiny. Metaphysics owes both its name and meaning to a change of direction alone. If *Stimmung* enables the fulfillment of the overcoming of metaphysics—an overcoming that is also its *metamorphosis*—this is because it *imprints, while taking this curve, a new torsion and reversal.* If overcoming always comes down to being diverted from the very thing overcome, overcoming metaphysics comes down to overcoming the overcoming itself, in an overcoming to the second power that grants to the concept of transcendence its authentic meaning.

Metamorphosed metaphysics is thus no longer the act of thought that consists in turning away from beings toward another conception of them (toward being understood as beingness) but the very detour of this detour, the turning around toward the other of

every being, toward being in its astonishing strangeness (*Befremdlichkeit*). By grace of this metamorphosis, metaphysics becomes what it is: overcoming, a
movement of turning toward *something else* and *other*.
This is why the Heidegger of the period of "What Is
Metaphysics?" still calls metaphysics the outcome of
the metamorphosis of metaphysics. It is a question
of metaphysics led back to its ground, truth, and
essence, of *metaphysics metamorphosed into itself.*
It is in this way that asking "what is metaphysics?"
comes down, in a sense, to asking "what is metamorphosis?" *This question, you have to admit, brings
into play something entirely different from the one that
amounts to asking, "what is modification?"*

Time's Forms, Crossing the Depths

Yet can such a clear demarcation between modification
and *W, W, & V*, you ask, really be established? We
will start from the analysis of boredom developed in
The Fundamental Concepts, where something immediately grabs our attention: boredom is presented
there as taking three "forms" that correspond to its
"degrees of depth." The passage from each form to
the other—the "descent" from surface to bottom—is
treated as both a "modification" and a "transformation [*Wandlung*]" or "change [*Wandel*]." It is right
here, on this lexical hybridity, that the border you
are questioning me about is drawn.

The analysis of boredom, Heidegger tells us, must
begin by "recording provisionally these moments of
distinction with respect to depth [*die Momente des
Unterschiedes der Tiefe*]."[36] Boredom's three "forms
[*Formen*]"—"becoming bored by something," "being
bored with something and the kind of passing the

time belonging to it," and "profound boredom as 'it is boring for one'"[37]—are organized into the hierarchy of a "becoming deeper [*Tieferwerden*]."[38] This becoming corresponds to an intensification that is as much ontological as affective, since each of boredom's "degrees" is also a degree of authenticity.

So in a sense, the passage from one "form" or "degree" of boredom to another is brought about through modification and causes *Dasein* to cover, through the rhythm of the mobility we already examined in *Being and Time*, the impalpable but real distance separating its authentic potential to be from its inauthentic potential to be. Nonetheless, the introduction of the motif of depth considerably changes the analysis, as it allows for another perspective on the "structural whole." Heidegger affirms that "comprehending the genuine context [*der echte Zusammenhang*] for these transformations of boredom" is of the greatest import; this "transformation . . . is not some arbitrary, free-floating changing of forms [*kein beliebiges, freischwebendes Verändern von Formen*], but bound to the occurrence [*Geschehen*] of *Dasein* in which boredom in each case arises in such and such a way and thereby clings to the surface or finds its way back into the depths."[39] *The schema of articulation cedes its place here to a schema of difference of altitude. Existence is "historicalized" between distance and depth.*

Each time a form is transformed, it is not just the partition between *Dasein*'s different modes of being that is displaced but also the *historical* distance separating man from the *Dasein* tensed up inside it. *In boredom, man and* Dasein *bore (from inside) each other such that it would appear that the difference between the forms of boredom is never only the gamut of possible relations deployed between man and* Dasein. *Between man and* Dasein, *two different modalities of presence intersect and exchange without blending, and become bored in this contact—the metaphysics of presence become bored.*

"In truth and fundamentally, a corresponding displacement [*Verlegung*] of man's existence always occurs in advance here—either toward the surface and into the realm of his busy activities [*Umtreiben*], or into the dimension of *Dasein* as such [*in die Dimension des Daseins als solchen*], that of existing proper [*des eigentlichen Existierens*]."[40] *Man becomes the surface of* Dasein, *and* Dasein, *the bottom of man, a gap hollowed out between them. They cross past each other in boredom, avoiding each other from not knowing what to do (with each other).*

The transformation of the intensity of Stimmung, *then, is always at the same time* Dasein's *transformation as it leaves behind the essence of man.* The degrees of boredom's depth do not, in effect, reveal only the "depths [*Tiefe*]" of *Dasein* itself.[41] Hence each form of boredom, inasmuch as it is revealed to be a "changed form [*gewandelte Form*]"[42] of the preceding, has already "changed [*gewandelt*] *Dasein*."[43] *Stimmung* is in this sense the "*basis of a transformation of* Dasein *itself [aufgrund einer Verwandlung des Daseins selbst*]."[44]

"We now know . . . that these structural moments," says Heidegger of boredom's forms, "are in each case transformed [*jeweils gewandelt*], that they are not rigid standards [*starre Maßstäbe*], not a fixed framework [*ein festes Gerippe*] that we can lay at the basis of every form of boredom."[45] Yet these "supple" forms, which modulate the partition, are also the supple forms permitting for the figuration not of another man, but of the other of man.

STIMMUNG AND TEMPORALITY

This cleavage brings us to time. Boredom, in fact, is "how times resonates" within *Dasein*.[46] All the exchanges, passages, transformations, and differences of degree and altitude find their foundation in temporality. Boredom is a *"relation to time*, a way in which we stand with respect to time, a feeling of time. Boredom and the question of boredom thus lead us to the problem of time."[47] Without being either "fickle" or "inconstant," time sometimes merges with its "capacity for transformation": "time can oppress us or leave us in peace, sometimes in this way, sometimes in that. This is ultimately bound up with its own capacity for transformation [*ihr eigene Wandlungsfähigkeit*]."[48] In reality, *Stimmung* manifests in its changes only the manner "in which we stand with respect to time," the way in which "our own temporality temporalizes itself [*sich zeitigt*]."[49] A strict connection links temporalization and changes of temperament in their essences. "Becoming bored and boredom in general are then evidently entirely rooted in this enigmatic essence of time. What is more—if boredom is an attunement, then time and the way in which it is as time [*wie sie als Zeit ist*], i.e. the way in which it temporalizes [*zeitigt*] itself, plays a peculiar part in *Dasein*'s being attuned in general."[50]

The analysis of boredom begins with time that "becomes drawn out" and "long," a dull monotony that will progressively gain in depth.[51] The first "form" of boredom, the most "superficial," corresponds to the feeling of "being held in limbo" and "left empty" as "time drags."[52] The example Heidegger gives of it is a four-hour wait in a small train station where there is nothing to do: "We read the timetables or study the table giving the various distances from this station to other places we are not otherwise acquainted with at all. We look at the clock—only a quarter of an hour has gone by."[53] We try to find some "pastime"—we seek, in reality, to "overcome the temporalization of time" (to kill time).[54]

Boredom's second form—"being bored with something and the kind of passing the time pertaining to it"[55]—"transforms" the first to the extent that it deprives the mood of an object. In the first form, *Dasein* has the impression that its boredom comes from the station itself. Yet in the boring dinner party Heidegger now discusses, no being can really be incriminated. "We have been invited out somewhere for the evening," he writes. "We do not need to go along. Still, we have been tense all day, and we have time in the evening. So we go along. There we find the usual food and the usual table conversation, everything is not only tasty, but tasteful as well. Afterward people sit together having a lively discussion, as they say, perhaps listening to music, having a chat, and things are witty and amusing. And already it is time to leave. The ladies assure us, not merely when leaving, but downstairs and outside too as we gather to leave, that it really was very nice, or that it was terribly charming. Indeed. There is nothing at all to be found that might have been boring about this evening, neither the conversation, nor the people, nor the rooms. Thus we come home quite satisfied. We cast a quick glance at the work we interrupted that evening, make a rough assessment of things and look ahead to the next day—and then it comes: I was bored after all this evening, on the occasion of this invitation."[56] A little later, we are told why: we were "leaving ourselves behind," and the "emptiness" that so "forms [*bildet*]" is thus an "abandoning [of] ourselves," of, "namely, our proper self."[57] The prevailing feeling is of having wasted time.

The third form, finally—"profound boredom as 'it is boring for one'"[58]—is even more indeterminate. "Passing the time," we read, "*is missing* in this boredom."[59] Such boredom is quite close to anxiety. "'It is boring for one,'" Heidegger says for example, "to walk through the streets of a large city on Sunday afternoon."[60] There is a feeling, as during anxiety, of beings recoiling in their entirety, an "indifference enveloping beings as a whole."[61] In it, *Dasein*'s possibilities seem to be "left unexploited"[62] such that it does not know what to do with itself. *Dasein* seems here, Heidegger says, to drift, and "feels timeless"— "removed from the flow of time."[63]

The trait common to all three of boredom's forms is the fact that time seems to be in each of them at once stuck in the now (which is set on not passing) and irreducible to this same punctuality—it drags, narrows, changes intensity, and sees "transformations" that show it to be, of course, unmeasured. It is here that the ambiguity constitutive of boredom emerges. Boredom seals off every possibility; but at the same time, in shutting possibles away, it reveals them as "given to be free."[64] There is, between rigidity and slackness, the possibility of a *fluctuation—the fluctuation between man and* Dasein. *Man at once holds* Dasein *in place and lets it out. He quite simply gives to it this way the time of being possible:* "being held in limbo" is "being impelled toward the *originary possibilization* [*Ermöglichung*] of Dasein *as such.*"[65] At once stuck to man and dissociated from him, like a now that lasts too long while no longer being able to take place, *Dasein* can resolve and concentrate itself in the original, authentic point of the *Augenblick*, or "instant."[66] Thus "the *Dasein* in us oscillates out into the expanse of the temporal horizon of its temporality and thus is able only to oscillate into the instant [*Augenblick*] pertaining to essential action. This oscillating in between [*dieses Schwingen im Zwischen*] such expanse [*Weite*] and such extremity [*Spitze*] is our being attuned, this boredom as attunement."[67]

The different forms and transformations of boredom, which in fact correspond to temporal modifications, enable *Dasein* to undergo the experience of a strange kind of doubling. In effect, it is not really *Dasein* but the man in *Dasein* and, reciprocally, the *Dasein* in man, who is bored. The two forms bore each other from opposite sides of the affective partition. This dimension of metaphysical and historical doubling, though, is absent from *Being and Time*. Heidegger shows there the tight correlation uniting the modifications of *Dasein*'s comportments to the modification of time itself; in effect, it is always the passage from originary temporality to leveled or "derived" time that provides, in reality, the rhythm of the circulation of the modes of being. The "tempo" between the expanse and the point appears in *Being and Time* as the mutual modification of authentic temporality and vulgar time,[68] and it is thus always "temporality that permits modification,"[69] and on temporality that the properness and improperness of *Dasein* is ontologically grounded. In spite of this, however, *Stimmung* is not yet treated in *Being and Time* as an affective fracture splitting *Dasein* from man. From his "the primordial phenomenon of originary, authentic temporality is the future," Heidegger does not yet conclude that *Dasein* is the future of man. It will still take time, that of a metamorphosis and migration, and the establishment of *W, W, & V* in thought, for that.

The Event of Existence

"Going beyond beings occurs in the essence of
Dasein [*das Hinausgehen über das Seiende geschieht
im Wesen des Daseins*]."[70] You are now able to understand this phrase and to see just how considerable
the change from modification to metamorphosis and
migration is. We come back, once more, to boredom.
Having illumined its different forms, Heidegger now
states that "[h]itherto we have dealt with boredom
in its various forms" and "have even dealt with a
profound boredom, with one form thereof, but we
have not at all dealt with what is decisive, *with the
boredom that today perhaps determines our* Dasein
here and now."[71] The fundamental question that
arises here is, in other words, "has man today in the
end become boring to himself?"[72] What the question
gets at is not whether people today are bored by
certain things or more bored than they were in other
eras but the historical (*geschichtlich*) determination
of boredom: is boredom, in other words, the *Stimmung* of our epoch? A major dimension of *Stimmung*
is exposed here, which is its *epochal* signification:
"the fundamental attunement of metaphysics in a
specific case, and the manner and measure of its
attunement, is a matter of fate [*Schicksal*], that is,
something which can change [*wandelt*] and does not
remain binding for every era."[73]

Yet what is it that reveals *Stimmung* today? Why
is there boredom *today*? Just why should man and
Dasein be separated on account of this boredom? Heidegger's response is that *the meaning of existence has
been transformed*: "we find ourselves," he says, "forced
to adopt another language because of a fundamental
transformation [metamorphosis] of existence [*wir sind
zu eiener anderen Sprache gezwungen aufgrund einer*

Verwandlung der Existenz]."[74] This "metamorphosis of existence" is not a new existence but existence *less metaphysics* (less, that is, the metaphysical concept of existence), which gets detached from it through an unappealable ontological and historical boredom. Boredom is the affect of a historical [*geschichtlich*] rupture. Today, existence for itself, existence on recess from man, is the genuine event, *Ereignis*. It is "suddenly unveiled."[75]

What is "suddenly unveiled" is also at the same time the answer to our initial question. Isn't structure, we asked, the term most suited to the dividing line we have sought to characterize from the start, the line between metaphysics and its other, between being (*Sein*) and be-ing (*Seyn*), man and *Dasein*, and existence and its metamorphosis? Our reading of *Being and Time* sent us back, finally, to structure as a *possible master term for change.* No structure, indeed, is thinkable apart from its modifiability, its articulation being the profound mark of its variability. In relating the triad to its past as modification, I took the risk of retrospectively illumining the entire course of our journey in light of this structural mutability. The two axes of the Heideggerian cineplastic—continuous, contiguous change and sharp rupture—correspond, perhaps, to two modes of being of one and the same structure. Perhaps the withdrawal of being is itself a structure, just as much as giving's sequencing and the possibility of passing from one mode of presence to the other are. After all, nothing, as you will now acknowledge, is ever shattered in Heidegger. From the outset, migration and metamorphosis proceed without rending anything apart and operate according to a logic of replacement that has neither an inside nor outside and that works *right on* what it replaces. This logic being, moreover, the task proper to technology.

We should not forget, then, that migration and metamorphosis started with a *modification*. Heidegger did not in all likelihood forget this; for him, *everything* can change since for him it is *only everything* (in other terms, the structural whole itself) that is capable of changing. Structure's modification is the ineffaceable memory of metamorphosis.

At the same time, a movement by which structure says farewell to itself will always be evident in Heidegger. Modification exceeds itself. Inexorably. And very quickly after *Being and Time*. Very quickly, each time we modify ourselves. Very quickly, each time we incline structure in one direction or another, toward each of our acts, so to speak. Modification *qua* the structure from which it is inseparable is structurally destined to be modified, which is to say, first, to be undone—unglued, that is, and dissociated from itself. There is something else besides us in us. Which is another change. An entire history in the structure. A locus of exchange that distends the unity of the latter. In effect, the division between the proper and improper modes of being ends up substituted for by the division between metaphysics and the other thought. The whole secret is knowing whether these four terms form a chiasm, whether they match up or if there is, instead, a distance between them that can never be crossed. The difference between modification and *W, W, & V* is situated in precisely this distance.

Retrospectively confronting modification with the triad allows both the coexistence and incompatibility of these four terms to be tested. But can the synonymy between, on the one hand, the improper and the metaphysical and, on the other, the proper and the ultrametaphysical really be so summarily addressed? The answer is both *yes and no*, which explains the simultaneously *fecund* and *sterile* character of the motif of structure in Heidegger: it is a jointure uniting everything as much as an irreducible gap that fragments this unity.

This fecundness and sterility or strength and insufficiency, which allows *and* prohibits the Heideggerian problematic of change *qua* structural adventure, forms the locus of an everyday experience, the everydayness of *Dasein* itself historically and retrospectively understood. *The vibrancy and waning of structure is in us; it is the telescoping together of the existential (modes of being) and the historical (the metaphysical and ultrametaphysical) in us. And it is this play between the structure that we are and are not—this circulation between the four terms of the proper, the improper, man, and* Dasein—*that opens the space where the deployment of the metamorphosis of existence, the heir and absolute other of modification, can occur.*

Conclusion

The W, W, & V of an Alternative

No "revolution" is sufficiently "revolutionary."

—Heidegger, *Geschichte des Seyns*

In setting out from the first (ex)change conceived as the constitution and progressive metamorphosis of both the form of metaphysics and the shape and switchbacks of its route, then exploring after that the migratory and metamorphic articulation of the second (ex)change as manifested in giving—the self-passing of being—*qua* substitutional economy and essential porosity of beings (whose milieu is the *Gestell*), and in relating, finally, the triad of change to its past, in *Being and Time*, as modification and showing, too, that the line of change dividing everything is inscribed in the furthest intimacy of *Dasein*, I have only this whole time been developing with you the terms of one and the same question.

At issue is knowing if philosophy can, at the end of the day, endure the trial of its own experience, the becoming visible—fantastically visible—of *ontological transformability*; if it can accept the revelation of its destiny, which turns it into the schematic device or imaginary apparatus (in the profoundly metamorphosed sense Heidegger gives this term) that governs both the occlusion and appearing of this visibility throughout the Western tradition; if it can welcome its own truth, which is that being is nothing . . . but its mutability, and that ontology is therefore the name of an originary migratory and metamorphic tendency, the aptitude to give change (and throw off the trail) whose strange economy we have from the start been attempting to characterize; if philosophy can acknowledge that ontology is nothing besides an economy, the long adventure of the (ex)changing of the currencies of the essential.

What is at stake is whether philosophy can at the end of the day endure the announcement it makes to itself of a "metamorphosis without rest," along with its knowledge that the constitution of the announcement finds itself affected by the very thing it announces; that the eschatological, the apocalyptic, and even the messianic are structures of the originary transformation of presence. Everything announced is changed at the origin; everything announced (ex)changes what it announces, and announces change alone. Remember: I am what I am—*changed in advance.*

The whole question is of knowing if philosophy can at the end of the day cease evading what it has nonetheless never ceased to teach itself—the originary metamorphic and migratory condition. Even Nietzsche, who came very close to this teaching, recoiled when faced with the radicality of ontological convertibility by maintaining the traditional conception of essence *qua* immutable instance.

But what, in the end, do we do with Heidegger? We have attempted to show that philosophy was sent with him down the path of its metamorphosis. Yet at the same time, the threatening prospect that change could become impossible, or (what amounts to the same thing) of metamorphosis in perpetuity, cast its shadow over each phase of our journey. I insisted, as we saw, that Heidegger offer proof of a *plastic* power, of the capacity to bring to light an unprecedented concept, an ultrametaphysical determination of *form* lacking which philosophy would simply be, or end up, unable to put the strength and resistance of its metabolism to the test.

This much we have seen: *everything depends on the destiny of form*. And the two alternatives developed in the second part of this book (and at the exact midpoint of our inquiry) is the radicalized, aggravated expression of an anxiety that runs throughout it. *Everything depends on the destiny of form*—on the convertibility of an imago, on a non-ideal origin, on the vibratile intensity of a partition or attunement.

Flexibility and Plasticity

Perhaps form remains form (the form of metaphysics) such that it would not manage to exceed its (traditional) form or structure. In which case what takes place with Heidegger is but a supplementary *reformulation* of metaphysics, merely one more epochal metamorphosis or migration, and philosophy, in its *imaginal* consummation, dies out from remaining hopelessly identical to itself—the imago remaining the imago, and form form, as tributary to the idea and the constancy of essence. In which case the evidence that has emerged for the transformability of being (for being as nothing else but its transformability) simply indicates the onset of a new ontological bricolage. Man, stamping his seal everywhere, would be made master of the infinite fashionability of essences, and engage in, without completely deciding to, a series of metamorphoses in which one and the same form would be reformed, and the same pathway followed. If such is the case, the revelation of ontological mutability marking the fulfillment of metaphysics does not allow for the latter's supersession, and modern technology simply closes the loop of a generalized equivalence where everything is of equal value (*alles gilt gleich*) and everything possible—every manipulation, bargain, direction, and ideological advance.

Perhaps form can cross the line. In that event, everything is different. Form would then *double presence*, surpass *its* presence, and give change. Philosophy would become *the other thinking* in the sense of a *different thinking of form* whose source lies in an ancient, so far unnoticed link between *Gestell* and *Gestalt*, a source so archaic that the ἰδέα itself results from it, along with, therefore, all the typological metaphors—stamp, imprint, seal, and so on. *Form can cross the line* so that things are altogether different. If form "shoots out from the originary domain of *Gestell*," then essence effectively changes so that it is no longer the ideal pattern of things but the fragile point, the incision of the other in them, what enables them to leave themselves and cross with each other. Form becomes, then, the *nonphenomenological*, irreducibly shifting mode of appearance of the fragile round of exchange; the suffering minimum of all things, which stays ever small. *An infant gathering.*

Form can cross the line such that ontological transformability cannot be conflated with the possibility of fashioning or creating from scratch an essence, a god, a man, a thinking, a mode of speech, or a relation to being. This transformability is, rather, the revelation of an essential fragility that disarms metaphysics and lets the poverty and precariousness of the favor appear—the supple, changing core in each thing that does not allow itself to be seized hold of but that nonetheless is neither unattainable nor transcendent. The ontological infancy of originary mutability is exactly what authorizes me to speak of a Heideggerian ethics corresponding to Heidegger's thinking of plasticity.

Effectivity and Revolution

Perhaps form remains form such that we would be authorized to see it, as Philippe Lacoue-Labarthe did, as Heidegger's political symptom. Despite everything, didn't the latter believe in the possibility of *forming an essence*, of *sculpting one or striking it out as a coin would be?* Conceived from such a perspective, metamorphosis and migration, even when decked, as I put it, in the beautiful hues in which I have tried to clothe them here, doubtlessly lead in one way or another to the philosophical and spiritual fabrication of exemplary incarnations—such as those of a new *Dasein* or a people.

It is quite true that Heidegger at a very specific point conceived of Nazism in terms of a philosophical and historical *Wandel, Wandlung,* and *Verwandlung.* It is also true that he greeted Nazism as the promise of renewal, mutation, and the long awaited enactment of a spiritual metabolism. "I believe that I only know," he wrote in a note to Elizabeth Blochmann on September 19, 1933, "that we are preparing ourselves for a great spiritual transformation [*daß wir uns auf große geistige Wandlungen vorbereiten*], which means that we should raise [*heraufführen*] ourselves up toward it."[1] In the *Address on the German University* of August 15–16, 1934, he also speaks of "the spirit of the front [*Frontgeist*]" as a "creative metamorphosis of the war [*eine schöpferische Verwandlung des Krieges*],"[2] and a section of this speech is even entitled "The Essence of the National Socialist Revolution as Metamorphosis of German Actuality [*das Wesen der nationalsozialistischen Revolution als Verwandlung der deutschen Wirlichkeit*]."[3] Heidegger did not fail to consider whether change, transformation, and metamorphosis could be incarnated in particular *Daseins*—those, for him, of the Führer and the German people[4]—and he thereby shut the door on what the triad otherwise enabled him to discover. This translation of the triad is aggravated by the question we are ending with: *that of knowing if and in that case how it would be possible to grasp and endure, all the way and without the slightest compromise, the immense question of ontological transformability.*

Perhaps form can cross the line. In that event, change changes meanings so that it can no longer be tied to the coming of a new historical *effectivity.* And Heidegger knew this *as well,* and even renounced the above understanding of change—which was nevertheless definitely his at his worst moments. In several instances, he emphasizes the impossible situation philosophy finds itself in when it desires to foment *a change of historical form*: "such expectations and requirements demand too much of the capability and essence of philosophy. One says, for example, that because metaphysics did not contribute to preparing the revolution [*Revolution*], it must be rejected. That is just as clever as saying that because one cannot fly with a carpenter's bench, it should be thrown away. Philosophy can never directly supply the forces and create the mechanisms and opportunities that bring about a historical state of affairs."[5] In the *Der Spiegel* interview, he further states both that "philosophy will not be able to effect an immediate change in the present state of the world [*keine unmittelbarre Veränderung des jetztigen Weltzustandes bewirken können*][6] and that "if one thinks in different terms, a mediated effect is possible, but not a direct one [that would say that] thinking, as it were, can usually change [*Veränderung*] the situation of the world."[7]

I do not believe that these statements can be regarded as expressions, as Habermas put it, of "passivity."[8] What is in question, instead, is another change. *Another change that is underway.* Philosophy cannot, of course, *cause* upheaval in the effectivity or actuality of the present of the world. But it paradoxically enough only owes the impossibility of its doing so to its *power of metamorphosis.* Why does philosophy, Heidegger asks in *An Introduction to Metaphysics*, remain unable to initiate an immediate mutation of the condition of the world? "Because philosophy is the direct concern of the few. Which few? The ones who transform [metamorphose] creatively, who unsettle things [*die schaffend Verwandelnden, die Umsetzenden*]."[9] Philosophy is directed, as Heidegger confided to the Japanese interlocutor of "A Dialogue on Language," "toward a transformation of thinking [*in einer Verwandlung des Denkens*]—which, however, cannot be established as readily as a ship can alter its course [*Kurzänderung*], and even less can be established as the consequence of an accumulation of the results of philosophical research. The transformation occurs as a migration [*die Wandlung geschieht als Wanderung*] in which one site is left for another."[10] Yet this migration is neither "ineffective" nor inactual. Those who truly understand, "who come a long way on their own ground, . . . are the ones who bring much with them in order that they may thoroughly metamorphose [*um viel zu verwandeln*]."[11]

This is how, finally, "thought does not 'work its effect' in that it leaves behind particular consequences for later times. Rather, when it is thought, when the one who is thinking it stands [*stellt*] firm in this truth of beings as a whole, when thinkers who are of such a nature are, then beings as a whole also undergo metamorphosis [*verwandelt sich auch schon das Seiendes im ganzen*]."[12]

What, then, is this metamorphic and migratory power whose effects "come a long way" and that is scarcely perceivable but nonetheless indisputable? *Just what is change when history is no more?* This is precisely the question Heidegger—the other Heidegger—raises. I am altogether confident that this question, as I stressed during the first stage of our journey, cannot be divorced from a critique of capitalism. For Heidegger, capitalism and metaphysics connect together and buttress each other by constituting, as we saw, a logic of exchange that occludes the meaning of originary exchangeability. The ordeal of a metamorphosis of beings as a whole undergone by those who "thoroughly metamorphose" is also, necessarily, the experience of an overturning of the material circulation of things. At stake is an experience granted by an inclusion of the thinker both in what is thought and in the truth of beings; at stake is being among or in the midst, of the trial of engaging with the gift.

Ereignis, it should be recalled, *is the appropriating event that suspends the proper* while in the same move rendering thought susceptible to a break with the logic of appropriation conceived as servitude. But this rupture does not lead thought to transcend the economic or exit the sphere of exchange and substitution. The announcement of the other (ex)change has nothing to do with the aneconomic coming of god knows what nonpromising promise or nongiving gift. A proximity between Heidegger and Marx indeed exists, and it doubtlessly lies in the possibility of the ontological and the economic coinciding within the definition of exchange, of exchange and mutability, of the metamorphosable and displaceable character of value, and of the impossibility of transgressing all this plasticity. Even if the terms of this proximity remain to be elaborated, what is clear is that the absence of transcendence, in the sense of a resolutely dissymmetrical alterity or a radical beyond of being, reconciles Heidegger's thinking, much more than is commonly believed, with a certain dialectical understanding of transformation that bars both the extradition or exodus of transformable instances from transformation itself and the constitution of a transcendental reserve—of a place out of play.

Reciprocally, the true point of rupture in relation to revolutionary dialectics concerns the Heideggerian affirmation of the itinerant character of metabolic teleology. Where ontological metabolism affirms itself as being *without history* (which it has been doing for a very long time now), it reveals the absence of an aim of the accomplishment, the absence of the accomplishment of accomplishment, and perhaps even the absence of revolution—unless migration and metamorphosis first of all effect, for Heidegger, revolution itself. We will not forget that *W, W, & V* alone are what "thoroughly metamorphose," precisely through detaching transformation from the logic of historical effectiveness, which is to say from the inefficacious imperialism of philosophical decision *cum* dead letter—of ("philosophical") "change the world!" and "revolution!"

The world nevertheless keeps changing . . . and the triad of change is on one essential side of itself revolutionary movement, the genius of Heidegger then consisting in having inscribed the possibility of revolution not in a future event to come but in the fact (so modest, slight, and tiny) *of being-there, of still being there after the accomplishment that was never accomplished. Of being,* as are we all, *opened by de(con)struction and divided between two presences, two modes of being, and two regimes of (ex)change—the metaphysical and the ultrametaphysical, which are also, therefore, the capitalist and the ultracapitalist. The mark of revolution is the fracture constituting us. We always have the possibility of flight, of "slipping away" from the thin partition. But we also always have the possibility of thinking it and making our way out of the shadows.*

Every modification of *Dasein,* as we envisaged at the finish, has the meaning and value of a *surpassing.* Heidegger shows how each one of our gestures and attunements is itself an improbable, unprecedented transgressive power. Existence itself surpasses metaphysics. If Heidegger felt it necessary to modify modification, it was no doubt because he wanted to radicalize this surpassing power, and turn it into something far more extensive than a simple existential phenomenon—to make it *law* itself. *The economic law of being: each thing, beginning with being itself, is constantly exchanged with itself, moved between presence and presence, value and value, and properness and disappropriation.* The least technological object shows this: each thing is breached by *an ultrametaphysical secretion of itself,* each thing, everything, all of it. Everyday, the most stupid people pass over the line; they surpass metaphysics everyday, mistaking for its shadow that which never stops crossing it and is in fact the double of its heart, or second heart—*Dasein.*

Those who "transform creatively" deliver transformation from stupidity (stupidity as such as well as their own), and create the conditions of visibility of the subdued revolution of the reality—the everyday, affective, technological, philosophical, and economic reality—of the destruction of metaphysics. This reality is one that can only appear to some people, because it takes an entirely novel gaze, cast under a wholly new light, to understand it: *we started a revolution without at all realizing we were.*

Form can cross the line, becoming precisely the other of the idea—a non-ideal form that is at once both the condition and the result of change. Form can cross the line . . . and the line becomes form, creative minds *giving form* to the line; the form of a life that is from here out revolutionized, reversed, and opened in its middle: a market of (ex)changes, an agora, the negotiating table between two changes, *a space of responsibility.* What is change—how to change—when history is no more?

The End of All History (of Being)

No (more) history. The summary of the seminar on *Time and Being* contains what after its enunciation became a celebrated question—"Does the entry into appropriation [*Ereignis*] mean the end of the history of being?"—and addresses it as follows: "A similarity with Hegel seems to exist here which must, however, be regarded against the background of a fundamental difference. Whether or not the thesis is justified that one can only speak of an end of history where—as is the case with Hegel—being and thought are really identified, remains an open question. In any case, the end of the history of being in Heidegger's sense is something else [*etwas anderes*]."¹³ In view of these questions, how could one not evoke Hegel? If the exigency of form and the true sense of the Heideggerian critique of history and teleology are to be understood, it will be, contrary to what a too hasty consideration of the problem could lead one to think, absolutely necessary to read the motifs of the end of history and the entry into *Ereignis qua* end of the history of being in light of each other.

Pretending to be able to think one without the other boils down, first of all, to lacking the *event-dimension* of the achievement of historical *telos*. Heidegger alone knew how to give absolute knowledge its veritable meaning: that, in fact, of an *event*, that of an event irreducible to all others as well as to the very concept of the event, an event that cannot anymore belong to history but that is not for that a "pure event" that would somehow miraculously rip open the historicity of history. The end of history, it must be repeated, is *an appropriating and disappropriating event* that binds the change, transformation, and metamorphosis of the event and of history right at events and history themselves, in accordance with the cineplastic simultaneity of continuity and farewell.

Such pretending also comes down, secondly and inversely, to severing *Ereignis* from its genesis, the achievement of the historical *telos* that therein allows for its emergence. If it is true, as we saw, that *Ereignis* does not mark the inauguration of a new epoch and is not on account of that inscribed within any teleological horizon, this does not preclude the "wealth of transformation"—being's "epochal abundance of transformations"—from being what alone enables its coming. *Understanding what it is that changes once history is over necessarily entails* holding *together* the process of teleologically-oriented spiritual development (the history of metaphysics in its characterization here as the deployment of the first change) and the *event of telos* itself, which is unfastened in some fashion from its proper itinerary—via a leap, bridge, or relay—so that it *ends up standing in, an improvised replacement, for absolute knowledge. In Heidegger,* Aufhebung/*sublation and* einspringen—*the latter being our "leaping into the breach" or "improvised replacement"—are metamorphosed and displaced into each other, this being the enigma of their fratricidal complicity.*

Why and owing exactly to what, then, is "the end of the history of being in Heidegger's sense something else [*etwas anderes*]"? In *Means Without End,* Giorgio Agamben declares apropos this question that "Heidegger tried to address . . . with the idea of an *Ereignis,* . . . an ultimate event in which what is seized and delivered from historical destiny is the being-hidden itself of the historical principle, that is, historicity itself. Simply because history designates the expropriation itself of human nature through a series of epochs and historical destinies, it does not follow that the fulfillment and the appropriation of the historical *telos* in question indicate that the historical process of humankind has now cohered in a definitive order. . . . It indicates, rather, . . . that now human beings take possession of their own historical being, that is, of their own impropriety."[14]

This analysis is sound in that it rightfully insists on the profound bond uniting the proclamation of *Ereignis* and the end of history. Where it becomes debatable, however, is in its affirmation of *Dasein*'s need to reappropriate its historical identity, as this reappropriation is purely and simply impossible.

Heidegger instead insists, it seems to me, on the necessity of taking cognizance of the definitive departure from this identity—an unappealable expropriation of the historical being of *Dasein*—and on the importance of *creating the form of this recess or "time away."*

Who were we in the epoch of history? While the question is legitimate, this "who" remains unappropriatable (not re-appropriatable), quite obviously displaced, metamorphosed, and unrecognizable from the second it is approached. The who, in other words, takes a new form. If form passes over the line, it is precisely the mode of being of this transformation, the manifestation of the vertiginous distance that both suddenly and step by step wrenched our historical being from us, the distance that each of us, in one way or another, experiences *everyday*, as though from under billowing, too-large clothes. This emptiness, which I risked calling here the crossing or living tissue of exchange(s)—is precisely, again, the place of passage of the two presences, regimes of the event, and modalities of change. In each thing, which is to say in everything, there is (do not forget it) a parting of the historical waters. A border, as Jean-Luc Nancy puts it, between "presence . . . and the distancing whereby the truth of presence itself goes absent," a place of exchange involving "tangency without contact," "commonality without mixing," and "proximity without intimacy."[15] Between us and our being-historical there is no possibility of reappropriation. *We cross (with) ourselves without touching.*

So that if Hegel and Heidegger cross, they no longer touch each other: they are exchanged while remaining forever separate. This is the way it is for everything sharing the line—for all sides, halves, and doubles. Yet man and *Dasein,* being and be-ing, metaphysics and its other, the historical determination and ultrahistorical fate of ontological metabolism, Hegel and Heidegger . . . *are not strangers to each other.* We said this: the point of rupture is also a point of suture. This suture, simply put, is not made through contact but via an *articulation,* as though a jointure, hinge, or *partition* separated each term of these pairs from the other side of their metamorphoses, held these apart while bringing them close, and distanced them in uniting them. When form steps over the line, it becomes the form of a new familiarity, a new kinship between these exchanges or passers-by; it becomes likeness, family resemblance, as-yet unseen aspect. The "truly creative" spirits—the artist-thinkers—show that metamorphosed *Dasein* has a physique: its face, its very body, and its "identity" attest to the force of transformation of post-historical plasticity. In a certain sense, the contemporary claims of absolute self-fashioning—the priority of molding over generic determination—manifest this plasticity. Being, as Heidegger says, is *befremdlich,* astonishing. Couldn't this word also be translated as queer? So that it would convey the strange and bizarre but also, as we know, another gender or genre? Couldn't one regard Heidegger as having revealed, well before any militancy of political or sexual identity did, the originary mutability of genres that is now making it possible to call them deeply into question? This mutability, once more, is seen, and sees itself—on faces, modes of being, forms of life—and is *the fantastic reality of the consummation of metaphysics. There can be no reappropriation, then, of our being-historical . . . just the formation of its disappearance.*

The Duplicity of Self-Transformation

Despite what could be believed of it, the end of
history does not oversaturate the horizon of transformability but instead stretches it to infinity. Who
today can resist transformation? Who today fails to
feel that a profound mutation, having neither a limit
nor a historical goal or meaning, is taking place?
Habermas rightly declares *"the self-transformation
of the species"* to be right now underway.[16] Yet this
self-transformation—at once genetic, political, and
cultural—seems to be the exact substitute of history; it is the actual occurrence of originary ontological transformability, which is, as we have seen,
completely indifferent to itself, and thus senseless.
We affirmed this upon leaving the cavern: ontological mutability presupposes the originary economy of
an exchange prior to exchange and economy. Prior
to money, price, and sex; prior to commerce, and
prior even to history itself. This *pure* migratory and
metamorphic deployment is not directed toward any
telos, save for the one that consists in turning it from
its proper essence by fulfilling this. But this indifference of ontological difference, the impassiveness
of the metabolism of being, offers no justification for
"passivity" and instead commits *Dasein,* as we indicated, to its *responsibility. Dasein* and *Dasein* alone,
Heidegger tells us, is the *guardian* of this metabolism
of which it is one of the essential instances.

*Everything depends on the destiny of form. Per-
haps form remains form,* and *Dasein's* responsibility
would simply be to decide to re-engage the space
opened in each and every thing by the division of
presence into the "of value for"—the simulacrum of
appropriation and alienation. The self-transformation
of the species would in that case be committed to

the road of an experimentation driven by the flexibility of all that is. Form would remain form, and
we could, at best, but stamp out our modes of being
and life, and be left believing that our (physical,
social, sexual, familial, and parental) identities can
be constructed from scratch and kept within the
infinite play of equivalence.

Perhaps form passes over the line, and it is in
that event true that we remain ignorant of *where*
Dasein *goes when it leaves man behind,* and that
attempting to fill in this emptiness or gap in our
knowledge would only be in vain. If it is true that
we do not, since we are caught in metamorphosis
and migration without respite, know where we are
headed and whence transformation goes, this errancy
can become, *for itself,* a reason to live. Form is the
chance randomness of this path—*the new theory of
itinerary/the plasticity of errant roaming.*[17] It is not
(or is no longer) a matter of sculpting an identity
or unrelentingly transforming everything—*plasticity, again, is not flexibility*—but of entering into the
errancy of genres and reaching the point where every
genre and essence leave themselves—the interregnum of mutant kin, gathering or assembled mobiles,
an exchange involving neither domination nor the
sacralization of the gift but that respects, instead, the
suffering minimum. *We know next to nothing about
where* Dasein *goes when it leaves man. But what we
can nevertheless do,* between being-there (*da-sein*)
and being-away (*weg-sein*), *is love its uncertain path
for itself, and watch over it.*

In every presencing there is an itinerary, an *Irrtum*
or errancy, that is mixed in with the idea, contained
in the Aristotelean concept of μεταβολή, of "installation
in the aspect." "For Aristotle," as Heidegger puts it,
"all movedness is the throwing of something [*Umschlag*

von etwas zu etwas], the passage by which, through the continuity of a single throw, something is brought from . . . to."[18] This throwing takes place in such a way that "in the passage [*Umschlag*], the very act of passage breaks out into the open [*zum Außschlag*], i.e. comes into the appearance [*d. h. im Vorschein kommt*]."[19] Hence μεταβολή renders the very passing of the passage sensible; it orders the visibility of the very passing of the passage to the point that it would be impossible, whether the throwing is underway or through, to say (both of the passage and that which passes) what truly changed. Everything that enters presence passes—is migrated, put *en route*, and in the same move installed in the very form of its passage. Presencing is indissociable, precisely, from a μορφή.

We have changed—this much is certain—and we will keep changing. If form passes over the line, we ought to think the μεταβολή *of a new time*. It is up to us, that is, to enter into the form of our transitions and make them appear; up to us to contend with the visibility of our metamorphoses and migrations—*to imagine them as they are*. And what, in the end, are they? The *W, W, & V* of man, of god, of the relation to being, of being itself, of beings, and of essence. The *W, W, & V* of speech and philosophy. These changes, though, do not again give birth to "fantastic creatures." There is not a figure in Heidegger comparable to Freud's Sandman, Kafka's Odradek, Kleist's marionette, Nietzsche's Zarathustra, or Cronenberg's fly. *Metamorphosis and migration are here metamorphoses and migrations of the whole world.* The fantastic is being like everyone. *The fantastic is the new face of the entire world.* Migration, metamorphosis, and the new form all depend upon the very particular visibility of the fine, tenuous, and modest line (the "existential fontanelle") I perceived taking shape in *Being and Time*, and that we all share, and that divides us all, as a shell's ages do its calcite. The nonwounding scar from the gash the destruction of metaphysics tore into our faces. It is there in the very line of this fissure, the fantastic visibility of the place of exchange of essences, that something happens, which is the arrival, *Ankuft*, and flight, *Flucht*, of the other. The flashes and streaks of God in *Dasein*, of *Dasein* in being, and of being in beings—of porous beingness. There is no superman, only akin mutants. *Mutantkin.*

Heidegger's Change in the Balance

The Heidegger Change—have we at last made it? *Everything, Heidegger as well, depends on the fate of form. Perhaps form remains form.* In that case, Heidegger remains Heidegger, and there is nothing to be done with him—nothing else to make of or from him, no other (in) Heidegger. Nothing could change and the shadow of Gregor Samsa would return to obscure the meaning of *W, W, & V.*

Perhaps form steps over the line, metamorphosis and migration in that event entering Heidegger's philosophy into a transformation that carries it so far away from itself that it can finally, beyond all its weaknesses, all the paralyzing identifications of it, and all its coteries, sects, and jargon, become what it is: the great thinking of being as (ex)change that has since Nietzsche (who was its instigator) been waiting for the figure of its thinker. The great thinking of ontological mutability, which can finally help us understand what it is that happens and arrives; the great thinking of migration and metamorphosis whose signature is visible, and fantastically so, on

the real itself, which it at once discovers and transforms—discovers transformed. The great thinking of
ontological imagination. Perhaps form passes over
the line and *The Heidegger Change*, it too, becomes
what it is: the name of what Heidegger, and he alone,
changed.

But why, you ask, are the alternatives so sharply
drawn? Does this not at bottom indicate, in spite of
what has been borrowed from "On the Question of
Being," an impossibility of deciding that runs straight
against your assurance from the beginning: "the
Heidegger change: It is done! It is decided!"? Why so
much vacillating at the close, and why make everything hang on the destiny of the concept of form?

I perfectly well understand your surprise. My
words indeed seem to be trembling, as if they suspended their response or opened to the bad infinity
of a "perhaps" bound up with a capriciousness of
form that is much like a tolling bell. I understand
this "perhaps . . . perhaps . . ." is a bit shocking to
you, since it resembles neither the rest of our text nor
Heidegger nor even myself anymore. But let me offer
you some reassurance: there is not even a shadow
of hesitation in me. The migratory and metamorphic
power of Heidegger's thinking is not at all in doubt
for me, and cannot be because *W, W, & V* never
failed, for the whole length of this long, solitary, and
perilous path, to keep their promises and to bear me
along in some way. I end this book well aware of its
deficiencies while being at the same time persuaded
of having pursued, as I had hoped to, an adventure
of thought distinctly my own, and of having given
The Future of Hegel the future it lacked.

If I am putting, in closing, everything *in the
balance*, this is not (however it might appear) out

of hesitation but in order to bring off a conversion. Not only because *The Heidegger Change*, elaborated as it is on the basis of *W, W, & V*, can only in the end be valid if you (all of you) who are reading me are converted—if you accept having the scales of your reading tipped in one direction and one alone—but also because the balance is the purest and simplest convertor, *the very figure of risk.* In one of his most beautiful text, "What Are Poets For?," Heidegger writes apropos Rilke that "Whoever is in being at a given time is what is being risked. Being is risk pure and simple [*das Sein ist das Wagnis schlechthin*]. It risks us, us humans [*es wagt uns, die Menschen*]. It risks the living beings [*es wagt die Lebewesen*]. The particular being is, insofar as it remains what has ever and always been risked."[20]

Being at risk is to "hang in the balance [*in der Wage*]. In the Middle Ages the word for balance, *die Wage*, still means about as much as hazard or risk [*Gefahr*]. This is the situation in which matters may turn out one way or the other. That is why the apparatus which moves by tipping one way or the other is called *die Wage*, the balance. It plays and balances out. The word *Wage*, in the sense of risk and as name of the apparatus, comes from *wägen*, *wegen*, to make a way, that is, to go, to be in motion. *Bewägen* means to cause to be on the way and so to bring into motion: to shake or rock, *wiegen*. What rocks [*wiegt*] is said to do so because it is able to bring the balance, *Wage*, into the play of movement, this way or that."[21]

Of what, then, do the alternatives consist? What rests on each pan of the balance? Man, Heidegger responds, "lives essentially by risking his nature in the vibration of money and in the currency of values

[*der Vibration des Geldes und des Gelten der Werte*].
As this constant trader and middleman [*Wechsler und Vermittler*], man is the 'merchant.' He weighs and measures constantly, yet does not know the real weight of things. . . . But at the same time, man who is outside all protection can procure safety by turning unshieldedness as such into the Open and transmuting it into the heartspace of the invisible [*dem Herzraum des Unsichtbaren einverwandelt*]. . . . The balance of danger then passes out [*übergeht*] of the realm of calculating will over to the Angel."[22]

Being in the balance, as you doubtlessly understood, does not at all here mean *ignorance about which side to take*. No longer is balance a waiting game. The messianic horizon, as I put it, is never pure but always changed in advance, and the angel, as Heidegger saw, is metamorphosed at the origin. The balance is the form expressing the coexistence of the two (ex)changes: the first, the game of the "of value for," and the second, the open economy of the "favor." *Making the sides oscillate, breaking the flat evenness between them: the form to come puts into movement shared-divided forms.*

If am asking you, at last, which side you are now tipping toward, it is not in order to render relative all the things I spent so much time showing but out of an effort to construct with you the figural balance that can bring before our gaze the equilibrium and the disequilibrium mobilizing *our two beings*.

I am asking you, at last, which side you are tipping toward because I have hope, deep inside me, that you no longer recognize Heidegger, and can now begin to imagine him.

Notes

Translator/Editor's Preface

1. Jacques Derrida and Catherine Malabou, *Counterpath*, translated by David Wills, Stanford University Press, 2004.

2. Catherine Malabou, *The Future of Hegel: Plasticity, Temporality, Dialectic,* translated by Lisabeth During (New York: Routledge, 2005), 192.

3. Ibid.

4. Catherine Malabou, What Should We Do With Our Brain? Translated by Sebastian Rand (Bronx, New York: Fordham University Press, 2007), 31.

Introduction

1. *The Essence of Truth: Plato's Allegory of the Cave and Theaetetus* (New York: Continuum, 2002), 77. *Vom Wesen der Wahrheit: Zu Platons Höhlengleichnis und Theaetetus. G.A.,* Bd. 34, 106.

2. The title, in other words, elides the preposition *de,* as happens in instances of the Old French genitive, such as *hôtel-Dieu* or the French title of Joseph Conrad's *Almayer's Folly—La Folie Almayer.*

3. *Das Zuspiel* and *der Sprung* are the titles of the third and fourth parts (or "jointures"—*Fügungen)* of *Contributions to Philosophy* (Bloomington: Indiana University Press, 1989). *Beiträge zur Philosophie: Vom Ereignis. G.A.,* Bd. 65. Hereafter cited as CP.

4. It is intentional and with awareness of the fact that my decision is somewhat arbitrary that I have chosen to translate, for the sake of consistency, *Wandel, Wandlung,* and *Verwandlung* as, respectively, "change," "transformation," and "metamorphosis."

5. "What Is Metaphysics?" in *Pathmarks* (Cambridge: Cambridge University Press), 89. *"Was ist Metaphysik?,"* in *G.A.,* Bd. 9, 113. Hereafter cited as WM?

6. CP §7, 19 (26), §41, 58 (84); §53 (113).

7. "Introduction to 'What Is Metaphysics?'" in *Pathmarks* (Cambridge: Cambridge University Press, 1999) 279. *"Was ist Metaphysik? Einleitung,"* in *G.A.,* Bd. 9, 368. Hereafter cited as IWM?.

8. *What Is Philosophy?*, translated by William Kluback and Jean T. Wilde (Oxford: Rowan and Littlefield, 1956) 71. *Was ist das, die Philosophie?* (Pfullingen: Neske, 1956), 33–34. Hereafter cited as WP?

9. "The End of Philosophy and the Task of Thinking," in *Time and Being*, translated by Joan Stambaugh (Chicago: The University of Chicago Press, 2002), 60. "Die Ende der Philosophie und die Aufgabe des Denkens," in *Zur Sache des Denkens* (Tübingen: Niemeyer, 1961), 67. Hereafter cited as EP.

10. CP §5, 10–11 (14).

11. CP §37, 129 (184).

12. CP §36, 54 (77–78).

13. "On the Question of Being," in *Pathmarks* (Cambridge: Cambridge University Press), 71; translation modified. "Zur Seinsfrage," *G.A.,* Bd. 9, 73. Hereafter cited as QB.

14. *Sojourns*, translated by John Panteleimon Manoussakis (Albany: SUNY Press, 2005), 3. *Aufenthalte* (Frankfurt am Main: Vittorio Klostermann, 1989), 10. Hereafter cited as S.

15. Roger Caillois, *Cohérences aventureuses* (Paris: Gallimard, 1973), 77. Hereafter cited as Caillois.

16. Caillois, 173.

17. IWM?, 281 (370).

18. Ibid.

19. CP §166, 202 (288). Translation modified.

20. CP §166.

21. CP, §39, 57 (82).

22. *Hölderlin's Hymn "The Ister"* (Bloomington: Indiana University Press, 1996), 39. *Hölderlins Hymne "der Ister."* *G.A.,* Bd. 53, 39. Hereafter cited as HHI.

23. As in the phrase *das Schiff wenden*—"the boat turns or tacks." *Winden*, similarly, means "turning, winding," and *die Wendung*, "screw thread."

24. The Dudden dictionary. A *Verwandlungskünstler*, moreover, is an illusionist or "quick-change artist."

25. Dudden dictionary.

26. "Age of the World Picture," in *The Question Concerning Technology* (New York: HarperCollins, 1977). *Die Zeit des Weltbildes* in *Holzwege* (Tübingen: Vittorio Klostermann, 1950), 99. Hereafter cited as AWP.

27. CP §38, 55 (79).

28. Migration, moreover, is sometimes used in biology to indicate the displacement of an organism during the course of its development or metamorphosis.

29. CP §213, 237 (338).

30. CP, 3 (3).

31. CP §1, 4–5 (5). Translation modified.

32. S, 4. Translation modified.

33. CP §256, 288. (409).

34. *Time and Being*, translated by Joan Stambaugh (Chicago: University of Chicago Press, 2002) 51. "Zeit und Sein," in *Zur Sache des Denkens* (Tübingen: Niemeyer, 1961), 56. Hereafter cited as TB.

35. Ibid.

36. TB, 52 (56).

37. TB, 52–53 (56).

38. TB, 53 (56–57).

39. Saying much more about these questions than the following works already do would be difficult: Otto Pöggeler, *Der Denkwerk Martin Heideggers* (Stuttgart: Neske, 1963); Jean Grondin, *Le Tournant dans la pensée de Martin Heidegger* (Paris: PUF, 1987); and Marlène Zarader, *Heidegger et les paroles de l'origine* (Paris: Vrin, 1986).

40. Habermas, for example, treats a series of "transformations" (*Wandlungen*) in Heidegger's thinking as the fruit of mere opportunism. See his preface to the celebrated work of Victor Farias, *Heidegger und der Nazional-Socialismus* (Frankfurt am Main: Fischer Verlag, 1989), 11–37. (This text does not appear in the English translation of Farias's book.) In effect, these "transformations" essentially result, following the political engagements of 1933 and *Contributions*, in the elaboration of "a philosophy of passivity" destined to relieve philosophy of "all responsibility." The *Kehre*, Habermas declares, is the first sign of this "change" to passivity after an initial—"ideological" and "neoconservative"—turn that began in 1929. "In 1929 . . . there begins [in Heidegger]

a transformation [*Wandlung*] of the theory of ideology. It
is during this period that themes tied to a confused diag-
nostic of the epoch and a neoconservative style insinuate
themselves into the heart of his philosophy" (23). This
"transformation" issues from "internal deficits . . . immanent to *Being and Time*" (25). Remarkably enough, these
"deficits" are tied to the conception of an "invariable condition of *Dasein* [*invariante Grundverfassung des Daseins*]"
that kept Heidegger from "moving from historicity to real
history" in his thought. In other words, Habermas points
toward the absence of a thinking of change in Heidegger:
Dasein, ostensibly "invariable" and closed in on itself, ends
up removed from the domain of true transformation—the
sociohistorical—and Heidegger, not having an authentic concept of change, is "unable to oppose fascism." Heidegger's
change would simply be a function of his circumstances. If
"the vision of the philosopher itself changes [*wandelt*]" and
"the existentials metamorphose themselves [*verwandeln sich
die Existentialen*]," the invariable "ground" of *Being and Time*
remains intact (21). It would moreover be for this reason
that "Heidegger, who declared himself in favor of National
Socialism in 1933, . . . interpreted Hitler's accession to
power via the fundamental and unchanged concepts of his
analysis of *Dasein*" (ibid.).

    41. *On the Way to Language* (New York: HarperCol-
lins, 1982), 57. *Unterwegs zur Sprache. G.A.,* Bd. 12, 149.
Hereafter cited as OWL.

    42. EP, 70–71 (66). In 1954, the Plato specialist Paul
Friedländer developed a critique of Heidegger that showed
that ἀλήθεια did not mean "unveiledness" or "unhiddenness"
even in Homer, and that it instead already corresponded to
our "coherence" and "correctness." "The Greek concept of
truth," he concluded, "did not undergo a mutation transforming the unhiddeness of being into the correctness of
perception." In "The End of Philosophy and the Task of
Thinking," Heidegger is obviously acknowledging this criti-
cism, but without calling into question the mutability of
being or truth.

Part I

    1. "Plato's Doctrine of Truth," in *Pathmarks* (Cam-
bridge: Cambridge University Press, 1999), 177. "Platons

Lehre von der Wahrheit," in *G.A,.* Bd. 9, 231. Hereafter cited as PDT.

2. Ibid.

3. Ibid.

4. PDT, 176.

5. *What Is Called Thinking?* (New York: HarperCollins, 1968), 45. Hereafter cited as WT? *Was Heißt Denken?* (Tübingen: Niemeyer, 1954), 60.

6. WT?, 45.

7. ". . . Poetically Man Dwells . . ." in *Poetry, Language, Thought* (New York, HarperCollins, 2001), 223. ". . . *Dichterisch Wohnet der Mensch . . .*" in *Vörtrage und Aufsätze, G.A.,* Bd. 7, 204. Hereafter cited as PMD.

8. "Metaphysics as History of Being," in *The End of Philosophy*, translated by Joan Stambaugh (Chicago: The University of Chicago Press, 2003), 11. *Nietzsche II, G.A.,* Bd. 6.2, 374. This passage is found in the section entitled "*Der Wandel der* ενεργεια *zur actualitas.*" Heidegger also here says about this change that "even though the linguistic formulations of the essential constituents of being change, the constituents—so it is said—remain the same."

Chapter 1

1. Heidegger, *What Is Philosophy?*, translated by Jean T. Wild and William Kluback (Rowan and Littlefield, 2003), 61 (28). Hereafter quoted as WP?

2. WP?, 89–90 (37).

3. CP §34, 52 (75).

4. *Basic Questions of Philosophy: Selected Problems of "Logic"* (Bloomington: Indiana University Press: 1994), 61. My translation. *Grundfragen der Philosophie: Ausegwählte "Probleme" der Logik G.A.,* Bd. 45, §18, 67.

5. "On the Question of Being," in *Pathmarks* (Cambridge: Cambridge University Press, 1999), 298. Hereafter cited as QB. (395).

6. *Hegel, G.A.,* Bd. 68, 16.

7. QB, 299 (395).

8. "Overcoming Metaphysics," in *The End of Philosophy*, translated by Joan Stambaugh (Chicago: The University of Chicago Press, 2003), 90 (75). Hereafter cited as OM.

9. CP §117 ("Leap"), 162 (229).

10. CP §119, 164 (232) "The first beginning and its end encompasses the entire history of the guiding question, from Anaximander to Nietzsche [*Der erste Anfang und sein Ende umfaßt die ganze Geschichte der Leitfrage von Anaximander bis zu Nietzsche*]."

11. CP §119, 164 (232). Translation slightly modified.

12. Ibid. Translation slightly modified.

13. *Nietzsche, vol. II*, 230, translation modified. (266).

14. "On the Essence and Concept of φύσις: Aristotle's Physics B," in *Pathmarks* (Cambridge: Cambridge University Press, 1999), 190. Hereafter cited as OECP. "Vom Wesen und Begriff der φύσις: Aristotles, Physik B" in *G.A.*, Bd. 9, 248.

15. You will notice that this occlusion—the change of the Greek concept of change, i.e., the reduction of the metabolic to the phoronomic—is expressed in terms of the triad of change. Heidegger makes use of *W, W, & V* in order to characterize the transition from the Greek to the modern concept of change: "Herein there appears an essential transformation [*change*] of the concept of *physis* [*wesentliche Wandlung des Physisbegriffes*]." *What Is a Thing?*, translated by W.B. Barton, Jr., and Vera Deutsch (Chicago: Henry Regnery Co., 1969), 85. *Die Frage nach dem Ding, G.A.*, Bd. 41, 84. Hereafter cited as WTh?. Also, further down: "Corresponding to the change of the concept of place [*Wandlung des Ortbegriffes*], motion is only seen as a change of position [*Lageänderung*] and relative position [*Lagebeziehung*]." WTh?, 87 (88).

16. CP § 158, 198 (281).

17. *Basic Concepts of Ancient Philosophy* (Bloomington: Indiana University Press, 2008), chap. 4 ("The Later Philosophy of Nature: Empedocles, Anaxagoras, and Atomism"), §25 ("Being and the multiplicity of changing beings in the latter philosophy of nature"), 64–65. *Die Grundbegriffe der antiken Philosophie, G.A.*, Bd. 22, 78–79.

18. In *Being and Time*, Heidegger analyzes the role of the *capax mutationum* in Descartes in terms of an invariable variability: "what constitutes the being of the *res corporea* is *extensio*, the *omnitudo divisibile, figurabile et mobile*, what can change in every kind of divisibility, plasticity [*Gestaltung*], and motion, the *capax mutationum*, what persists throughout all these changes [*Veränderun-*

gen], *remanet.* In a corporeal being what is capable of such a *remaining constant* is its true being, in such a way that it characterizes the substantiality of substance." *Being and Time*, trans. Joan Stambaugh (Albany: SUNY Press, 1996) §19, 85. *Sein und Zeit, G.A.,* Bd. 2, 122–23.

19. QB, 300 (397).

20. QB, 300 (215).

21. "The Ontotheological Constitution of Metaphysics," in *Identity and Difference* (Chicago: University of Chicago Press, 2002), 56. Hereafter cited as OTCM. *"Die Onto-Theo-Logische Verfassung der Metaphysik,"* in *Identität und Differenz* (Stuttgart: Neske, 1999), 47. Hereafter cited as OTCM.

22. "Introduction to What Is Metaphysics?" in *Pathmarks*, 287 (379). Hereafter cited as IWM?.

23. Ibid., 287–88 (379).

24. OTCM, 71 (306).

25. IWM?, 288 (379): "As the truth of beings as such, metaphysics has a twofold character [*Zweigestaltung*]."

26. "Hegel's Concept of Experience," in *Off the Beaten Track*, 132 (214).

27. AWP, 57 (75).

28. AWP, 57 (75).

29. AWP, 79 (104). The same characterization can be found in *Nietzsche* IV, 92: "A fundamental metaphysical position may be determined by: 1. By the way in which man as man is *himself* and thereby knows himself; 2. By the projection of beings on being; 3. By circumscribing the essence of the truth of beings, and 4. By the way in which each respective man takes and gives 'measure' for the truth of beings."

30. *The Principle of Reason*, 93 (139).

31. Martin Heidegger, *The Fundamental Concepts of Metaphysics: Word, Finitude, Solitude* (Bloomington: Indiana University Press, 1995) §41, 175 (259). *Die Grundbegriffe der Metaphysik: Welt-Endlichkeit-Eisamkeit, G.A.,* Bd. 29–30.

32. AWP, 74–75 (99).

33. AWP, Off the Beaten Track, 75 (99).

34. Cf., for example, §18 of WTh?, whose title is "The Change of Natural Science [*Wandel der Naturwissenschaft*]."

35. *"Et il n'est pas possible à quiconque est un jour monté sur ce grand trottoir roulant que sont les pages de Flaubert, au défilement continu, monotone, morne, indéfini,*

de méconnaître qu'elles sont sans précedent dans la littéra-ture." Marcel Proust, *Sur Baudelaire, Flaubert, et Morand* (Paris: Éditions Complexe, 1987), 65.

36. CP §166, 203 (289).

37. *Aristotle's Metaphysics Theta 1–3*, 22. Aristotles, *Metaphysiks Θ 1–3: Von Wesen und Wirklichkeit der Kraft. G.A.,* Bd. 33, 27.

38. WTh?, 106 (106). Translation slightly modified.

39. NIII, 93 (120).

40. OM, 95 (81). Translation slightly modified.

41. QB, 299 (395). I am intentionally using *Form* and *Gestalt* interchangeably since Heidegger, as we will discuss, sees little reason to distinguish between them.

Chapter 2

1. PDT, 155 (203).

2. *Parmenides,* trans. André Schuwer and Richard Rojcewicz (Bloomington: Indiana University Press, 1992), 45. Translation modified. *Parmenides. G.A.,* Bd. 54, 66. Hereafter cited as P.

3. PDT, 176 (230).

4. PDT, 176 (230).

5. The appearances of this particular change— *"Wandel der Wahrheit," "Wandel des Wesens der Wahrheit," "Wesenswandel der Wahrheit"*—are numerous. They are most developed in the 1932 course on Plato, *On The Essence of Truth: Plato's Cave Allegory and Theaetetus,* translated by Ted Sadler (New York: Continuum, 2002) (*G.A.,* Bd. 34), *Nietzsche,* and the 1948 course, *Nietzsche: Der Europaïsche Nihilismus* (*G.A.,* Bd. 48).

As Alain Boutot indicates in the preface to his trans-lation of *The Essence of Truth*: "Heidegger contends [here] that a new conception of truth attempts to manifest in Plato, or rather that an original, earlier conception cedes its place to another, derived one that will be from that point on preponderant. 'Logical' truth, conceived as the agreement of proposition and thing, is substituted for the 'ontological' truth conceived by the Presocratics and Heraclitus as outside the withdrawal of beings."

Parmenides (1942–43) is where Heidegger's most extensive development of the motif of the change of essence of truth is to be found. He conceives of it in terms of a double historical articulation: Greek—the change of the essence of truth achieved with Plato's philosophy—and Roman: the change accomplished with the romanization of ἀλήθεια, which is to say the interpretation of "exactitude" (*Richtigkeit*) as accuracy, justice, and uprightness. See also the title of §3, which is "Clarification of the transformation [*Wandels*] of ἀλήθεια (*veritas, certitudo, rectitudo, iusticia, Wahrheit, Gerechtigkeit*)." The opposition of the true and false becomes the opposition between the just and unjust and is fully achieved in the Roman determination of the imperium. On these changes, see the analyses of Didier Franck, *Nietzsche et l'ombre de Dieu* (Paris: PUF, 1998), 39–52.

The two volumes of Nietzsche are rife with discussions of the thematic of the change of the essence of truth. See in particular chapter 20 of part I of book 3 of the English edition, which is entitled "The Uttermost Transformation of Metaphysically Conceived Truth [*Der aüßerte Wandel der metaphysisch begriffen Wahrheit*]," See also the text from the second German volume (available in *The End of Philosophy* in English), "Metaphysics as History of Being," whose initial chapters are "Whatness and Thatness in the Essential Beginning of Metaphysics: ιδεα and ενεργεια," "The Change of *energeia* to *Actualitas*," and "The Transformation of υποκειμενον into *subjectum*." See finally, part III of the 1948 course, "*Der Wesenwandel der Wahrheit und des Seins als der verborgene Grund des Vorrangs der Subjektivität und ihrer Entfaltung*"—"The Change of the Essence of Truth and of Being as the Foundation . . . the Primacy of the Subject and its Deployment."

    6. PDT, 167 (218).

    7. PDT, 167 (218).

    8. PDT, 170 (215).

    9. PDT, 165. (215–16).

    10. "Thinking goes μετ᾽ έχεινα 'beyond' those things that are experienced in the form of mere shadows and images, and goes εις ταυτα, 'out toward' those things, namely, the 'ideas.'" PDT, 180 (235).

    11. PDT, 180 (235).

12. PDT, 180 (235).

13. *"Bildung,"* Heidegger specifies, "means forming [*Bilden*] someone in the sense of impressing [*Prägung*] on him a character that unfolds. But at the same time this forming someone "forms" (or impresses [*prägt*] a character on) someone by antecedently taking measure in terms of some paradigmatic image [*an einem maßgebenden Anblick*], which for that reason is called the proto-type [*Vorbild*]. Thus at one and the same time "formation" [*Bildung*] means impressing a character on someone and guiding someone by a paradigm [*Geleit durch ein Bild*]." PDT, 166–167 (217).

14. QB, 299 (395).

15. PDT, 166 (216).

16. PDT, 177 (230).

17. PDT, 175 (227).

18. PDT, 164 (214).

19. PDT, 181 (236).

20. PDT, 167 (218). Translation modified.

21. PDT, 181 (236).

22. PDT, 168 (218).

23. Ibid.

24. PDT, 181 (236).

25. PDT, 180 (235).

26. PDT, 181 (237).

27. PDT, 181 (236).

28. P, 51 (75).

29. CP §110, 151 (216).

30. PDT, 180 (235).

31. PDT, 180 (235).

32. PDT, 180–81 (235).

33. PDT, 178 (233).

34. PDT, 167 (218).

35. PDT, 176 (230). Translation slightly modified.

36. PDT, 177 (231).

37. PDT, 167 (217).

38. PDT, 167 (218).

39. PDT, 181 (237).

40. PDT, 182 (238).

41. PDT, 177 (231).

42. PDT, 164 (213).

43. "On the Essence of Truth," in *Pathmarks*, 153. *Vom Wesen der Wahrheit*, G.A. Bd. 9 201. Hereafter cited as ET.

44. ET, 154 (202).

45. ET, 154 (202).

46. ET, 143 (185).

47. ET, 154 (202).

48. See *Die Geschichte des Seyns*, 1938–1940 (*G.A.*, Bd. 69), §31, 30: "the metamorphosis of humanity in meaning, which is, and only means: the 'essence' of the truth of be-ing [*die Einverwandlung des Menschentums in den "Sinn," d. h. hier und heißt nur: die Wesung der Wahrheit des Seyns*]."

49. P. 55 (80); translation slightly modified. (*"'Die Geschichte,' wesentlich begriffen, und d. h. aus dem Wesengrund des Seins selbst gedacht, ist der Wandel des Wesens des Wahrheit. Sie ist 'nur' dieses."*)

50. P, 42–43 (63). (*"Die Rede vom 'Wandel der Wahrheit' ist freilich ein Notbehelf; denn sie spricht noch gegenständlich von Wahrheit und nicht aus der Weise, wie sie selbst west und die Geschichte 'ist.'"*)

51. ". . . Poetically Man Dwells . . ." in *Poetry, Language, Thought*, translated by Albert Hoftsader (New York: HarperCollins, 2001), 223 (204). Hereafter cited as PMD.

52. See the 1927–28 lecture course *Phenomenological Interpretation of Kant's Critique of Pure Reason* (Bloomington: Indiana University Press, 1997), 283 (*Phänomenologische Interpretation von Kants Kritik der reinen Vernunft*, *G.A.*, Bd. 25, 417), where Heidegger says that "the power of imagination is . . . ontologically creative, in that it freely forms the universal horizon of time as horizon of . . . objectness. . . . Thus the productive power of imagination is original; that is, in its enactment it gives freely, it is a free power of invention [*Dichtung*]." The same characterization of the productive imagination can be found in *Kant and The Problem of Metaphysics* (Bloomington: Indiana University Press, 1997): "if in the imagination the . . . appearance of an object is freely composed [*frei gedichtet*], then . . . the power of imagination is called 'productive'" (*Kant und das Problem der Metaphysik*, *G.A.*, Bd. 3, 130). On the difference between the reproductive

and creative imaginations, see Jean-Louis Vieillard-Baron, *Hegel et l'idéalisme spéculatif* (Paris: Vrin, 1999), especially page 77.

First Incision

1. "This change [*Wandel*] in the essence of truth is present as the all-dominating fundamental reality—long-established and thus still in place—of the ever-advancing world history of the planet in this most modern of times." PDT, 181–82 (237).

2. "Anaximander's Saying," in *Off the Beaten Track* (Cambridge: University of Cambridge Press, 2002), 274. "Der Spruch des Anaximander," in *Holzwege,* 364. Hereafter cited as AS.

3. Ibid.

4. AS, 275 (365).

5. PDT, 182 (237).

6. "Postscript to 'What Is Metaphysics?'" in *Pathmarks* (Cambridge: Cambridge University Press, 1999), 235. "Nachwort zu: 'Was ist Metaphysik?'" in *G.A.,* Bd. 9, 308–9. Hereafter cited as PWM?. Heidegger also says here that "such thinking lets all being count only in the form of what can be set at our disposal and consumed [*nur in der Gestalt des Beistellbaren und Verzehrlichen zur Geltung bringt*]."

Chapter 3

1. Friedrich Nietzsche, *The Gay Science* (Cambridge: Cambridge University Press, 2001), 12.

2. Martin Heidegger, *Nietzsche Volume I: The Will to Power as Art*, translated by David Farrell Krell (San Francisco: Harper San Francisco, 1991), 148–49. *Nietzsche G.A.,* Bd. 6.1, 151. Hereafter cited as NI.

3. Martin Heidegger, *What is Called Thinking?,* translated by J. Glenn Gray (Harper: San Francisco, 1968), 69. Hereafter cited as WT?.

4. WT?, 68 (66).

5. NII, x (417).

6. WT?, 51 (21).

7. NI, 211 (213).

8. NI, 200–201 (203).

9. *Nietzsche III: The Will to Power as Knowledge and as Metaphysics*, translated by David Farrell Krell (Harper-Collins: New York, 31), 31. *Nietzsche G.A.,* Bd. 6.2, 456. Hereafter cited as NIII.

10. NIII, 31 (456).

11. NIII, 30 (455).

12. NIII, 28 (453).

13. NIII, 24 (449).

14. NIII, 29 (454).

15. NIII, 24 (454–55).

16. NIII, 29 (454).

17. NIII, 95–96 (526).

18. NIII, 96 (526–27).

19. NIII, 119 (551).

20. NI, 115 (115).

21. NI, 135 (137).

22. NI, 61 (57).

23. NI, 136 (138).

24. NI, 136 (138).

25. NI 61, (57).

26. NI, 73.

27. NI, 118 (118).

28. NI, 119 (118–19).

29. NI, 120 (120).

30. NII, 183 (401).

31. NI, 51 (49).

32. NII, 30 (249).

33. NII, 34 (254).

34. NII, 231. "Wer ist Nietzsches Zarathustra?," in *Vörtrage und Aufsätze, G.A.,* Bd. 7, 121–22.

35. "Nietzsche's Word: God Is Dead," *Off the Beaten Track* (Cambridge: Cambridge University Press, 2002), 193. Hereafter cited as GID. "Nietzsches Wort: 'Gott ist tot,' in *Holzwege* (Frankfurt am Main: Klostermann, 1950), 262.

36. Ibid.

37. On the relation between the Overman and the metamorphosis of man, see NI, 208.

38. NII, 158 (252).

39. NII, 47 (266–67).

40. NII, 59 (279).
41. NII, 32 (252).
42. QB, 299 (396).
43. Ibid.
44. Ibid.
45. QB, 300 (398).
46. QP, 300 (397). My emphasis.
47. QB, 301 (398).
48. NIII, 228 (275).
49. *Nietzsche Volume IV: Nihilism*, translated by David Farrell Krell (New York: HarperCollins, 1991), 205. *Nietzsche, G.A.,* Bd. 6.2, 309. Hereafter cited as NIV.
50. NIII, 230. (277) See on this point the analysis of the links between Protagoras's position—man as measure—and Descartes' *cogito.* Jünger's *Der Arbeiter* is inscribed, according to Heidegger, in the main line of this ambiguous relation: the domination of the worker corresponds to the mode of representation, visible everywhere, of its "figure of measure"—a new, self-certain will to power.
51. NII, 231 (122).
52. CA, 173.

Chapter 4

1. NII, 22 (241).
2. Gilles Deleuze and Félix Guattari, *Kafka: Toward a Minor Literature*, translated by Dana Polan (Minneapolis: University of Minnesota Press, 1986), 7. Hereafter cited as KML.
3. On this power, see in particular, Friedrich Nietzsche, *Twilight of the Idols* (Cambridge: Cambridge University Press, 2005) §10, 196–97: "The contrasting concepts of Apollonian and Dionysian that I introduced into aesthetics—what do they mean, as types of intoxication? Apollonian intoxication stimulates the eye above all, so that it gets the power of vision. Painters, sculptors, poets are visionaries *par excellence.* In the Dionysian state, on the other hand, the entire system of affects is excited and intensified: so that it discharges its modes of expression at once, releasing the force of presentation, imitation, transfiguration, transformation, and all types of mimicry and play acting, all at the same time. The

essential thing is the ease of metamorphosis, the inability not to react (—similar to certain hysterics who can take on *any* role at the drop of a hat). It is impossible for a Dionysian to fail to understand any suggestion, he will not miss any affective signal, he has the most highly developed instinct for understanding and guessing, just as he possesses the art of communication to the highest degree. He enters into any skin, into any affect: he constantly transforms himself."

4. See on this point Marcel Détienne and Jean-Pierre Vernant, *Cunning Intelligence in Greek Culture and Society* (Chicago: University of Chicago Press, 1991), especially the discussion of the metamorphoses of Zeus and Proteus.

5. On Heidegger's relation to Kafka, see chap. 8, note 15, below.

6. "We won't try to find archetypes that would represent Kafka's imaginary, his dynamic, or his bestiary (the archetype works by assimilation, homogenization, and thematics, whereas our method works only where only a rupturing and heterogeneous line appears). . . . We believe only in a Kafka experimentation." KML, 7.

7. Élie Faure, "De la cinéplastique," in *L'Arbre d'Eden* (Paris: Crès, 1922). The text is also reprinted in his *Fonction du cinéma* (Paris: Gonthier Méditations, 1964), 16–36.

8. CP §8, 20 (28).

9. CP §1, 3 (4).

10. CP §1, 4 (5). Translation modified.

11. CP §40, 57 (83).

12. CP §7, 19 (26).

13. CP §32, 50 (72).

14. CP §160, 198 (282).

15. CP §259, 306 (434).

16. CP §92, 131 (186).

17. CP §85, 122 (173).

18. "The talk of the end of metaphysics should not mislead us into believing that philosophy is finished with 'metaphysics'" [*Die Rede von Ende der Metaphysik darf nicht zu Meinung verleiten, die Philosophie sei mit der 'Metaphysik' fertig*]." Ibid.

19. CP §38, 55 (78).

20. CP §89, 124.

21. CP §116, 162 (227).

22. CP §82, 119 (169).

23. CP §91, 129 (184).

24. Ibid.

25. CP §23, 41 (59). Translation slightly modified.

26. CP §117, 162 (229): *"Das ganz Andere des anderen Anfangs gegen den ersten läßt sich verdeutlichen durch ein Sagen, das scheinbar nur mit einer Umkehrung spielt, während in Wahrheit sich alles wandelt."*

27. CP §125, 171 (242): *"Seine Wesung muß wie ein Stoß erwartet werden."*

28. CP §92, 130 (186).

29. CP §92, 131 (186).

30. "Hebel—der Hausfreund," in *Aus der Erfahrung des Denkens, G.A., Bd.* 13, 137–38. My translation. Hereafter cited as HHf.

31. NI, 61 (58).

32. The verb *einrücken* means both "to go back (into)" [*rentrer*] and "to go (in)" [*entrer*].

33. CP §213, 237 (338).

34. CP §91, 130 (185).

35. CP §91, 128 (183).

36. WT?, 8–9 (5–6).

37. CP §157, 197 (280).

38. CP §259, 298 (422). Translation slightly modified. (*"Dieses Denken darf nie in eine Gestalt des Seienden flüchten und in ihr alles Lichte des Einfachen aus dem gesammelten Reichtum seines gefügten Dunkels erfahren. Dieses Denken kann auch nie der Auflösung in das Gestaltlosen folgen. Dieses Denken muß diesseits von Gestalt und Gestaltlosem (was ja nur im Seienden ist) im Abgrund des Gestaltgrundes den Wurfschwung seiner Geworfenheit auffangen und in das Offene des Entwurfs tragen."*)

39. Ovid, *Metamorphoses*, translated by David Raeburn (New York: Penguin Books, 2004), 5. Hereafter cited as OM.

40. See also, for example, Minerva's transformation of Ariadne into a spider (OM VI, 1–145) or the Lycian peasants who are turned into frogs (OM VI, 331–38).

41. OM, X, 243–97.

42. On the importance of the motif of flight in the *Metamorphoses*, see Jacqueline Fabre-Serris, *Mythe et poésie dans les Métamorphoses d'Ovide* (Paris: Klincksiek,

1995), 225. For a description and analysis of representations of the *Metamorphoses* in Renaissance painting,
sculpture, and gardening, see this remarkable work:
Michel Jeanneret, *Perpetuum mobile: Métamorphoses des
corps et des oeuvres de Vinci à Montaigne* (Paris: Macula,
1997), especially its fifth chapter, "*Grotesques et corps
monstrueux.*"

43. FCM, 25 (39).

44. Ibid.

45. See Johann Wolfgang von Goethe, *The Metamorphosis of Plants* (Cambridge: MIT Press, 2009), §4, 6: "the
process by which one and the same organ appears in a
variety of forms has been called *the metamorphosis of
plants.*" The metamorphosis of plants is ordinarily conceived
of as the process of their internal differentiation into parts
like flower, petal, stamen, and pistil; for Goethe, it is one
and the same primordial form—*Urform* or *Urgestalt*—that
appears in the infinite multitude of individual plants and
that particularizes itself in them. Goethe's project is, as
Rudolph Steiner says in his commentary on the text, to
develop "into a plastic image . . . this primordial form
nature plays with."

46. The biologist Marcel Abeloos declares that "among
the spectacles offered by the development of animal forms,
none arouses our curiosity more than metamorphosis. As
common as they are, the transformations of the caterpillar
into the butterfly and the tadpole into the frog seem to
defy the ordinary rules of life. Out of a larva capable of
leading for some months an independent existence suddenly arises a completely different being; and its sexual
reproduction makes it so that each generation can be seen
repeating this same sequence. If it is admitted that there
is a general tendency to imagine the course of ontogenesis as the preparation of an adult adequately equipped
for its particular type of life, how is it conceivable that a
larva, living its specific kind of life, could be the outline
of an organism destined for a completely different kind
of existence? What is the meaning of these erasures of
embryogenesis, where life undoes what is has engendered
in order to reconstitute it on a new plane?" Marcel Abeloos, *Les Métamorphoses* (Paris: Armand Colin, 1956), 5.

47. CP §11, 23 (32). It is most often through his dialogues with Nietzsche (both explicit and not) that Heidegger develops his reflections on the figure of the bridge. In *What is Called Thinking?*, he emphasizes that Nietzsche thinks passage and transition as the bridge to the superman: "three simple matters . . . seem to suggest themselves by the word 'superman' understood in its plain meaning: 1. The passing over [*das Übergehen*] 2. The site from which the passage leaves [*Von wo weg der Übergang geht*] 3. The site to which the passage goes [*Wohin der Übergang geschieht*]" (WT?, 60). He also says, right after this, that "the superman goes beyond [*über*], overpasses man as he is, the last man. Man, unless he stops with the type of man he is, is a passage, a transition; he is a bridge; 'he is a rope strung between the animal and the superman.' The superman, strictly understood, is the figure and form [*Gestalt*] of man to which he who is passing over passes over. Zarathustra himself is not yet the superman, but only the very first to pass over to him—he is the superman in the process of becoming." (WT, 60) Finally, also: "The superman constitutes a transformation [*Verwandlung*] and thus a rejection [*Abstoßen*] of man so far." (WT, 70) Nonetheless, the crossing of this bridge remains for Heidegger a far too continuous/continuist motif; this is why, for instance, he never presents the metamorphosis of man as a bridge leading from the *animal rationale* to *Dasein*.

48. CP §5, 11 (14).

49. WT?, 12 (48).

50. WT?, 41–42 (16–17).

51. PR, 50 (75–76).

52. PR, 51 (76); translation modified. The passage this phrase comes from reads: "Ground/reason remains at a remove from being. Being 'is' the abyss in the sense of such a remaining-apart of reason from being. To the extent that being as such grounds, it remains groundless. 'Being' does not fall within the orbit of the principle of reason, rather only beings do."

53. PR, 53 (77).

54. PR, 53 (79).

55. PR, 60 (80).

56. CP §256, 288 (410).

57. Ibid. Translation slightly modified.

58. PR, 53 (80).

59. PR, 54–55 (81–82).
60. PR, 56 (83).

Part II

1. QB, 322 (425–26). The phrase "true equivalents" is taken here from a passage from Goethe that Heidegger places at the end of this text: "If someone regards words and expressions as sacred testimonials, rather than bringing them into quick and fleeting circulation [*schnellen, augenblick Verkehr*] like tokens [*Scheidemünze*] or paper money [*Papiergeld*], seeking instead to employ them as true equivalents in intellectual exchange [*im geistigen Handel und Wandel*], then one cannot chide him."

2. TB.

3. TB, 27 (29).

4. EP, 78 (78).

5. TB, 8 (8).

6. PR, 56 (100–101).

7. Cf. CP §7 (26): "*diese übereignende Zueignung ist Ereignis.*"

8. The economy of the "of value for" makes an appearance in *Contributions* in §132, where Heidegger says that essence, or beingness, "is made of value [*sich geltend macht*] for being" and beingness "of value for οὐσία, ἰδέα" and also, consequently, for "objectness . . . as condition for the possibility of the object." CP §132, 176 (25).

Chapter 5

1. "*Von dieser Bedeutung von Wandlung, die im Hinblick auf die Metaphysik gesagt ist, bleibt jene scharf zu unterschieden, die in der Rede gemeint ist, daß das Sein verwandelt wird—nämlich in das Ereignis.*" TB, 52 (56).

2. TB, 2 (2). Here at the end of the prologue to "Time and Being," Heidegger declares that "the point [here] is not to listen to a series of propositions, but rather to follow the step of an approach that shows [*sondern dem Gang des Zeigens zu folgen*]." Translation slightly modified.

3. TB 6 (6). Translation modified.

4. TB, 2 (2).
5. TB, 6 (5–6).
6. TB, 6 (5–6).
7. TB, 5 (5).
8. TB, 5 (5).
9. TB, 6 (6).
10. TB, 6 (6).
11. TB, 52 (56).
12. TB, 7–8 (7).
13. TB, 8 (7–8).
14. TB, 8 (8).
15. Fission: the division of an atomic nucleus into two or several nuclides then capable of undergoing a series of transmutations.
16. TB, 9 (9).
17. TB, 9 (9).
18. TB, 8 (8).
19. TB, 10 (10).
20. TB, 12 (12). Translation modified
21. TB, 12 (12). Translation slightly modified.
22. TB, 12 (12).
23. TB, 15 (16).
24. TB 16 (16).
25. TB, 17 (18).
26. TB 40–41 (22): *"Eine aufgewandelte Auslegang des Seins."*
27. TB, 19 (19).
28. TB, 19 (20).
29. TB, 19 (20).
30. TB, 19–20 (20). Translation slightly modified.
31. TB, 20 (21).
32. TB, 40–41 (44).
33. TB, 21 (22).
34. TB, 41 (44). Translation slightly modified.
35. TB, 22 (22–23).
36. TB, 27 (24).
37. TB, 5 (5).
38. TB, 5–6 (5–6).
39. TB, 8–9 (9).
40. TB, 17–19 (18–20).
41. TB, 45 (48–49).

42. Jean-Luc Marion, *Being Given: Toward a Phenomenology of Givenness*, translated by Jeffrey L. Kosky (Stanford: Stanford University Press, 2002). Hereafter cited as BG.

43. Cf. TB 22 (22): "Being vanishes in Appropriation [*Ereignis*]."

44. BG, 36.

45. BG, 37.

46. BG, 34.

47. BG, 37.

48. BG, 38.

49. BG, 37.

50. BG, 35.

51. See, for example, CP §164–66. Heidegger writes in the last of those sections that "essence here is only the other word for being (understood as beingness). And accordingly essence means *Ereignis*. . . . Occurrence of the truth of be-ing—that is essential swaying [*Wesen ist hier nur das andere Wort für Sein (verstanden als Seiendheit). Und demgemäß meint Wesung das Ereignis. . . . Geschehnis der Wahrheit des Seyns, das ist Wesung*]." CP §166, 202 (288). See also, in the "Summary," the reproduction of this statement from "The Letter on Humanism": "For the 'It' which gives here is being itself." TB, 43.

52. TB, 41 (44).

53. TB, 6 (6).

Second Incision

1. TB, 8 (8).

2. TB, 9 (9).

3. TB, 41 (44).

4. PWM? 236 (310).

5. Ibid. Translation slightly modified.

6. "The Thing," in *Poetry Language, Thought* (New York: HarperCollins, 2001), 174. "Das Ding," in *Vorträge und Aufzätze, G.A.,* Bd. 7, 178. Hereafter cited as TTh.

7. Heidegger reproduces this sentence in FCM, 72 (108).

8. See Jacques Derrida, *Given Time I: Counterfeit Money*, translated by Peggy Kamuf (Chicago: University of Chicago Press, 1992), 7.

9. BG, 114.

Chapter 6

1. CP §5, 11 (14).

2. CP §32, 49 (70); translation slightly altered: *"Das Sein selbst, das Ereignis als solches erstmal sichtbar."*

3. CP §139, 183 (260). *Anfall* means assault or attack as well as beginning and debut.

4. The *"Pacte Civil de Solidarité" (PACS)* is a new form of civil union that was established by French law in 1999. It grants certain rights once only associated with marriage to couples who do not wish to marry or are not legally allowed to. A PACS is established through a contract drawn up by two individuals and then certified through a brief appearance before a judicial official, and can be dissolved fairly easily.

5. CP §32, 49 (72).

6. CP, §107, 144 (207).

7. CP, §32, 50 (72).

8. "The Turning," in *The Question Concerning Technology* (New York: HarperCollins, 1977), 38; translation modified. "Die Kehre," in *Die Technik und die Kehre* (Stuttgart: Günther Neske, 1962), 38. Hereafter cited as TT.

9. TB, 53 (56–57).

10. The Christian God is a "god who commands [*ein befehlender Gott*]." See P, 40 (58).

11. See on all these points the 1955 lecture "Die Frage nach der Technik," which reprises and further develops the 1949 lecture "Das Gestell" (*G.A.*, Bd. 79, *Bremer und Freibürger Vorträge*). The former appears in *Die Technik und die Kehre* (Pfullingen: Neske, 1962), and can be found in English in *The Question Concerning Technology* under the same title ("The Question Concerning Technology"). Hereafter cited as QT.

12. QT, 17.

13. QT, 16 (16).

14. Ibid.

15. QT, 15 (15).

16. "Die Gefahr," in *G.A.*, Bd. 79, *Bremer und Freiburger Vorträge . . .* , 52. *"Das Ge-stell läßt, den Bestand*

bestellend, das Abtsandlose herrschen. Alles gilt gleich."
Hereafter cited as DG.

17. QT, 26 (25).

18. TT, 37 (37). Translation modified.

19. TT, 38 (38).

20. TT, 37 (37).

21. QT, 38 (38).

22. DG, 51. *"Das Gestell ist das Wesen der modernen Technik. Das Wesen des Ge-stells ist das Sein selber des Seienden; nicht überhaupt und nicht von jehrer, sondern jetzt, da sich die Vergessenheit des Wesens des Seins vollendet. Das Ereignis dieser Vollendung der Seinsvergessenheit bestimmt allererst die Epoche, indem jetzt das Sein in der Weise des Ge-stells west."*

23. DG, 52.

24. DG, 54.

25. TT, 42 (40).

26. TT, 44 (42); my translation.

27. TT, 43 (42). Translation slightly modified.

28. QT, 30 (26).

29. QT, 30 (26).

30. QT, 38–39 (37).

31. QT, 20 (19).

32. QT, 28. The passage in its entirety reads: "The essence of technology, as a destining of revealing, is the danger. The transformed meaning of the word 'enframing' [*Gestell*] will perhaps become more familiar to us now if we think enframing in the sense of destining [*Geschick*] and danger [*Gefahr*]."

33. TT, 41 (40); translation modified.

34. Ibid. Translation again modified.

35. TT, 43 (42).

36. TT, 43 (42).

37. Tth, 183 (22). Translation modified.

38. TT, 41 (40).

39. "The Principle of Identity," in *Identity and Difference* (Chicago: University of Chicago Press, 2002), 35–36. "Der Satz der Identität", in *Identität und Differenz* (Stuttgart: Neske, 1999), 269–270. Hereafter cited as PI.

40. QT, 30 (29).

41. QT, 29 (28).

42. QT, 30 (29).

43. Ibid.
44. DG, 53.
45. PI, 36 (26).
46. DG, 52.
47. PI, 37 (26).
48. DG, 52.
49. See PI, 23–24 (9).
50. PI, 24 (10–11).
51. DG, 52.
52. Cf. the analysis of the *Befremdlichkeit* of being in *Contributions to Philosophy*, and §121 in particular.
53. BC, 44.
54. PI, 39 (28).
55. PI, 40 (28).
56. QT, 30 (30).
57. C §110, 146 (209).
58. NI, 147 (149).
59. NI, 147–148 (137). Translation modified.
60. NI, 148 (139).
61. Ibid.

Chapter 7

1. QB, 303 (401).
2. TTh, 177 (179).
3. See in particular WM?.
4. I develop this point in "Pierre Loves Horranges: Levinas-Sartre-Nancy—An Approach to the Fantastic in Philosophy" (*Umbr(a)* no. 1: 2006, 99–114), where I characterize the philosophical fantastic as the appearance in reality of the ontological difference. Specifically, I attempt to show how Sartre conceived *the real effect of existence* in both *Being and Nothingness* (in "Quality as a Revelation of Being") and *Nausea*: a modification of things, like the roots of a chestnut tree, that cause them to reveal, as their new form, the ontico-ontological difference.
5. See TTh, 177 (181).
6. Two passages from Deleuze and Guattari are relevant here. The first concerns "becoming-imperceptible," and comes from *A Thousand Plateaus: Capitalism and Schizophrenia*, vol. 2., trans. Brian Massumi (Minneapolis:

University of Minnesota Press, 1987), 279: "The imperceptible is the immanent end of becoming, its cosmic formula.
For example, Matheson's *Shrinking Man* passes through the
kingdoms of nature, slips through molecules, to become an
unfindable particle in infinite meditation on the infinite. Paul
Morand's *Monsieur Zéro* flees the larger countries, crosses
the smallest ones, descends the scale of states, establishes
an anonymous society in Lichtenstein of which he is the
only member, and dies imperceptible, forming the particle
0 with his fingers: 'I am a man who flees by swimming
underwater, and at whom all the world's rifles fire. . . . I
must no longer offer a target.' But what does becoming-
imperceptible signify? . . . Becoming-imperceptible means
many things. What is the relation between the . . . impe-
ceptible, the . . . indisernible, and the . . . impersonal?
A first response would be: to be like everybody else." The
second passage is from *Kafka: Toward a Minor Literature*
and concerns "becoming-minor," which is defined in these
terms: "finding his own point of underdevelopment, his
own patois, his own third world, his own desert." KML, 18.

    7. C, §32, 49 (70).
    8. QT, 30 (31).
    9. QT, 33 (34).
    10. TTh, 178 (182).
    11. Ibid.
    12. Ibid. In "On the Question of Being," the "crossing
out" of being is also treated as an index of exchange: "the
sign of this crossing through cannot, however, be the merely
negative sign of a crossing out. It points, rather, toward
the four regions of the fourfold and their being gathered
in the locale of their crossing through" QP, 311 (412).
    13. TT, 43. See also the last chapter.
    14. C §125, 171 (242).
    15. μεταβολικός: (1) concerning change: supple; flex-
ible, changing, inconstant; of variable quantity. (2) Of or
pertaining to exchange, markets, bargaining.
    16. OECP, 190 (249).
    17. Ibid.
    18. OECP, 191 (249).
    19. OECP, 211. Translation modified.
    20. OECP, 210 (275).
    21. OECP, 211 (276).

22. OECP, 239 (345)
23. OECP, 211 (276).
24. QP, 299 (395).
25. QB, 305 (404).
26. QB, 305–306 (404).
27. QB, 303 (400–401).
28. QB, 303 (400–401). Translation modified.
29. Lacoue-Labarthe coins the expression "ontotypol-ogy" to characterize Heideggerian destruction. According to him, Heidegger's thinking of the history of being largely draws its resources from the metaphysical conception of form (as *Form, Gestalt, Bildung, Prägung,* etc.) that it nonetheless pretends to destructure or destroy. So for Heidegger, "politics is derived from a plastic operation." See *Heidegger, Art, and Politics: The Fiction of the Political* (Cambridge, Massachusetts: Blackwell, 1990), here-after cited as FP. In *Heidegger and the Politics of Poetry* (Champagne-Urbana: the University of Illinois Press, 2009), Lacoue-Labarthe again characterizes Heidegger's thinking of fiction/figuration (*plassein/fingere*), fashioning, striking (*Schlag*), and typing as ontotypology.
30. FP, 86.
31. It is not known, Heidegger writes in *Contributions,* whether the last god is "one or many": *"ob eines Einen oder Vieler."* CP §259, 308 (437).
32. *Discourse on Thinking* (New York: Harper & Row, 1966), 49 and 55. *Gelassenheit* (Neske, 1992), 16. Here-after cited as DT.
33. Cf. PI, 9 (9): "When thinking attempts to pursue something that has claimed its attention, it may hap-pen that on the way it undergoes a change [*daß es sich unterwegs wandelt*]."
34. DT, 55 (24). Translation slightly modified.
35. DT, 55 (24). My translation.
36. HHf., 138–39. Translation mine.

Third Incision

1. *Hölderlin's Hymn "The Ister,"* translated by William McNeill and Julia Davis (Bloomington: Indiana University Press, 1996), 30. Translation slightly modified. *Hölderlins*

Hymne "Der Ister." G.A. Bd. 53, 35. Hereafter cited as TI.

2. Ibid.

3. Ibid.

4. TI, 33 (39).

5. Lacan, as we know, elaborates a concept of the real as resistance to symbolization—to idealization, that is.

6. C §192, 219 (312). Translation slightly modified.

7. Marie-José Fourtanier, *Ovid, Metamorphosis, Commentaire* (Paris: Bertrand-Lacoste, 1995), 107.

Part III

1. The texts that precede *Being and Time* attest to this. See in particular the 1912 *Neuere Forschungen über Logik, G.A.,* Bd. 1, the 1925 *History of the Concept of Time: Prolegomena,* trans. Theodor Kisiel (Bloomington: Indiana University Press, 1992) (*Prolegomena zur Geschichte des Zeitbegriffs, G.A.,* Bd. 20), and *Logic: The Question of Truth,* translated by Thomas Sheehan (Bloomington: Indiana University Press, 2010) (*Logik, die Frage nach der Warheit, G.A.,* Bd. 21), from 1925–26.

2. This, according to the *Index zu Heideggers "Sein und Zeit"* (Tübingen: Niemeyer, 1968) and Rainier A. Bast and Heinrich P. Delfosse, *Handbuch zum Textstudium von Martin Heideggers "Sein und Zeit," Bd. 1: Stellenindizes Philologisch-kritischer Apparat* (Stuttgart: Fromann-Holzboog, 1979).

3. Cf., for example, §42 of *Contributions,* "From Being and Time to *Ereignis,*" where Heidegger thematizes the necessity of a change of the ground and soil (*Wandeln aus Grund*) of the question of the meaning of being by relating the latter to the site he assigns it to in *Being and Time.* CP, 58 (84).

4. Jean Grondin, *Le Tournant dans la pensée de Martin Heidegger* (Paris: Presses Universitaires de France, 1987), 9.

5. CP §5, 10 (14).

6. See *Contributions* §43, 60–61 (87), where Heidegger speaks of "the danger of misinterpreting *Being and Time*

in this direction, i.e., 'existentiell-anthropologically' [*die Gefahr, 'Sein und Zeit' in dieser Richtung 'existenziell'- 'anthropologisch' zu mißdeuten*]." The "ground of *Dasein* [*die Gründung des Da-seins*]," he says, requires something else besides "the moral-anthropological [*das 'Moralisch-Anthropologische'*]." In §272, 346 (492), Heidegger lays out the traditional metaphysical determinations of the concept of man—"the thinking animal [*denkende Tier*], as extant source of passions, drives, goals, and value-settings, fitted out with a character, etc. [*vorhandene Quelle der Leiden-schaften, Triebe, Ziel- und Wertsetzungen, ausgestaltet mit einem Charakter usf.*]"—which *Being and Time* did not entirely overcome."

7. The concept of structure is itself also partly taken from the phenomenological lexicon. On this point, I would like to refer the reader to my article "Une différence d'écart: Heidegger et Lévi-Strauss," which analyzes the provenance and meaning of structure in *Being and Time*. See *La Revue Philosophique* 4: 403–16.

8. BT §30, 131 (186).

9. BT §38, 167 (186).

10. FCM §49, 203 (298). Translation slightly modified.

Chapter 8

1. Kafka, "The Metamorphosis," in *Selected Short Stories of Franz Kafka* (New York: Modern Library, 1952), 53. Hereafter cited as M.

2. We will see in the course of this analysis that Heidegger often resorts to the term *Umschlag* to express "change" and to have a synonym for modification. Remember that Heidegger elsewhere uses *Umschlag* to translate μεταβολή.

3. BT §5, 16 (19).

4. BT, §7, 28 (32).

5. BT §33, 148 (159).

6. BT §7, 29 (33).

7. BT §44, 205 (223).

8. Ibid.

9. Jean-Luc Nancy, "The Decision of Existence," in *The Birth to Presence* (Stanford: Stanford University Press, 1993), 94. Hereafter cited as BP.

10. BT §7, 31; translation modified.

11. Cf. this statement from §27, 122: "the sameness of the authentically existing self is separated ontologically by a gap from the identity of the I maintaining itself in the multiplicity of its 'experiences' [*Erlebnismannigfaltigkeit*]."

12. BT § 42, 183 (261).

13. This, in any event, is what can be concluded from reading his correspondence with Hannah Arendt. In a letter dated June 27, 1950, Heidegger writes the following: "The Kafka volumes have arrived. Thank you so much for this great gift. I started to leaf through them, but I could tell that it will take a great deal of work to really read them." The letter from September 24, 1967, in which Arendt again insists on the importance of Kafka goes unanswered. See Hannah Arendt and Martin Heidegger, *Letters 1925–1975*, translated by Andrew Shields (New York: Harcourt, 2004), 91 and 97 (*Hannah Arendt–Martin Heidegger, Briefe 1925–1975* (Frankfurt am Main: Klostermann, 1998).

14. M, 19.

15. See the analysis of fear in BT §30, 133–134: "We are familiar with further varieties [*Abwandlungen*] of fear, such as timidity, shyness, anxiety, misgiving. All modifications of fear [*Modifikationen der Furcht*] as possibilities of attunement point to the fact that *Dasein* as being-in-the-world is 'fearful.'" Heidegger also says here that "the factors constitutive of the full phenomena of fear can vary [*können variieren*]." (This is also referred to in chap. 4, note 5, above.)

16. BT §69, 464 (464).

17. BT §39, 170 (241).

18. See Part One, chapter VI: "Care as the Being of *Dasein*," particularly §39–41.

19. See Part Two, chapter III: "The Authentic Temporality Potentiality-for-Being-a-Whole of *Dasein*, and Temporality as the Ontological Meaning of Care."

470. BT §65, 300–301 (327).

21. The three fundamental existentials, moreover, appear only after the analysis of the everydayness of *Dasein* has been elaborated (via being-in-the-world).

22. BT §13, 58 (62).

23. BT §13, 58 (62).

24. BT §38, 167 (238).

25. BT §27, 122 (173).

26. BT §27, 121 (171).

27. BT §7, 32 (36).

28. BT §60, 274 (394–95).

29. BT §31 (37).

30. BT §41 (182).

31. The analysis of temporality again clearly demonstrates this. "The problem," writes Heidegger, "is not *how does 'derivative,'* infinite time 'in which' objectively present things come into being and pass away, *become primordial/originary*, finite temporality, but rather, how does *in*authentic temporality, as *in*authentic, temporalize an infinite time out of finite time." BT §65, 304 (330–31).

32. Modification is most present in §54 ("The Problem of an Attestation of an Authentic Potentiality-of-Being"), §60 ("The Existential Structure of the Authentic Potentiality-of-Being Attested in Conscience"), §64 ("Care and Selfhood"), §65 ("Temporality as the Authentic Meaning of Care"), §67 ("The Basic Content of the Existential Constitution of *Dasein*, and the Preliminary Sketch of Its Temporal Interpretation"), and §69 ("The Temporality of Being-in-the-World and the Problem of the Transcendence of the World").

33. BT §65, 303 (329).

34. BT §27, 122 (130).

35. BT §54, 247 (267).

36. M, 27.

37. M, 57.

38. Maurice Blanchot, *De Kafka à Kafka* (Paris: Gallimard, 1981), 73.

39. Françoise Dastur, *Heidegger and the Question of Time*, translated by François Raffoul and David Pettigrew (Atlantic Highlands, N.J.: Humanities Press, 1998), 23. Hereafter cited as HQT.

40. Dastur rightfully recalls that *Eigentlichkeit* and *Uneigentilichkeit* are terms that emerge in "*The Logical Investigations* of Husserl, who himself found the distinction between the authentic mode of intuitive thought and the inauthentic mode of symbolic thought in the work of his master Brentano (see . . . the Sixth Logical Investigation). This latter text—which for Heidegger represents the height of Husserlian phenomenology—demonstrates how the 'empty' intentionality of symbolic thought, which

largely represents our way of thinking, can be fulfilled by an intuition, becoming thereby an 'authentic' thought. Transposed to *Dasein* as a whole, this distinction accounts for the non-substantial character of *Dasein*." HQT, 23.

41. Ibid.

42. BP, 82–83.

43. BT §38, 167 (179).

44. BP, 99.

45. Ibid.

46. Ibid.

47. Quoted by Nancy on 401, and originally found in Emmanuel Levinas, "Mourir pour . . ." in *Heidegger: Questions Ouvertes* (Paris: Collège International de Philosophie-Osiris, 1988), 261.

48. *"On disparaît sur place . . ."* The pronoun *on* corresponds in French translations of Heidegger's thought to German *das Man*, which is rendered as "the they" in English.

49. BT §54, 248 (268).

50. BT §44, 204 (222).

51. BT §54, 248 (268).

52. BT §54, 248 (268).

Chapter 9

1. M, 61.

2. BT §57, 256 (369).

3. BT §57, 255 (369).

4. BT §57, 256 (369).

5. BT §57, 256–257 (369).

6. BP, 106.

7. Gilles Deleuze, *Francis Bacon: Logic of the Sensible*, translated by Daniel W. Smith (Minneapolis: University of Minnesota Press, 2002), 68. Hereafter cited as LOS.

8. LOS, 68.

9. LOS, 67.

10. BT §38, 167 (178). The full passage where this phrase is found reads: "The phenomena pointed out of temptation, tranquilizing, alienation, and self-entangling (entanglement) characterize the specific kind of being of falling prey. We call this kind of 'movement' of *Dasein* in

its own being the plunge [*Absturz*]. *Dasein* plunges out of itself into itself, into the groundlessness and nothingness of inauthentic everydayness."

11. For Heideger's analysis of stress, see his *Zollikon Seminars: Protocols—Conversations—Letters*, translated by Franz Mayr (Evanston, Ill.: Northwestern University Press, 2001), 132–43. *Zollikoner Seminare* (Frankfurt am Main: Klostermann, 1987).

12. BT §42, 184 (262).

13. BT §42, 184 (263).

14. BT §42, 185 (263).

15. BT §16, 69 (100).

17. BT §69, 330 (477–78). Translation slightly modified.

17. BT §47, 221 (317). Translation modified.

Chapter 10

1. FCM, 21 (31).

2. WM, 89 (113).

3. BT §42, 183 (261).

4. FCM, 350 (509).

5. FCM, 150 (225).

6. FCM, 124–25 (187–88).

7. FCM, 135–36 (204).

8. BT §41, 182 (196).

9. FCM, 82 (123).

10. FCM, 67 (101).

11. FCM, 77 (116).

12. WM, 93 (110).

13. BT §41, 178.

14. FCM, 88 (132).

15. BT §29, 126–27 (134).

16. Ibid.

17. OECP, 191 (249).

18. FCM, 68 (102).

19. FCM, 67 (101).

20. BT §29, 128 (135).

21. FCM, 19 (28).

22. This inclusion of questioner and question in each other corresponds to the awakening of a basic attunement

allowing for this "gripping" (which is both a gripping and being gripped). See FCM, 7 (9).

23. FCM, 6 (9).

24. IWM, 282–83 (372).

25. IWM, 279 (368).

26. IWM, 87 (110).

27. WM, 88 (111–12)

28. WM, 90 (113).

29. WM, 89 (112–13).

30. WM, 91 (115)

31. "Profound boredom, drifting here and there in the abysses of our existence like a muffling fog, removes all things and human beings and oneself along with them into a remarkable indifference. This boredom manifests beings as a whole." WM, 87.

32. Didier Franck, *Heidegger et le Problème de l'Espace* (Paris: Éditions de Minuit, 1986), 73–74.

33. WM, 89 (113).

34. FCM, 38 (58).

35. FCM, 39 (58).

36. FCM, 130 (196).

37. These three phrases are, respectively, from the headings for chapters 2, 3, and 4 of *The Fundamental Concepts of Metaphysics.* —Trans.

38. Ibid., translation modified. The title of §28, from which this material comes is entitled, in part, "The becoming deeper of the second form of boredom [*das Tieferwerden der zweiten Form der Langweile*]." FCM, 128 (194).

39. FC, 155–56 (233).

40. FCM, 157 (233).

41. "It is not a matter of taking a definition of boredom home with you," Heidegger writes, "but of learning and understanding how to move in the depths of *Dasein.*" FCM, 131 (198).

42. "[T]he second form of boredom has the structural moment of being left empty, albeit in a transformed [changed] form [*in gewandelter Form*] and not so conspicuously as the first." FCM, 122 (185).

43. FCM, 135–36, translation modified. Note that the French translator of the seminar sometimes renders "gewandelt" as "modifié" (as is precisely the case in §25), and sometimes, as he does in this passage, as "transformé".

44. FCM, 352 (511).
45. FCM, 137 (206).
46. FCM, 80 (120).
47. FCM, 80 (120).
48. FCM, 98 (148–49). We can see here how time, as Jean-Louis Vieillard-Baron puts it, "detaches" from its "concept" (*Begriff*) and becomes confounded with its own transformability. See his *Le Temps: Platon, Hegel, Heidegger* (Paris: Vrin, 1978).
49. FCM, 127 (191).
50. FCM, 98 (149).
51. FCM, 78 (118).
52. These terms are repeated throughout FCM, 99–105.
53. FCM, 93 (140). Notice that the examples for each of the three forms of boredom (the train station, the dinner party, and the city) are all place of encounters, crossings, and exchanges.
54. FCM, 98 (148).
55. FCM, 106 (160).
56. FCM, 109 (165).
57. FCM, 119 (180).
58. FCM, 132 (199).
59. FCM, 135 (204).
60. FCM, 135 (204).
61. FCM, 138 (207–8).
62. FCM, 141 (213).
63. FCM, 141 (213).
64. FCM, 149 (223).
65. FCM, 144 (216).
66. FCM, 151 (226).
67. FCM, 151 (227).
68. Cf. BT §65.
69. BT §67, 307 (396). My translation.
70. WM, 96 (121).
71. FCM, 157 (235–36).
72. FCM, 161 (242).
73. FCM, 182 (270).
74. FCM, 203 (298).
75. Jean-Paul Sartre, *Nausea,* translated by Lloyd Alexander (New York: New Directions Publishing, 2007), 127. In a sense, the only thing the novel contends with is this metamorphosis of existence into an event. "So

a change has taken place," says Roquentin. "[A] small crowd of metamorphoses accumulate in me without my noticing it, and then, one fine day, a veritable revolution takes place" (4–5). Also: "I had never understood what it means to exist "(127, translation modified), and "to exist is simply *to be there*" (131).

Conclusion

1. *Reden und andere Zeugnisse eines Lebensweges,* G.A., Bd. 16, 169. Hereafter cited as R. Where the relations between Heidegger's biographical, philosophical, and political life are concerned, I have made frequent reference to both Hugo Ott, *Martin Heidegger: A Political Life* (New York: Fontana, 1994) and Rüdiger Safranski, *Martin Heidegger: Between Good and Evil,* translated by Ewald Osers (Boston: Harvard University Press, 1999).

2. R, 300.

3. R, 302.

4. In *Of Spirit,* Jacques Derrida underscores the structural tie joining the motifs of force, imprint, and spirit in "The Rectorship Address." "Heidegger . . . confers the most reassuring and elevated spiritual legitimacy on everything in which, and on all before whom, he commits himself, on everything he thus sanctions and consecrates at such a height. One could say that he spiritualizes National Socialism." See Jacques Derrida, *Of Spirit: Heidegger and the Question* (Chicago: University of Chicago Press, 1989), 47. Heidegger also sees National Socialism, Derrida notes, as "the imprint (*Prägung*) . . . of the German people," which is to say its form and force: "Heidegger says sometimes *Prägekraft* or *prägende Kraft*" (40).

5. IM, 10–11 (12).

6. Martin Heidegger, "Only a God Can Save Us: *Der Spiegel's* Interview," in *Martin Heidegger: Philosophical and Political Writings,* edited by Manfred Stassen (New York: Continuum, 2006), 38. "Spiegel-Gespräch mit Martin Heidegger (23. September 1966)," in *Reden und andere Zeugnisse eines Lebensweges,* 671. Hereafter cited as DS.

7. *DS,* 39 (673). See just as much, on page 41 (676): "I know of no paths to the immediate transformation of

the present situation of the world, assuming that such a thing is humanly possible at all."

8. Jürgen Habermas, *The Philosophical Discourse of Modernity: Twelve Lectures,* translated by Frederick Lawrence (Cambridge: MIT Press, 1993), 160.

9. IM, 11 (12).

10. WL, 42 (130). Translation modified.

11. NII, 142 (361).

12. NII, 131 (353).

13. *TB,* 49–50 (53). Translation slightly modified.

14. Giorgio Agamben, *Means Without End: Notes on Politics,* translated by Vincenzo Binetti and Cesare Casarino (Minneapolis: University of Minnesota Press, 2000), 110.

15. Jean-Luc Nancy: *Noli me tangere: On the Raising of the Body,* translated by Sarah Clift, Pascale-Anne Brault, and Michael Naas (New York: Fordham University Press, 2008), 23–25. I regret that I cannot discuss at length here the ties between metamorphosis, migration, and resurrection as they are treated in "The Gardener," the admirable chapter of the book devoted to the "unrecognizable" face of the resurrected Christ. Jesus, Nancy writes, is "the same that is no longer the same; the aspect is dissociated from the appearance; the visage is made absent right in the face; the body is sinking into the body, sliding under it. The departing [*la partance*] is inscribed onto presence, presence is presenting its vacating. He has already left; he is no longer where he is; he is no longer as he is. . . . He is properly only his impropriety" (28). Is metamorphosis the past or future of resurrection?

16. Jürgen Habermas, *The Future of Human Nature* (London: Polity Press, 2003), 29.

17. The latter formula—*plasticité d'errance*—is found in Thierry Davila's very original work *Marcher. Créer. Déplacements, flâneries, derivés dans l'art de la fin du XXe siècle* (Paris: Éditions du Regard, 2002), 22–23.

18. OECP, 190 (249).

19. OECP, 217 (285). Translation modified.

20. "What Are Poets For?," in *Poetry, Language, Thought* (New York: HarperCollins, 2001), 99. "Wozu Dichter?," in *Holwege,* 279. Hereafter cited as WPF?

21. WPF?, 101 (281). Translation slightly modified.

22. WPF?, 132–33 (314–15).

Bibliography of Cited Works by Heidegger

The titles of German works follow those of their English counterparts, and when relevant, abbreviations for English titles come at the end of each entry. References to a specific volume, or *Band* (Bd.), of Heidegger's complete works are to the German edition: *Gesamtausgabe* (*G.A.*) (Frankfurt am Main: Vittorio Klostermann, 1975 to the present). Listed works are limited to those cited in the text.

"Anaximander's Saying," in *Off the Beaten Track*, trans. Julian Young and Kenneth Haynes (Cambridge: University of Cambridge Press, 2002). "Der Spruch des Anaximander," in *Holzwege* (Frankfurt/Main: Klostermann, 1950). Hereafter cited as AS.

"Age of the World Picture," in *The Question Concerning Technology*, trans. William Lovitt (New York: HarperCollins, 1977). *Die Zeit des Weltbildes* in *Holzwege* (Tübingen: Vittorio Klostermann, 1950).

Aristotle's Metaphysics Theta 1–3: On the Essence and Actuality of Force, trans. Walter Brogan and Peter Warnek (Bloomington: Indiana University Press, 1995). *Aristotles, Metaphysiks Θ 1–3: Von Wesen und Wirlichkeit der Kraft, G.A.,* Bd. 33.

Basic Concepts of Ancient Philosophy, trans. Robert D. Metcalf and Mark B. Tanzer (Bloomington: Indiana University Press, 2008). *Die Grundbegriffe der antiken Philosophie, G.A.,* Bd. 22.

Basic Questions of Philosophy: Selected Problems of "Logic," trans. Richard Rojcewicz and André Schuwer (Bloomington: Indiana University Press: 1994). *Grundfragen der Philosophie: Ausegwählte "Probleme" der Logik, G.A.,* Bd. 45.

Being and Time, trans. Joan Stambaugh (Albany: SUNY Press, 1996). *Sein und Zeit, G.A.,* Bd. 2. Cited as BT.

Contributions to Philosophy, trans. Parvis Emad and Kenneth Maly (Bloomington: Indiana University Press, 1989). *Beiträge zur Philosophie: Vom Ereignis. G.A.,* Bd. 65. Hereafter cited as CP.

Discourse on Thinking, trans. John Anderson and E. Hans Freund (New York: Harper & Row, 1966). *Gelassenheit* (Pfullingen: Neske, 1992). Cited as DT.

The Essence of Truth: Plato's Allegory of the Cave and Theaetetus, trans. Ted Sadler (New York: Continuum, 2002). *Vom Wesen der Wahrheit: Zu Platons Höhlengleichnis und Theaetetus, G.A.,* Bd. 34

"The End of Philosophy and the Task of Thinking," in *Time and Being,* trans. Joan Stambaugh (Chicago: The University of Chicago Press, 2002). "Die Ende der Philosophie und die Aufgabe des Denkens," in *Zur Sache des Denkens* (Tübingen: Niemeyer, 1961). EP.

The Fundamental Concepts of Metaphysics: Word, Finitude, Solitude, trans. William McNeill and Nicholas Walker (Bloomington: Indiana University Press, 1995). *Die Grundbegriffe der Metaphysik: Welt-Endlichkeit-Eisamkeit, G.A.,* Bd. 29–30. Hereafter cited as FCM.

"Die Gefahr," in *Bremer und Freiburger Vorträge, G.A.,* Bd. 79. Hereafter cited as DG.

Die Geschichte des Seyns, 1938–1940, G.A., Bd. 69

"Hebel—der Hausfreund," in *Aus der Erfahrung des Denkens, G.A.,* Bd. 13

"Hegel's Concept of Experience," in *Off the Beaten Track,* trans. Julian Young and Kenneth Haynes (Cambridge: Cambridge University Press, 2002). "Hegels Begriff der Erfahrung," in *Holzwege* (Frankfurt am Main: Klostermann, 1950).

Hölderlin's Hymn "The Ister," trans. William McNeill and Julia Davis (Bloomington: Indiana University Press, 1996), 39. *Hölderlins Hymne "der Ister," G.A.,* Bd. 53. Hereafter cited as HHI.

History of the Concept of Time: Prolegomena, trans. Theodor Kisiel (Bloomington: Indiana University Press, 1992). *Prolegomena zur Geschichte des Zeitbegriffs, G.A.,* Bd. 20.

"Introduction to 'What Is Metaphysics?'" trans. Walter Kaufmann, in *Pathmarks* (Cambridge: Cambridge University Press, 1999). "Was ist Metaphysik? Einleitung," *G.A.,* Bd. 9, 368. Hereafter cited as WM?.

Kant and the Problem of Metaphysics, trans. Richard Taft (Bloomington: Indiana University Press, 1997). *Kant und das Problem der Metaphysik, G.A.,* Bd. 3.

Logic: The Question of Truth, trans. Thomas Sheehan (Bloomington: Indiana University Press, 2010). *Logik, die Frage nach der Wahrheit. G.A.,* Bd. 21.

"Metaphysics as History of Being," in *The End of Philosophy,* trans. Joan Stambaugh (Chicago: The University of Chicago Press, 2003).

Nietzsche Volume II, G.A., Bd., 6.2.

Mindfulness, trans. Parvis Emad and Thomas Kalary (New York: Continuum, 2006). *Besinnung, G.A.,* Bd. 66.

Nietzsche Volume I: The Will to Power as Art, trans. David Farrell Krell (San Francisco: Harper San Francisco, 1991). *Nietzsche G.A.,* Bd. 6.1. Hereafter cited as NI.

Nietzsche Volume II: The Eternal Recurrence of the Same, trans. David Farrell Krell (San Francisco: Harper San Francisco, 1991). *Nietzsche, G.A.,* Bd. 6.1. Hereafter cited as NII.

Nietzsche Volume III: The Will to Power as Knowledge and as Metaphysics, trans. David Farrell Krell (HarperCollins: New York, 31). *Nietzsche, G.A.,* Bd. 6.2. Hereafter cited as NIII.

Nietzsche, Volume. IV: Nihilism, trans. David Farrell Krell (New York: HarperCollins, 1991). *Nietzsche,. G.A.,* Bd. 6.2, 309. Hereafter cited as NIV.

"Nietzsche's Word: God is Dead," *Off the Beaten Track,* trans. Julian Young and Kenneth Haynes (Cambridge: Cambridge University Press, 2002). "Nietzsches Wort:

'Gott ist tot,'" in *Holzwege* (Frankfurt am Main: Klostermann, 1950), 262.

Neuere Forschungen über Logik, G.A., Bd. 1.

"On the Essence and Concept of φυσις: Aristotle's Physics
B," trans. Thomas Sheehan, in *Pathmarks* (Cambridge:
Cambridge University Press, 1999). "Vom Wesen und
Begriff der φυσις: Aristotles, Physik B" in *G.A.,* Bd.
9. Cited as OECP.

"On the Essence of Truth," trans. John Sallis, in *Pathmarks.*
"Vom Wesen der Wahrheit," *G.A.,* Bd. 9. Cited as OET.

"On the Question of Being," trans. William McNeill, in
Pathmarks (Cambridge: Cambridge University Press,
1999). "Zur Seinsfrage," *G.A.,* Bd. 9. Cited as OQB.

On the Way to Language, trans. Peter D. Hertz (New York:
HarperCollins, 1982). *Unterwegs zur Sprache, G.A.,*
Bd. 12. Cited as OWL.

"Only a God Can Save Us: *Der Spiegel*'s Interview," in
*Martin Heidegger: Philosophical and Political Writ-
ings,* ed. Manfred Stassen (New York: Continuum,
2006). "Spiegel-Gespräch mit Martin Heidegger (23.
September 1966)," in *Reden und andere Zeugnisse
eines Lebensweges.*

"The Ontotheological Constitution of Metaphysics," in
Identity and Difference (Chicago: University of Chicago Press, 2002). "*Die Onto-Theo-Logische Verfassung
der Metaphysik,*" in *Identität und Differenz* (Stuggart:
Neske, 1999), 47. Cited as OTCM.

Parmenides, trans. André Schuwer and Richard Rojcewicz
(Bloomington: Indiana University Press, 1992). *Parmenides, G.A.,* Bd. 54. Cited as P.

*Phenomenological Interpretation of Kant's Critique of Pure
Reason,* trans. Richard Rojcewicz (Bloomington:
Indiana University Press, 1997). *Phänomenologische
Interpretation von Kants Kritik der reinen Vernunft,
G.A.,* Bd. 25.

"Plato's Doctrine of Truth," trans. Thomas Sheehan, in
Pathmarks (Cambridge: Cambridge University Press,
1999). "Platons Lehre von der Wahrheit," *G.A.,* Bd.
9. Cited as PDT.

". . . Poetically Man Dwells . . ." in *Poetry, Language,
Thought,* trans. Albert Hofstadter (New York, HarperCollins, 2001). ". . . Dichterisch Wohnet der

Mensch . . ." in *Vörtrage und Aufsätze, G.A.,* Bd 7. Cited as PMD.

"Postscript to 'What Is Metaphysics?,'" trans. William McNeill, in *Pathmarks* (Cambridge: Cambridge University Press, 1999). "Nachwort zu: 'Was ist Metaphyisk?'" *G.A.,* Bd. 9.

"The Principle of Identity," in *Identity and Difference* (Chicago: University of Chicago Press, 2002). "Der Satz der Identität," in *Identität und Differenz* (Stuggart: Neske, 1999). Cited as PI.

"The Thing," in *Poetry Language, Thought,* trans. Albert Hofstadter (New York: HarperCollins, 2001). "Das Ding," in *Vorträge und Aufzätze, G.A.,* Bd. 7. Cited as TTh.

"The Turning," in *The Question Concerning Technology* (New York: HarperCollins, 1977). "Die Kehre," *Die Technik und die Kehre* (Stuggart: Neske, 1962). Cited as TT.

Reden und andere Zeugnisse eines Lebensweges. G.A., Bd. 16. Cited as R.

Sojourns, trans. John Panteleimon Manoussakis (Albany: SUNY Press, 2005). *Aufenthalte* (Frankfurt am Main: Vittorio Klostermann, 1989). Cited as S.

Time and Being, trans. Joan Stambaugh (Chicago: University of Chicago Press, 2002). "Zeit und Sein," *Zur Sache des Denkens* (Tübingen: Niemeyer, 1961). Cited as TB.

"What Are Poets For?," in *Poetry, Language, Thought,* trans. Albert Hofstadter (New York: HarperCollins, 2001). "Wozu Dichter?," *Holwege* (Frankfurt am Main: Klostermann, 1950), 279. Cited as WPF?.

What Is Called Thinking?, trans. J. Glenn Gray (New York: HarperCollins, 1968). *Was Heißt Denken?* (Tübingen: Niemeyer, 1954). Cited as WT?.

"What Is Metaphysics?," trans. David Farrell Krell, in *Pathmarks* (Cambridge: Cambridge University Press, 1999). *"Was ist Metaphysik?,"* in *G.A.,* Bd. 9. Cited as WM?.

What Is Philosophy?, trans. William Kluback and Jean T. Wilde (Oxford: Rowan and Littlefied, Publishers, 1956). *Was ist das, die Philosophie?* (Pfullingen: Neske, 1956), 33–34. Cited as WP?.

What Is a Thing?, trans. by W. B. Barton, Jr., and Vera Deutsch (Chicago: Henry Regnery Co., 1969). *Die Frage nach dem Ding, G.A.,* Bd. 41. Hereafter cited as WTh?.

Zollikon Seminars: Protocols—Conversations—Letters, trans. Franz Mayr (Evanston, Ill.: Northwestern University Press, 2001). *Zollikoner Seminare* (Frankfurt am Main: Klostermann, 1987).

Other Works Cited

Abeloos, M., *Les Métamorphoses* (Paris:Armand Colin, 1956).

Agamben, G., *Means Without End: Notes on Politics*, trans. Vicenzo Binetti and Cesare Casarino (Minneapolis: University of Minnesota Press, 2000).

Bast, R. A und Delfosse, H. P, *Handbuch zum Textsudium von Martin Heideggers «Sein und Zeit»* (Stuttgart: Fromann-Holzboog, 1979).

Blanchot, M., *De Kafka à Kafka*, Paris, Gallimard, «Folio Essais», 1981.

Butor, M., *La Modification* (Paris: Editions de Minuit, 1957). *Second Thoughts* (UK title; trans. Jean Stewart, 1958) / *A Change of Heart* (U.S. title; trans. Jean Stewart, 1959).

Caillois, R., *Cohérences aventureuses* (Paris: Gallimard, 1973).

Dastur, F., *Heidegger And The Question Of Time,* trans. François Raffoul and David Pettigrew (Atlantic Island, N.J.: Humanities Press, 1998).

Davila, T., *Marcher, créer. Déplacements, flâneries, dérives dans l'art à la fin du XXe siècle* (Paris: Editions du Regard, 2002).

Deleuze, G., Guattari, F., *Kafka, Toward a Minor Literature*, trans. Dana Polan (Minneapolis: University of Minnesota Press, 1986).

———. *A Thousand Plateaus: Capitalism and Schizophrenia*, vol. 2, trans. Brian Massumi (Minneapolis: University of Minnesota Press, 1987).

Deleuze, G., *Francis Bacon: Logic of the Sensible*, trans. Daniel W. Smith (Minneapolis: University of Minnesota Press, 2002).

Derrida, J., *Otobiographies, L'enseignement de Nietzsche et la politique du nom propre*, Paris, Galilée, 1984.

———. *Of Spirit: Heidegger and the Question* (Chicago: University of Chicago Press, 1989).

———. *Given Time I: Counterfeit Money*, trans. Peggy Kamuf (Chicago: University of Chicago Press, 1992).

———. With Catherine Malabou, *Counterpath*, trans. David Wills (Stanford: Stanford University Press, 2004).

Détienne, M. et Vernant, J. P., *Cunning Intelligence in Greek Culture and Society* (Chicago: University of Chicago Press, 1991).

Fabre-Serris, J., *Mythe et poésie dans les* Métamorphoses *d'Ovide* (Paris: Klincksieck, 1995).

Farias, V., *Heidegger und der Nazional-sozialismus* (Frankfurt/Main: Fischer, 1989).

Faure, E., «De la cinéplastique», in *Fonction du cinéma* (Paris: Gonthier Médiations, 1964).

Fourtanier, M. J., *Ovide*, Métamorphoses, *Commentaire* (Paris: Bertrand-Lacoste, 1995).

Franck, D., *Heidegger et le problème de l'espace* (Paris: Editions de Minuit, 1986).

Goethe, J. W., *Metamorphose der Pflanzen,* in *Naturwissenschaftliche Schriften* I, herausgeben von Dorothea Kuhn und Rilke Wankmüller, *Hamburger Ausgabe*, 1958, Bd 13. *The Metamorphosis of Plants* (Cambridge: MIT Press, 2009).

Grondin, J., *L'Horizon herméneutique de la pensée contemporaine* (Paris: Vrin, 1983).

———. *Le Tournant dans la pensée de Martin Heidegger* (Paris: PUF, 1987).

Habermas, J., *Heidegger—Werk und Weltanschauung*, Foreword to Victor Farias's *Heidegger und der Nazionalsozialismus* (Frankfurt/Main: Fischer, 1989), 11–37.

———. *The Philosophical Discourse of Modernity: Twelve Lectures*, trans. Frederick Lawrence (Cambridge: MIT Press, 1993).

———. *The Future of Human Nature* (London: Polity Press, 2003).

———. *Index zu Heideggers* Sein und Zeit (Tübingen: Niemeyer, 1961, 1968).

Jeanneret, M., *Perpetuum Mobile, Métamorphoses des corps et des œuvres de Vinci à Montaigne* (Paris: Macula, 1997).

Jünger, E., *Der Arbeiter* (Stuttgart: Klett, 1981).

———. Über die Linie (Frankfurt/Main: Klostermann, 1950) (Stuttgart: Cota, 1980).

Kafka, F., "The Metamorphosis," in *Selected Short Stories of Franz Kafka* (New York: Modern Library, 1952).

Lacoue-Labarthe, P., *Heidegger, Art and Politics: The Fiction of the Political*, trans. Chris Turner (Oxford: Blackwell Publishers 1990).

———. Heidegger and the Politics of Poetry, trans. Jeff Fort (Chicago: University of Chicago Press, 2007).

Levinas, E., «*Mourir pour*», in *Heidegger, Questions ouvertes* (Collège International de Philosophie-Osiris: Paris, 1988).

Malabou, C., *The Future of Hegel: Plasticity, Temporality, Dialectic*, trans. Lisabeth During (New York: Routledge, 2005).

———. "*Pierre Loves Horranges: Levinas-Sartre-Nancy. An Approach of the Fantastic in Philosophy*" (*Umbr(a)* no. 1: 2006, 9–114).

Maréchaux, P., *Premières leçons sur les* Métamorphoses *d'Ovide* (Paris: PUF, 1999).

Marion, J.L., *Being Given: Toward a Phenomenology of Givenness*, trans. Jeffrey L. Kosky (Stanford: Stanford University Press, 2002).

Nancy, J. L., *A Finite Thinking*, ed. Simon Sparks (Stanford: Stanford Univeristy Press, 2003).

———. *Noli me tangere: On the Raising of the Body*, trans. Pascale-Anne Brault, Sarah Clift and Michael Naas (New York: Fordham University Press, 2008).

Nietzsche, F., *Sämtliche Werke (S. W.), Kritische Studienausgabe*, herausgeben von G. Coli und M. Montinari.

———. *The Gay Science* (Cambridge: Cambridge University Press, 2001).

———. *Twilight of the Idols* (Cambridge: Cambridge University Press, 2005).

Pöggeler, O., *Der Denkwerk Martin Heideggers* (Stuttgart: Neske, 1963).

Proust, M., *Sur Baudelaire, Flaubert et Morand* (Paris: Editions Complexe, 1987).

Safranski, R., *Heidegger et son Temps*, Paris, Grasset, 1996.

Sartre, J. P., *Nausea*, trans. Lloyd Alexander (New York: New York Direction Publishing, 2007).

Vieillard-Baron, J. L., *Hegel et l'Idéalisme spéculatif* (Paris: Vrin, 1999).

————. *Le Temps: Platon, Hegel, Heidegger* (Paris: Vrin, 1978).

Marlène Zarader: *Heidegger et les Paroles de l'origine* (Paris: Vrin, 1986–1990).

Index Nominum

Index Rerum

339

Made in the USA
San Bernardino, CA
30 November 2012